Empowered lives.
Resilient nations.

EVALUATION
OF UNDP CONTRIBUTION TO
GENDER EQUALITY AND
WOMEN'S EMPOWERMENT

Independent Evaluation Office, August 2015
United Nations Development Programme

ACKNOWLEDGEMENTS

The Independent Evaluation Office (IEO) of the United Nations Development Programme (UNDP) would like to thank all those who contributed to this evaluation. The evaluation team, led by Chandi Kadirgamar and co-led by Ana Rosa Monteiro Soares, counted on the methodological guidance and support of Alexandra Pittman and on consultancy support in research and data collection and synthesis from Chelsey Wickmark, who was succeeded by Karen Cadondon. Thematic contributions were provided by Susan Bazilli (energy and environment), Christian Bugnion (crisis prevention and recovery), Minoli de Bresser (poverty and Millennium Development Goals), Charlotte Ørnemark (democratic governance), and Dana Peebles (institutional change). Contributions were also received from AlterSpark Corporation and the Statistical Cybermetrics Research Group at the University of Wolverhampton (cybermetric analysis) and Gabriela Byron (UN-SWAP assessment). Benoit Conti provided research support.

The evaluation was carried out with the invaluable assistance of UNDP colleagues whose insight, knowledge, advice and comments made this evaluation possible. We cannot acknowledge here all those who contributed, but would like to express our particular gratitude to Randi Davis, Raquel Lagunas and Rose Sarr and to all the gender advisors, past and present, in the Gender Team. Their willingness to candidly share views and ideas and provide feedback with patience and care was of great value to the evaluation team. In addition, we would like to particularly thank all the evaluation focal points in the regional bureaux and the staff in the country offices who provided advice, logistical support and administrative assistance. Without this input, the country visit component of this evaluation would not have been possible.

We wish to also extend our appreciation to IEO's Evaluation Advisory Panel members Michael Bamberger and Jayati Ghosh, who provided advice at key points throughout the process.

The quality enhancement and administrative support provided by our colleagues at the IEO was critical in the success of the evaluation. Michael Reynolds provided quality assurance and peer reviewed the draft report. Sonam Choetsho, Concepcion Cole and Antana Locs provided logistical and administrative support. Sasha Jahic managed the production and publication of the report.

FOREWORD

Gender equality remains an unfulfilled promise that affects all humanity. The Universal Declaration of Human Rights set out the fundamental bases of universal freedoms, equality and rights in 1948. During the 1970s and 1980s, discussions in civil society, governments and United Nations agencies focused on increasing attention, developing protection mechanisms and dedicating resources to advance women's equity and social justice. These debates on international norms and standards led to the adoption of the Convention on the Elimination of All Forms of Discrimination against Women in 1979. It established a critical reference point underscoring the importance of gender equality in development, with an explicit focus on reducing discrimination against women. It was followed by the Beijing Platform of Action in 1995, which enshrined 'gender mainstreaming' as a central tenet of all development activity. But disappointingly, more than three decades later, gender equality remains an elusive goal.

UNDP has been in the forefront of responding to these developments since the 1970s. The first evaluation of UNDP's efforts, in 2006, concluded that UNDP had put in place policies and strategies to mainstream gender and that there were some "islands of success". However, it found that the organization lacked a systemic approach to gender mainstreaming. Most crucially, UNDP lacked leadership as well as commitment at the highest levels and capacity at all levels.

This report, the second evaluation of UNDP's contribution to gender equality and women's empowerment, picks up the thread from 2008 and traces the implementation of UNDP's first Gender Equality Strategy, which concluded in 2013. Overall, the evaluation concludes that there has been notable change and improvement in the UNDP approach to and implementation of policies to address gender. Gender mainstreaming is now a shared corporate priority, and UNDP has moved well beyond the "islands of success" finding of the 2006 evaluation. This evaluation also makes clear that UNDP is a learning organization that seriously absorbed and acted on the findings and recommendations of that evaluation.

Notwithstanding the progress in 'engendering' UNDP operations and programmes, the evaluation has found significant areas that will require concerted attention in the short and medium term. Most notable was the need to improve the quality and effectiveness of gender results: the evaluation finds that UNDP succeeded only partially in meeting the objective of the Gender Equality Strategy that called for the UNDP development contribution to be 'gender responsive'.

UNDP will therefore need to devote attention and significant resources if it is to make the attainment of deeper gender results a central objective of its next strategic plan and beyond. In this connection, the evaluation used two measurement instruments to assess the effectiveness and quality of development results: the Gender Results Effectiveness Scale and the Gender@Work framework. It is hoped that these instruments will prove useful to UNDP in deepening future assessments of its contributions to gender results.

Another area that will require attention is the application of a firm corporate policy to ensure that gender analysis is mandatory in all programming. Furthermore, UNDP will need to devote much more concerted attention to defining its thought leadership and strategic contribution in the area of gender. It should also explore new frontiers for engaging in gender issues that go beyond women's issues. Attaining gender parity at the critical middle levels of UNDP management is another area that will require vigilance. UNDP must also adopt a more active policy to address the organizational culture issues highlighted in the annual staff surveys. All of these will be crucial steps in achieving true gender equality.

UNDP is well positioned to take on these challenges. I hope the conclusions and recommendations of this evaluation provide useful pointers, particularly as the organization readies itself to undertake the midterm review of the current Strategic Plan as the first step in preparing the next one. This evaluation is part of an ongoing process of periodic assessments.

Indran A. Naidoo

Indran A. Naidoo
Director
Independent Evaluation Office of UNDP

TABLE OF CONTENTS

ACRONYMS

ADR	Assessment of Development Results
BCPR	Bureau for Conflict Prevention and Recovery
BDP	Bureau for Development Policy
BPPS	Bureau for Policy and Programme Support
CEDAW	Convention on the Elimination of All Forms of Discrimination against Women
DFID	UK Department for International Development
FAO	Food and Agriculture Organization of the United Nations
GEPMI	Global Gender and Economic Policy Management Initiative
GEF	Global Environment Facility
GES	Gender Equality Strategy
GEWE	Gender equality and women's empowerment
GSIC	Gender Steering Implementation Committee
GRES	Gender Results Effectiveness Scale
IDEA	Institute for Democracy and Electoral Assistance (Haiti)
IEO	Independent Evaluation Office
ILO	International Labour Organization
IUCN	International Union for Conservation of Nature
LDC	Least-developed country
MAF	MDG Acceleration Framework
MDG	Millennium Development Goal
NGO	Non-governmental organization
OECD	Organisation for Economic Co-operation and Development
OHR	Office of Human Resources
PBSO	Peacebuilding Support Office
RBA	Regional Bureau for Africa
RBAP	Regional Bureau for Asia Pacific
RBAS	Regional Bureau for Arab States
RBEC	Regional Bureau for Europe and the Commonwealth of Independent States
RBLAC	Regional Bureau for Latin America and the Caribbean
ROAR	Results-oriented Annual Report
UN	United Nations
UNCT	United Nations country team
UNFPA	United Nations Population Fund
UNICEF	United Nations Children's Fund
UNDP	United Nations Development Programme

UN-REDD	United Nations Collaborative Initiative on Reducing Emissions from Deforestation and Forest Degradation
UN-SWAP	UN System-wide Action Plan (on gender mainstreaming)
UN-Women	United Nations Entity for Gender Equality and Women's Empowerment
WEDO	Women's Environment and Development Organization
WID	Women in development

EXECUTIVE SUMMARY

INTRODUCTION

Gender equality remains a crucial and unfulfilled human right. Together with the empowerment of women, it is a major theme in the global commitments emerging from the world conferences of the 1990s and the first decade of the twenty-first century. These include the Millennium Declaration and Millennium Development Goals and their reviews; Security Council resolution 1325 (2000) on women, peace and security; and the United Nations 2005 World Summit. Gender equality is recognized as integral to successful human development.

In response, UNDP has adopted gender mainstreaming for all its activities across the board. It developed a Gender Equality Strategy for the period 2008–2013 aiming to: (a) develop capacities, in-country and in-house, to integrate gender concerns into all programmes and practice areas; (b) provide gender-responsive policy advisory services that promote gender equality and women's empowerment in all focus areas, including in country programmes, planning instruments and sector-wide programmes; and (c) support specific interventions that benefit women and scale up innovative models.

In 2014 and early 2015, the UNDP Independent Evaluation Office conducted a thematic evaluation of the UNDP contribution to gender equality and women's empowerment. The evaluation, undertaken in response to Executive Board decision 2010/15, used as its frames of reference the UNDP Strategic Plan, 2008–2013, approved by the Executive Board in 2008, and the Gender Equality Strategy, which was "designed to complement and reinforce [the] UNDP strategic plan … by defining in more detail how attention to gender equality and women's empowerment will strengthen action in all areas of our work".[i]

As the second IEO exercise[ii] dedicated to the theme, this evaluation assesses the overall performance of UNDP in mainstreaming gender and the organization's contribution to development results and institutional change in terms of gender equality and women's empowerment. The purposes of the evaluation are to: (a) provide substantive support to the Administrator's accountability function in reporting to the Executive Board; (b) support greater accountability to stakeholders and partners; (c) serve as a means of quality assurance for UNDP interventions; and (d) contribute to learning at corporate, regional and country levels.

BACKGROUND

The objectives of the evaluation were to: (a) assess the contributions of UNDP to gender equality and women's empowerment during the period 2008–2013; (b) assess the extent to which the gender equality strategy functioned as an integrating dimension in implementation of the Strategic Plan, 2008–2013; and (c) provide actionable recommendations of relevance to implementation of the current UNDP Gender Equality Strategy (2014–2017). In addition, it is expected that the findings, conclusions and recommendations of the evaluation will be relevant to formulation of both the next strategic plan and the next gender strategy.

---

i   UNDP, 'Empowered and Equal: Gender Equality Strategy 2008–2011', New York, 2008.

ii   The first was the 2006 'Evaluation of Gender Mainstreaming in UNDP'.

The scope of the evaluation is aligned with the vision of the 2008–2013 Strategic Plan. It addresses mainstreaming of gender at global, regional and country levels throughout the four UNDP focus areas of poverty reduction, democratic governance, crisis prevention and recovery, and energy and environment. The evaluation covers two distinct but interlinked results areas as framed in the strategy: development results and institutional results. Specifically, the evaluation assesses the extent to which the strategy functioned as "an integrating dimension of UNDP work"[iii] in implementation of the Strategic Plan. It is important to note that the strategy was framed as a means of providing guidance, so the evaluation does not address the content of the strategy as a stand-alone document. Instead, it is an inquiry into the extent to which the strategy played a role in guiding the institutional and development contributions that UNDP made to gender equality and women's empowerment during implementation of the Strategic Plan, 2008–2013.

The evaluation sought to answer the following questions:

(a) Has UNDP contributed to gender equality and women's empowerment development results?

    i.   How effective has UNDP been in contributing to development results being gender responsive?[iv]

    ii. To what extent has UNDP contributed to development results being gender transformative?[v]

    iii. What is the value added by UNDP in promoting gender equality and women's empowerment results?

    iv. How has UNDP used partnerships to promote gender equality and women's empowerment at the global, regional and national levels?

(b) Has UNDP integrated gender equality across the institution at the programme, policy, technical and cultural levels during the period 2008–2013?

    i.   How effective has UNDP been in implementing gender mainstreaming and contributing to institutional change results?

    ii. How effective has UNDP been in building in-house gender equality capacity and accountability frameworks?

    iii. To what extent is gender equality a priority in the culture and leadership of the organization?

(c) Where have UNDP's institutional change results been the most and least successful in improving gender equality and women's empowerment development results?

    i.   To what extent has UNDP gender mainstreaming strengthened the link between development results and institutional change?

    ii. What are the key factors contributing to successful gender equality and women's empowerment results?

    iii. To what extent has UNDP learned from past evaluation findings to strengthen gender equality results at the programme and institutional levels?

The evaluation also assessed UNDP's positioning in the area of gender and women's empowerment in relation to other United Nations agencies

---

iii   UNDP, 'Gender equality strategy 2008–2011', p. 2.

iv   Gender-responsive results address the differential needs of men and women and the equitable distribution of benefits, resources, status and rights, but they do not address the root causes of inequalities in their lives.

v   Gender-transformative results contribute to changes in norms, cultural values, power structures and the roots of gender inequalities and discrimination. The aim is to redefine systems and institutions where inequalities were created and maintained.

(United Nations Entity for Gender Equality and the Empowerment of Women [UN-Women] and others), and its contribution to advancing gender equality in the country context.

FINDINGS ON THE UNDP CONTRIBUTION TO GENDER EQUALITY AND WOMEN'S EMPOWERMENT (2008–2013)

ASSESSMENT OF INSTITUTIONAL CHANGE RESULTS IN UNDP

Planning and resources

The first UNDP Gender Equality Strategy was a significant step forward with regard to planning guidance on gender mainstreaming and programming. The strategy included programmatic and institutional guidance and a results framework, both of which are essential ingredients for strong gender mainstreaming. However, it was not endorsed by the Executive Board, making it a set of voluntary guidelines that weakened its potential impact and integration. In a context where there are multiple competing priorities, staff reported that they do not prioritize an issue unless a guidance document has been endorsed by the Executive Board or it is considered a mandatory and urgent directive from the Administrator.

UNDP did not establish clear, steady financial benchmarks and mechanisms in support of core gender team activities during 2008–2013.[vi] Despite a promising increase from $4.2 million in 2008 to an average of $6.13 million over the period 2009–2012, the expenditure of the Gender Unit was reduced to $4.16 million in 2013, a level even lower than that of 2008. In 2014, it was further reduced to $3.37 million. The expenditure of the Gender Unit also saw a growing share of non-core resources as a percentage of its budget, from 23 per cent in 2008 to 39 per cent in 2013. This also impacted the number of global team staff, which grew from 4 posts in 2006 to 23 posts in 2010, and then declined to 8 by 2013.

In terms of the gender architecture to support gender mainstreaming, gender practice leaders consistently were at the P-5 level in each regional bureau. Evidence suggests that the majority of country offices have received support from gender practice leaders and that this guidance has been valued. However, at the country level the gender function remained understaffed throughout the evaluation period. In 2013 only 45 per cent of country offices had gender focal team structures in place, signaling a relatively weak response to the indicators established in the Strategic Plan.

Previous evaluations and reports have pointed to a cross-unit gender focal team, led by a senior gender adviser, as the optimal arrangement in terms of promoting gender equality and women's empowerment. The evaluation found that gender focal points covered gender issues in 80 per cent of country offices. However, only 20 per cent of them worked full time on the issue, and these staff were at junior levels with little specialized gender training.

Innovations to promote gender mainstreaming

The Gender Strategy Implementation Committee (GSIC) is a mechanism that has evolved from a pro forma exercise to become a key instrument for senior managers at headquarters level to report on accountability for promoting gender equality. It has functioned mainly as a forum for sharing cross-bureau experiences. Regional GSICs, which were an explicit target in the strategy, have yet to become a uniform feature across all regions.

The Gender Equality Seal pilot is a unique initiative developed by UNDP and applied in around 30 country offices since 2010. The certification process has motivated staff and tapped a competitive vein among country offices volunteering to be part of the pilot process. While it is too soon to conduct a comprehensive assessment of the seal's impact on gender equality results, it is clear that it is motivating change and promoting gender mainstreaming as something tangible and achievable.

---

vi   It should be noted that during this period, there was an overall reduction in UNDP expenditures.

Tracking gender investments and reporting on results

The gender marker, which requires managers to rate projects on a four-point scale indicating their contribution to achievement of gender equality, was introduced in 2009. Making it mandatory at the budget submission stage has succeeded in heightening awareness of the need to consider gender at the initial budget allocation stage. Nevertheless, evidence suggests that the gender marker is not being used effectively as a planning tool and is disconnected from the workflow of the programme cycle. Furthermore, there are variations in the way the gender marker codes are assigned, which has compromised the accuracy of the information produced by this tool.

The Results-oriented Annual Report (ROAR) incorporated gender considerations beginning in 2008. As a mandatory requirement, it has become an important driver of promoting reporting on gender equality. However, this corporate reporting does not systematically track the quality or type of gender result. Nor has it systematically explored trends or how change happens in work on gender equality and women's empowerment.

Gender parity and organizational culture

UNDP has been working on internal gender parity issues since 1995 and has achieved gender parity at the aggregate level. However, it lags behind in parity at the senior (D-1/D-2) and middle management (P-4/P-5) levels, which is a serious concern. While many policies have been institutionalized to promote more female candidates, they have not yielded tangible results. Furthermore, no explicit steps are being taken to address the concerns of males about the effects of these pro-female policies on their career prospects.

While UNDP has instituted policies and mandatory mechanisms to promote gender equality and women's empowerment and sensitize staff on gender issues, its organizational culture of promoting these areas remains weak. Trends from the annual UNDP global staff survey indicate consistent differences in the way female and male staff members score issues dealing with empowerment, profes-sional growth, fairness/respect, work-life balance and conflict management. Women generally score these aspects less favourably than men.

Accountability and oversight

The 2009 UNDP handbook on planning, monitoring and evaluating for results does not provide adequate guidance on how to undertake gender-related evaluation and is limited to highlighting gender-targeting inputs such as the need for sex-disaggregated data. Furthermore, decentralized evaluations have not paid sufficient attention to ensuring that the gender dimensions of UNDP programmes are consistently covered in depth. In terms of audit, the practice of the Office of Audit and Investigations conforms to international standards based on risk assessment. The focus has been limited to assessing gender-parity levels in country offices, and there has been no systematic practice of undertaking gender-responsive audits.

Knowledge management and communication

UNDP developed a set of global and regional knowledge platforms and communities of practice on gender during the evaluation period, but these have not been sustained. The use of knowledge products was also not systematically tracked or monitored. Cybermetric analysis revealed that the UNDP network of websites is highly complex and potentially difficult for users to navigate overall. Furthermore, regional and country-level interviews stressed that the lack of gender materials in languages other than English posed a problem.

United Nations system coordination and partnerships on gender

UNDP country offices are members of United Nations country gender theme groups and participate in joint gender programmes. Evidence indicates, however, that programming in this context is still at a nascent stage in terms of the capacity of the United Nations system to absorb a joint modality. The relationship with UN-Women at country level is central to such coordination. As UN-Women establishes a firmer global footprint, a maturing partnership is emerging between the two agencies based on acknowledged comparative advantages that address country-specific contexts and needs.

With 62 entities currently participating, the United Nations System-wide Action Plan (UN-SWAP) on gender mainstreaming represents an advance in terms of accountability and coherence. While the framework relies on self-reported data and is susceptible to overrating, the UN-SWAP still provides a systematic means for collection of data on common performance indicators within UNDP and across the United Nations system. UNDP has been recognized by UN-Women as spearheading initiatives that propel progress on gender mainstreaming and gender equality.

ASSESSMENT OF THE UNDP CONTRIBUTION TO GENDER EQUALITY AND WOMEN'S EMPOWERMENT DEVELOPMENT RESULTS

OVERALL FINDINGS

To assess the effectiveness of gender results, the evaluation developed a five-point Gender Results Effectiveness Scale.[vii] Results from all focus areas except democratic governance were overwhelmingly gender targeted, limited to counting the number of women and men involved. Democratic governance was the only area that consistently

delivered on gender-responsive results (over 62 per cent), demonstrating more meaningful results by addressing the differential needs and priorities of women and men.

To assess the quality of gender results, the evaluation used the Gender@Work quadrants of change.[viii] With respect to the quality of gender results, the major UNDP contributions are in the areas of greater access to resources and opportunities; changed policies, laws and institutional arrangements; and strengthened consciousness and awareness-raising. A few results signal that UNDP has contributed to systemic changes in internal culture and deep structure, which are needed for transformative change.

UNDP faces many barriers to taking a strategic, longer term approach that would stimulate transformative change. Many project and programme cycles are short term, lasting a couple of years. UNDP tends to engage in programming that addresses practical needs for women and has not consistently leveraged the added value of its long-term presence in a country to tackle deeper structural change. Uniform categorizing for the capture and documenting of gender-responsive and gender-transformative change have also been challenging. Instances of backlash (barriers to or

---

vii Gender results effectiveness scale:

Gender negative: Result had a negative outcome that aggravated or reinforced gender inequalities and norms.

Gender blind: Result had no attention to gender and failed to acknowledge the different needs of men, women, girls and boys, or marginalized populations.

Gender targeted: Result focused on the number or equity (50/50) of women, men or marginalized populations that were targeted.

Gender responsive: Result addressed differential needs of men or women and equitable distribution of benefits, resources, status and rights but did not address root causes of inequalities in their lives.

Gender transformative: Result contributed to changes in norms, cultural values, power structures and the roots of gender inequalities and discriminations. The aim was to redefine systems and institutions where inequalities are created and maintained.

viii The Gender@Work framework draws from instruments developed by an international collaborative that helps organizations to build cultures of equality and social justice, with a focus on gender equality. The quadrants of change are:

Consciousness and awareness: Changes that occur in women's and men's consciousness, capacities and behaviour.

Access to resources and opportunities: Changes that occur in terms of access to resources, services and opportunities.

Formal policies, laws and institutional arrangements: Changes in terms of rules and adequate and gender-equitable policies and laws, which must be in place to protect against gender discrimination.

Informal cultural norms and deep structure: Changes in deep structure, implicit norms and social values that undergird the way institutions operate, often in invisible ways.

reversals of progress) were reported across all thematic areas, raising the issue of the sustainability of results. Gender analysis and monitoring and evaluation of gender results have not consistently tracked gender reversals.

The lack of gender analysis in programme design was evident in all focus areas. Dedicated funds are not regularly set aside for gender analysis at the design stage or for outcome monitoring and evaluation. Despite efforts to institutionalize gender thinking and the perception that the organization is now 'gender aware', the evaluation found a lack of deeper understanding of what gender means in relation to development programming. In practice, 'doing gender' in UNDP often comes down to a targeting perspective. Women are often framed in a context of vulnerability rather than as key actors in a transformative social and development change process.

UNDP is recognized for its ground-breaking and innovative contribution to human development through its Human Development Report and Gender Inequality Index. However, the evaluation found little evidence that UNDP has succeeded in integrating such thinking in programming at the country and regional levels. It is not recognized as a thought leader in the area of gender equality and women's empowerment, and it is more common for UNDP to be described as a facilitator, enabler and useful reference point on United Nations commitments.

GENDER RESULTS IN THE FOUR FOCUS AREAS OF THE STRATEGIC PLAN, 2008–2013

Poverty alleviation and achievement of the Millennium Development Goals. In the poverty portfolio, the majority of changes occurred in terms of increased access to resources and opportunities. Targeting women as the main beneficiaries of poverty reduction, often through microcredit and inclusive growth programmes, has rendered short-term results for gender equality and women's empowerment. In many cases, UNDP has lacked a comprehensive analysis that

paid attention to gender factors and dynamics that go beyond access to resources and opportunities. Success was more readily evident in programmes that adopted a long-term perspective.

In terms of increased knowledge and skills, the UNDP Global Gender and Economic Policy Management Initiative has provided capacity development and advisory services to government planning and policy experts. Data suggest that the initiative's approach is relevant and potentially sustainable, although further evidence is needed to assess its overall effectiveness and longer term impacts.

In terms of policy advice, UNDP developed and is currently implementing the Millennium Development Goal Acceleration Framework (MAF). This global approach aims to help countries overcome slow and uneven progress towards achievement of the Goals, including those on gender equality and women's empowerment and maternal health. To date, the MAF is present in over 50 countries, promoting gender equality in national action plans as well as in MAF planning processes.

UNDP programming in the area of HIV/AIDS has consistently advocated for a human development and human rights approach that strives to address deep change in cultural values and norms. It has also helped to move the HIV/AIDS paradigm away from a biomedical approach to one that addresses it as a broader development problem.

Democratic governance. The greatest change occurred in the outcome areas of policies, laws and arrangements. UNDP helped to strengthen national legal and institutional frameworks to advance women's rights, placing women and men on a more even footing. Compared to other focus areas, democratic governance had the most coverage in all of the four Gender@Work categories, supporting the potential for contributing to more gender-transformative results. Results in this area were more often gender responsive.

A shift in the consciousness and awareness of rights was a common result seen across UNDP programming in this area. A significant number of gender results were recorded with respect to changes in consciousness. Gender results were also prominent in the outcome area of access to resources and opportunities. By supporting women in political caucuses, providing access to civic education and establishing safe electoral spaces, UNDP has helped to open doors for women in the political realm. However, deeper shifts in attitudes and norms are needed to institutionalize both women's participation in political processes and equitable power distribution at a transformative level.

One of the factors that helps to explain the success in the democratic governance area has been UNDP's promotion of gender equality by using the neutrality of its mandate and its role as convener, knowledge broker, adviser and enabler supporting civil society, civic oversight actors and political parties as well as government. UNDP has done this in situations where there are high stakes and a multitude of actors with vested interests. However, not all results have been positive, and programmes that were well intended at times had negative consequences because of failure to analyse gender roles and power relations that would allow for full and equal participation of women. In other cases, despite the contribution of UNDP to creating an enabling environment, the presence of cultural norms and historical legacies of discrimination led to poor results.

Crisis prevention and recovery. Results from the Gender@Work framework found that overall gender results in crisis prevention and recovery contributed to changes in access to resources and opportunities, with programmes focused on gender-targeted economic recovery. Results in the areas of consciousness and policies were related to the UNDP role in raising sustainable development concerns and promoting income-generation activities that increased the productive role of women. In terms of promoting women's access to justice, UNDP succeeded in rebuilding legal structures and setting up support for survivors of sexual and gender-based violence. There were also instances of gender-blind programming with less positive results. The UNDP strategy known as the Eight-Point Agenda effectively formed the backbone of gender programming in crisis prevention and recovery and contributed to the Secretary-General's Seven-Point Action Plan on Gender-responsive Peacebuilding.

Energy and environment. Overall gender results for energy and environment were limited in all Gender@Work outcome areas. The results reported were largely gender-targeted increases in access to resources and opportunities. There were no changes in internal culture or deep structure, and very few changes relative to policies, laws and arrangements.

In 2012, UNDP adopted an environmental and social screening procedure for UNDP projects that addresses gender dimensions and fully complies with the Global Environment Facility (GEF) safeguards policy. The GEF standards seek to ensure that programmes do not cause undue harm to people or the environment. It is too early to make any conclusive assessment of whether programming has benefited from the gender dimensions of the screening procedure.

The GEF Small Grants Programme has reported good results in targeting gender issues. According to a recent evaluation, two thirds of the 30 country programme strategies reviewed have a relatively strong approach to addressing gender, including elaboration of the concrete steps that should be taken. The 2013 evaluation of the Global Gender and Climate Alliance found that significant progress had been made towards delivering the intended outcomes of the Alliance. Gender is now well reflected in the United Nations Framework Convention on Climate Change agreement texts and recognized as an official agenda item of the Conference of the Parties. It is also being included in the modalities for financing mechanisms. Furthermore, the foundation has been laid for delivering the intended outcomes through building capacities at regional and national levels. In contrast, a recent study on the United Nations collaborative initiative on Reducing Emissions from Deforestation and forest Degradation (REDD+) in developing countries, by Women Organizing for Change in Agriculture and Natural Resource Management, concludes that women are not key stakeholders or beneficiaries of REDD+ because of their invisibility in the forest sector.

CONCLUSIONS

Conclusion 1. There has been far-reaching change and a marked improvement in the UNDP approach to and implementation of policies to address gender mainstreaming since the last independent evaluation in 2006. UNDP has demonstrated greater awareness that gender matters to institutional and development results. It has produced a series of tools and established a number of institutional arrangements, which have helped to strengthen its contribution to gender equality and women's empowerment.

The first UNDP Gender Equality Strategy (2008–2013) was catalytic in promoting a number of instruments, tools and processes new to the organization since the 2006 evaluation of gender mainstreaming in UNDP. The GSIC, which is chaired by the Associate Administrator and involves all bureau heads, demonstrates senior-level attention and accountability. However, the extent to which GSIC deliberations and directions trickle down to influence staff in regional and country offices was less clear.

While the gender marker achieved global application, its contribution in terms of conveying valid gender-enlightened programming is uneven since there has been variability in its use and a lack of quality assurance. The Gender Seal certification pilot, which innovatively integrated institutional and programmatic aspects of gender mainstreaming, generated interest and deepened understanding that gender equality and women's empowerment will succeed only when it becomes an intrinsic part of the working life of every staff member.

Conclusion 2. While UNDP corporate messaging has highlighted the centrality of gender equality as having a multiplier effect across development results, it has yet to promote and fully resource gender as a main priority of the organization. Resource allocations dedicated to programming and staff to promote gender equality and women's empowerment decreased substantially during the period 2008–2014.

Dedicated resources at the global programme level for gender equality received an initial injection in 2009–2010 and declined in 2013 and 2014. Throughout the evaluation period, core allocations for gender were lower than for other focus areas. Non-core resources were also a significant part of the gender unit programming budget during the period 2008–2013.

While gender unit staffing reached a high of 23 posts in the early years of the strategic plan period, this had shrunk to 8 posts by 2013. In 80 per cent of UNDP country offices, gender is attended to by focal points who devote only 20 per cent of their time to this work. For gender equality to be recognized as a central priority of the organization, it must be consistently upheld as a point of departure for all core operating and programmatic engagements.

Conclusion 3. UNDP was only partially successful in meeting the objective of the Gender Equality Strategy that called for the UNDP development contribution to be gender responsive. The majority of results to which UNDP contributed were gender targeted. Furthermore, the finding that a small portion of results to which UNDP contributes could be described as gender transformative means that UNDP will need to make the attainment of deeper gender results a central objective of its next strategic plan and beyond. While the focus area of democratic governance has seen the most systematic progress in terms of contributing in a gender-responsive manner, the other three focus areas—poverty reduction and the Millennium Development Goals, crisis prevention and recovery, and energy and environment—will require concerted attention. Moving to resilient gender-transformative change will

require a longer lead time, and UNDP will need to make a sustained commitment, ensure adequate funding and undertake periodic quality checks and assessments of gender results, if it is to stay the course.

The evaluation found that the majority of UNDP gender results were gender targeted, meaning they most often focused on counting the number of men and women who participated in or benefited from programming in the areas of poverty, crisis prevention and environment. In contrast, nearly two thirds of results in the democratic governance focus area were gender responsive, addressing the different needs of women and men and the equitable distribution of benefits, but not the deeper root causes of inequalities in their lives. Very few gender-transformative results emerged from the analysis. This is understandable given that such results, which address the roots of inequalities and power imbalances, require time.

In terms of development results, UNDP had the most systematic approach and made the biggest difference in results in the areas of democratic governance and women's participation in political processes. Democratic governance had the most coverage in the four Gender@Work categories. This provides a promising foundation for contributing to more gender-transformative results in the future.

The other three focus areas will require concentrated support and attention to make progress on the continuum from gender-targeted to gender-transformative contributions supported by UNDP. In terms of poverty reduction, most results were gender targeted in nature, limited to mentioning the percentage of women and men who had benefited, with attention focused on women's economic empowerment at an individual level and in a few instances on the integration of gender considerations in the Millennium Development Goal processes.

Of the four focus areas, crisis prevention and recovery had the lowest number of gender results reported. Along with contributions in gender-targeted economic recovery, the integration of gender equality considerations in disaster risk management and attention to sexual and gender-based violence appear to be the most consistent areas of attention in the crisis prevention and recovery portfolio. The area of environment and energy reported the second lowest number of gender results. In community-based energy and environment projects, gender has not received broad-based, even attention and generally has been limited to the participation of women.

Conclusion 4. Pathways to achieving gender results are complex and depend on a variety of institutional and contextual factors. The evaluation learned that demonstrating a direct correlation between UNDP institutional reforms and development results was challenging for a number of reasons. Data constraints posed a key problem, but the far more important factor was the complexity of gender programming. Complexity is intrinsic to such programming, which addresses issues that are deeply rooted in cultural mores, values and belief systems at both the individual and societal levels, and where much of the achievement of results is dependent on factors outside the control of UNDP.

At a basic level, when gender mainstreaming was integrated into programming and addressed the differential needs, status and roles of women and men, it was more likely that the programme yielded gendered development results. When gender analysis and mainstreaming were lacking, it was more likely that gender-negative, gender-blind or gender-targeted results occurred.

Internal factors associated with gendered development results were attributable to leadership commitment, particularly at the country level, and to accountability structures, gender-enlightened staff with a rights-based mindset, and dedicated gender units promoting and monitoring performance. Other examples of the link between institutional and gendered development results were seen in programming which explicitly recognized and developed capacities to ensure that all stakeholders could consider themselves gender experts, which then were applied to programming and policy work. These programmes also actively sought to engage community members and women's groups in programme design and activities. Other programming elements included selecting partners who were gender aware and strategically adapting programming based on the changing needs on the ground.

An analysis of assessment of development results reports of 10 country offices with institutional results classified as gender responsive or gender transformative found that 8 of these country offices also had gendered development results. In all of these cases, gender-responsive or gender-transformative results were in the democratic governance focus area.

The evaluation found that some of the external factors of prime importance to gendered development results beyond the direct influence of UNDP included the sociopolitical context, national and donor interest, and the presence of opportunities as well as backlash (which often affected the timing and trajectory of progress on results). Working in a country context where the government was open to or supportive of gender equality and women's empowerment created an enabling environment for gendered development programming. This was considered a factor in some of the countries that were early winners of the Gold Seal in the Gender Equality Seal certification pilot. The presence of strong women's movements and civil society groups that advocated on behalf of gender issues was also key to gains in terms of development results that promoted gender equality and women's empowerment.

Conclusion 5. UNDP has yet to develop a firm corporate policy which ensures that gender analysis is a mandatory requirement in all programming. The lack of gender analysis explains to some extent why so many UNDP gender results are gender targeted, gender negative or gender blind. The tools and processes to make gender equality and women's empowerment relevant to the work of staff members in programme design, implementation, monitoring and evaluation have also not been sufficiently developed and applied. The gender marker and the ROAR, as well as monitoring and evaluation, require further refinements and a more consistent application if UNDP is to increase the quality of its gender interventions, reporting and the assessment of its contributions.

Programming for gender equality and women's empowerment requires strong, context-specific analysis in order to identify possible unintended effects and understand the potential for backlash when advances are made. These analyses should be evident at the country programme level and also in individual programme and project interventions. In this connection, the gender marker has the potential to play a useful role at the design and appraisal stage and during monitoring, assessment and evaluation.

Although the gender marker is used primarily to track trends in gender mainstreaming in UNDP programmes, it also aims to improve overall UNDP reporting and accountability on gender equality through tracking of budgeting and expenditures for gender equality results. However, as currently used, it does not capture financial expenditures and allocations in a consistent and reliable manner. Aggregation of the amounts of resources dedicated to gender equality does not provide a clear enough picture of how the resources are allocated and used. If it is to fulfil the goal of tracking expenditure, improving accountability and enhancing transparency, UNDP has yet to develop clear guidelines on how to allocate gender marker ratings at the project and country programme outcome levels, and ensure there is a clear, organization-wide understanding of how to apply this guidance. Better gender analysis and consistent gender marker practice could help to ensure that both the decentralized and independent evaluation functions, as well as audit, have a sounder basis for assessing the contribution of UNDP to gender equality and women's empowerment.

Conclusion 6. UNDP has demonstrated that the goal of gender parity is important, although results up to this point remain at a gender-targeted level. Gender parity has been successful in terms of equitable numbers of men and women occupying the lowest and highest positions in the organization. However, at the critical middle levels (P-4/P-5 and D-1/D-2), parity has not been achieved. Men enter the organization at higher levels and get promoted more quickly than women. The culture and unwritten rules about who gets promoted and valued, and whose voices are heard, require deeper attention to truly achieve gender equality.

Although the gender parity strategy is a step in the right direction in trying to address concerns, there is a lack of deeper analysis. Reflection that goes beyond a parity focus will be necessary if the organization is to arrive at a more complete picture of the power relationships and gender dynamics that are at play. The data from the annual global staff surveys consistently show gaps between men's and women's positive experiences with respect to empowerment, professional growth, openness, fairness/respect, work-life balance and office management. Gender parity is generally reported at the aggregate level at both the regional and headquarters levels, which may obscure a more differentiated picture of the situation in individual country offices and units.

Conclusion 7. Although UNDP has a historically close and often collaborative relationship with UN-Women that has matured as UN-Women has reorganized its organizational footprint globally, there is room for further clarification of partnership arrangements. UNDP has yet to define and communicate its comparative strengths on gender issues to ensure that its interventions are strategic and add value. The headquarters of both agencies could facilitate the clarification process, which ideally should also take place in regional and country contexts.

Formally clarifying the relationship between UNDP and UN-Women and specifying each agency's comparative strengths and different entry points could help to ensure smoother working relationships at all levels of both organizations. This should help both agencies to establish working arrangements, particularly in areas where they address similar development challenges and can add significant value to each other's initiatives. The establishment of improved working arrangements needs to acknowledge that a one-size-fits-all approach will be inadequate and that partnership is based on mutual understanding and a clear appreciation of contextual factors. Successful cases of joint initiatives could inform this process. These could also provide an opportunity for UNDP to communicate its thought leadership on and contributions to gender equality and women's empowerment to national governments, partners and donors.

RECOMMENDATIONS

Recommendation 1. UNDP should align its resources and programming with its corporate message on the centrality of supporting gender equality and women's empowerment as a means to 'fast forward' development results. Gender mainstreaming should also go beyond providing sex-disaggregated data for all results areas of the strategic plan. In this connection, the merits of integrating the gender equality strategy as part of the next strategic plan (2018 onwards) should receive serious consideration.

Given that the vision of UNDP is to achieve the simultaneous eradication of poverty and significant reduction of inequalities and exclusion, the organization should systematically undertake programming that addresses all facets of gender-based discrimination. UNDP needs to make further efforts to institutionalize a more complete understanding of gender, gender equality and women's empowerment that goes beyond targeting and be able to report accurately on financial allocations and expenditures on gender. If the gender marker is not suited for this level of specificity, it is recommended that a new tracking and benchmark system be established. Furthermore, as specific financial benchmarks have been established in the current UNDP gender equality strategy, 2014–2017, these should be closely monitored and reported to the Executive Board.

Moreover, UNDP should assess the merits and demerits of integrating the Strategic Plan and the Gender Equality Strategy and making key gender results mandatory. Additionally, guidance documents that promote alignment between the Strategic Plan and country programme documents should require a gender analysis to be done for all programming developed within country programmes that set out medium-term objectives (over a 5-10 year period) along with other contextual analyses. The gender analysis done in the country programme context should have corresponding indicators and monitoring, assessment and evaluation mechanisms at programme and project levels.

Deeper attention to gender equality issues and gender mainstreaming is required, especially in the focus areas on conflict prevention and recovery and energy and environment, which saw the lowest number of gender results and the highest rates of targeting. Work in the focus areas on poverty and the Millennium Development Goals and democratic governance can deepen intentions and action towards gender-responsive and gender-transformative results. All UNDP programming and policies should be attentive to framing women as agents and active citizens. If UNDP aims to contribute to transformative change, it will need to accelerate efforts in all focus areas to more strategically target the roots of inequalities, structures of unequal power, participation and relations, and address and transform unequal norms, values and policies.

Management Response: *The UNDP Strategic Plan, 2014–2017 has strongly integrated gender equality across its Integrated Results and Resources Framework (IRRF). In addition to a dedicated outcome for accelerating gender equality, it has mainstreamed gender equality across all other outcomes. The new Gender Equality Strategy, 2014–2017 is* *an accompaniment to the Strategic Plan and looks at how to mainstream gender in all outcomes of the plan. The strategy, which was approved by the Executive Board, has made financial and human resource commitments to ensure that gender mainstreaming is adequately resourced. This includes as a principal objective meeting the United Nations system-wide financial target of allocating 15 per cent of the organization's resources towards gender equality by 2017. The gender marker is tracking UNDP investments on gender and is aligned to UN-SWAP principles and standards. The gender marker is now being used as an accountability tool in the GSIC to track progress towards the 15 per cent target. UNDP will integrate the 15 per cent financial commitment into the guidelines for trust fund allocations, work with IEO to improve its evaluation of gender outcomes and draw on the gender marker findings. The merits of integrating the gender equality strategy into the next strategic plan (2018 onwards) will be considered as part of the midterm review of the current Strategic Plan, 2014–2017. Additionally, new quality assurance tools are being developed to ensure that gender analysis is integrated in all country programmes and programme documents. The text under this recommendation also suggested that UNDP strengthen its work on the crisis prevention and recovery and energy and environment focus areas. Tools and work processes will be developed to address this recommendation.*

Actions: *UNDP will expand the GSIC forum to include all central and regional bureaux, the Human Development Report Office and all professional homes, and utilize tools such as the gender marker to monitor compliance with corporate mandates and resource targets. The gender marker data will be broken down by region and Strategic Plan outcomes and outputs to make it a more precise monitoring tool. The gender marker data will also be incorporated into the corporate planning system. Improvements will be made to the gender marker to improve accuracy (please see key actions under recommendation 3). The merits of integrating the gender equality strategy into the strategic plan from 2018 onwards will be considered based on findings of the midterm review of the Strategic Plan, 2014–2017. UNDP standard operating procedures in crisis contexts, surge* and express staff rosters (terms of reference, capacities, training) and crisis response tools all are being reviewed to ensure that GEWE can be addressed at the onset of crises. To support the integration of gender in energy and environment programming, UNDP will develop: (a) a toolkit for UNDP staff on mainstreaming gender in environment programming; (b) a gender toolkit for GEF projects; and (c) tools for integrating gender into disaster preparedness and response.

Recommendation 2. Given the uneven performance in the four focus areas of the Strategic Plan, 2008–2013 in promoting gender development results, UNDP should ensure that future assessments pay specific attention to the progress, effectiveness and quality of gender development results in the seven outcome areas of the current strategic plan.

The upcoming midterm review of the Strategic Plan, 2014–2017 presents an opportunity to set in place a framework for such an assessment. The assessment can build on the limited data from the IRRF report cards that summarize UNDP progress and performance in 2014 and include a deeper, qualitative analysis of the UNDP contribution to gender results on the ground. Preliminary lessons of the Gender Equality Seal certification process, which has been completed in 28 country offices (and implemented on a non-certification basis in others) could also be a rich source of information.

Management Response: UNDP welcomes this recommendation and will develop guidelines for integrating gender development results in thematic assessments including reviews, and will work with IEO to improve the integration of gender in all evaluations.

Actions: Guidelines for integrating gender in reviews, assessments, decentralized and independent evaluations (drawing on existing tools including the IRRF, gender marker, etc.,) will be developed.

Recommendation 3. UNDP should focus on refining tools, instruments and processes

developed during the period 2008–2013 and focus on further internalizing the centrality of gender equality and women's empowerment to the achievement of all development goals among staff. Specific recommendations on these improvements and possible new areas of intervention are discussed below:

- **Gender analysis should become mandatory in all programming and be linked with justifying the gender marker rating of each UNDP intervention.** Revised gender marker guidance (2014) indicates that ideally a gender analysis should be done during the project design, before the coding, to determine the most effective strategies in a particular context and to identify results that support gender equality. However, gender analysis should go beyond being optional and become a required first step. This will contribute to more context-specific gender assessment and will minimize inaccurate gender marker ratings that will enhance the credibility of this tool. Furthermore, such analysis should specify the areas of change and the role and contribution of UNDP in the change process, on the spectrum from gender blind to gender transformative;

- **The gender marker should track allocations in a way that provides reliable aggregated data at different stages of the project cycle.** It should be subject to random external checks and also be systematically assessed by internal audit exercises. The new guidance should be monitored and assessed on an annual basis to make this a reliable instrument to measure progress in terms of UNDP programming. Furthermore, if the gender marker is not suited for tracking expenditures with a credible level of specificity at the project and outcome levels, it is recommended that consideration be given to developing a new tracking and benchmark system. Added benefits of an improved gender marker system could be its greater use for resource mobilization, accountability, gender-responsive budgeting and gender-informed management decision-making;

- **The Gender Seal requires senior management's attention in terms of its future role as a corporate certification initiative.** To facilitate this process, the Gender Seal pilot should be assessed by a team of independent advisers to guide its application as it enters a critical post-pilot phase. Such an assessment could be of value in documenting and assessing the pilot process. This could include aspects such as the methodology, the resources required and the sustainability of the Gender Seal country interventions (including recertification), and explore institutionalizing different options to the standard gold, silver and bronze seal process. The focus should be on lessons learned that should inform the choices, costs, opportunities and downsides the Gender Seal may encounter as it moves into post-pilot implementation. The Gender Seal approach could also be extended to national ministries and partners where opportunities, interest and needs are expressed;

- **Stronger attention should be placed on using the GSIC forum as a venue for organization-wide learning, problem solving and sharing of instructive practices.** All key organizational entities in UNDP should provide reports on progress in promoting gender equality and women's empowerment and participate in discussions during annual 'gender days'. The GSIC should play a more active role in assessing UNDP reporting to the UN-SWAP and taking stock of feedback received (from UN-Women) on UNDP performance in the UN-SWAP process. This should facilitate the review of instructive practices from other organizations that may be applied in UNDP. Additionally, there is a need to revitalize the functioning of regional GSICs as envisaged in the gender equality strategy (2008–2013). Consideration should be given to having a mandatory agenda item in regional bureaux cluster meetings on a regular basis;

- **The GSIC should ensure that the gender parity strategy is revised and a roll-out programme is articulated.** Attention should be paid to addressing the concerns expressed in the global staff surveys and in terms of the gaps between men's and women's positive experiences with respect to empowerment, professional growth, openness, fairness, respect, work-life balance and office management. Annual reports to the Executive Board should include more detailed information on problems and progress in terms of achieving parity targets and actions. It may also help to rename the strategy to signal a 'beyond parity' approach to addressing staff culture and morale;

- **UNDP should strengthen capacity development processes that focus on gender mainstreaming so they are relevant and apply to staff's daily work and needs.** Online training courses should be independently assessed to determine whether they are useful and should be continued. In addition, the mentorship programming implemented in the regional bureaux for Africa and Asia and the Pacific and the leadership programmes being made available are examples of targeted investments with coaching and benchmarks. The efficacy and impact of these recent initiatives should be carefully tracked, assessed and reported to the GSIC. Other initiatives for capacity-building and awareness development could include unit or country office training plans with focused gender sessions that encourage lively and open discussions and debates, and include critical analysis of the portrayal of men and women in the media, discussion of current events and guest lectures;

- **UNDP should consider exploring new frontiers for engaging in gender issues that go beyond women's issues, for example the 'masculinity' agenda.** UNDP should engage more fully in working with men and other populations that suffer from gender discrimination and consider undertaking research that addresses how exclusion negatively affects progress in development.

Management Response: UNDP management appreciates the recognition of past efforts, and notes that UNDP will continue to refine tools, instruments and processes with a focus on internalizing gender equality and women's empowerment towards the achievement of development goals.

■ *UNDP will ensure that **gender analysis is linked with the gender marker rating** of every UNDP intervention by integrating this analysis in existing and upcoming mandatory programme/project planning, monitoring and assessment processes such as programme/project quality assurance, social and environmental screening and revision of the project document.*

Actions: Mandatory environmental and social screening procedures will be established for all projects above $500,000 to ensure they have gender equality as a key principal. Gender analysis is a requirement of the mandatory project quality assurance process. Quality assurance guidelines for all country programmes and global/regional programmes will address GEWE.

■ *UNDP will include in the revised **gender marker** guidance note provisions for random assessments and integrated into internal audit exercises.*

Actions: The gender marker guidance note will be revised to provide more specific guidance to improve gender marker accuracy. The gender marker rating will be included in the cover note for project documents and integrated in the quality assurance guidelines. A sample of random gender marker audits will be undertaken each year to improve accuracy (ensuring regional balance). Guidelines for integrating gender in reviews, assessments, evaluations and audits (drawing on existing tools including IRRF, gender marker, etc.) will be developed.

■ *Management appreciates the recognition that the **Gender Equality Seal** approach can be of value to national ministries. UNDP welcomes and agrees with the recommendation for independent assessments to review, document and improve upon the experiences of the Gender Equality Seal.*

Actions: Independent assessment will be undertaken of the Gender Equality Seal to review, document and improve the tool.

■ *UNDP appreciates the recommendation for the **GSIC** to become a venue for learning, finding solutions and sharing of practices. UNDP has expanded the membership of the GSIC, and for the first time in 2015, all UNDP bureaux reported gender equality progress and results, shared lessons learned and identified overall and bureau-specific recommendations to take forward.*

Actions: The GSIC will continue to be strengthened with all bureaux reporting. Accountability tools such as the gender marker, ROAR data and gender parity data will inform its meetings. Its recommendations will be presented to the Executive Group to be reviewed for implementation by GSIC. It will refresh the UNDP gender parity strategy with a view to achieving a more holistic approach to gender parity issues in UNDP.

■ *UNDP agrees on the importance of **capacity development for gender mainstreaming** and will improve existing and upcoming training tools by including gender content.*

Actions: UNDP will review and improve training tools for policy and programme staff on gender mainstreaming in programming, monitoring and reporting. Greater focus will be put on improving capacity for gender analysis, accuracy and consistency in gender marker ratings and gender in areas of profession.

■ *UNDP will consider exploring new frontiers for **engaging in gender issues** that go beyond women's issues, for example the 'masculinity' agenda.*

Actions: UNDP plans to undertake research on 'masculinities' to better understand the linkages between masculinities and gender inequality, specifically gender-based violence.

Recommendation 4. Country offices should prepare gender plans that identify gaps and needs in technical support, capacity-building, joint action and advocacy, and collective monitoring that facilitate stronger gender programming. These plans should also help to identify areas where UNDP can draw on expertise and leverage the existing capacities of other United Nations agencies active on gender issues at

the country level. This process should be supported, monitored and reported upon annually by the respective regional bureaux to the GSIC.

Gender-capacity benchmarks have been set by the Executive Board in terms of in-country gender expertise, a welcome development that should promote better gender analysis, programming and results in the 40 countries that meet the criteria. However, to ensure more even attention to all countries and because country offices are expected to prepare gender plans, it is suggested that regional bureaux take specific measures to support the preparation of these multi-year, country-specific gender plans and monitor and report on their formulation and implementation to the GSIC. This process will provide an opportunity for offices to assess their needs and gaps at the country level and to articulate expectations for support from the regional service centres in promoting gender equality and women's empowerment.

Additionally, these plans may provide an opportunity for UNDP to define its comparative strengths in contributing to gender equality and women's empowerment and to explore partnerships with United Nations agencies, in particular the United Nations Children's Fund, the United Nations Population Fund and UN-Women (see conclusion 7 above for more details with reference to UN-Women).

Management Response: The Gender Equality Seal certification is the primary tool for strengthening country office capacity and ensuring collective monitoring for stronger gender programming. Currently, 29 countries have undertaken the Gender Seal certification process. This will be expanded to more countries. Regional bureaux and the GSIC will draw upon committee benchmarking to measure progress.

Actions: Gender Equality Seal benchmarking will be completed by all country offices in Africa and utilized as a tool for monitoring gender capacity. The next phase of the GSIC initiative will be launched, with approximately 30 country offices to be certified.

Recommendation 5. UNDP currently does not have a measurement standard to systematically track the type, quality and effectiveness of its contribution to gender results that also captures the context of change and the degree of its contribution to that change. In order to address this issue, UNDP should codify the way it wishes to monitor, report, evaluate and audit its contributions to gender, and this framework should be used for rigorously tracking results for gender equality and women's empowerment at the country, regional and global levels.

Overall, UNDP is currently using a number of different metrics, which may confuse rather than clarify future efforts for gender equality and women's empowerment. Action should be taken to harmonize various assessment scales in a manner that is most meaningful for corporate programming, reporting, evaluation and audit. These elements should be embedded in iterative learning systems that go beyond linear performance frameworks, which are limited to reporting on indicators focusing on sex-disaggregated data.

More attention to the quality of gender results and the context within which changes happen is required in UNDP monitoring and assessment systems. UNDP may want to reflect on the usefulness of having quality and type measures such as the Gender Results Effectiveness Scale and Gender@Work frameworks used in the evaluation. This would help to move beyond the tendency to focus on numbers of women and men and targeting strategies to more responsive and transformative results. The practice of gender audits should also become a more standard feature throughout the organization.

While UNDP has made significant improvements in tracking gender results at the country level through the ROAR, the system has limitations in terms of capturing diverse and non-linear change, which is often characterized as a 'two steps forward, one step back' phenomenon. UNDP should start systematically to track the types of organizations with which it partners to have a comprehensive picture of its partnerships at the global, regional and country levels. Monitoring and assessment should include tracking of backlash and efforts to maintain past gains and identify accelerators and barriers to change to better contextualize change processes and learn from what is working under different conditions and contexts. This will help UNDP to articulate its role, most importantly at the country level, which will remain the primary unit of analysis in terms of assessing the short-, medium- and long-term contribution of UNDP to gender equality and women's empowerment.

Management Response: *UNDP believes that it has a range of tools for measuring progress that are used for different purposes. These comply with a range of different inter-agency standards. Taken together, these give a good view of the gender mainstreaming taking place in a given business unit. However, management will take forward the recommendation* *to consider adopting measures such as the Gender@ Work framework to move beyond a focus on numbers of women and men towards more transformative results is worth consideration.*

Actions: *UNDP will begin an internal dialogue bringing experts from the Gender@Work network to explore how the organization can move beyond a focus on numbers of women and men towards more transformative results. This will include the development of a capacity-building strategy to support country offices and accelerate changes. In developing its monitoring policy, UNDP will integrate provisions for systematic tracking of the type, quality and effectiveness of its contribution to gender results. UNDP will bring the Gender@Work framework to be discussed at GSIC meetings. The feasibility of the Gender@Work framework to become part of the UNDP results-based management policy and processes to be considered in the midterm review of the Strategic Plan, 2013–2017.*

GENDER EQUITY TIMELINE

A snapshot of key developments in the international arena from 1948 through 2013

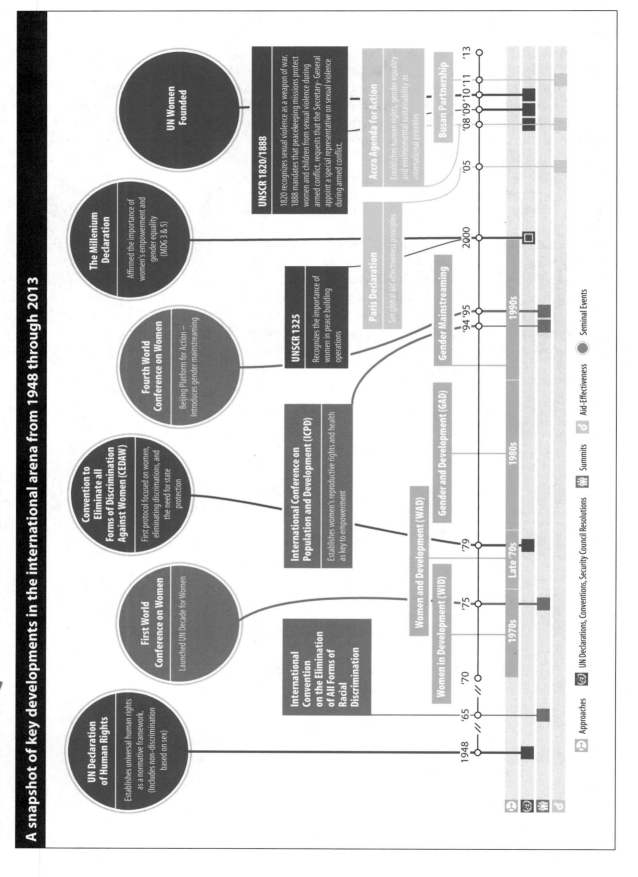

UN Declaration of Human Rights
Establishes universal human rights as a normative framework. (Includes non-discrimination based on sex)

First World Conference on Women
Launched UN Decade for Women

Convention to Eliminate all Forms of Discrimination Against Women (CEDAW)
First protocol focused on women, eliminating discriminations, and the need for state protection

Fourth World Conference on Women
Beijing Platform for Action — Introduces gender mainstreaming

The Millennium Declaration
Affirmed the importance of women's empowerment and gender equality (MDG 3 & 5)

UN Women Founded

International Convention on the Elimination of All Forms of Racial Discrimination

International Conference on Population and Development (ICPD)
Establishes women's reproductive rights and health as key to empowerment

UNSCR 1325
Recognizes the importance of women in peace building operations

UNSCR 1820/1888
1820 recognizes sexual violence as a weapon of war. 1888 mandates that peacekeeping missions protect women and children from sexual violence during armed conflict, requests that the Secretary-General appoint a special representative on sexual violence during armed conflict.

Paris Declaration
Set global aid effectiveness principles

Accra Agenda for Action
Establishes human rights, gender equality and environmental sustainability as international priorities

Busan Partnership

Women in Development (WID)

Women and Development (WAD)

Gender and Development (GAD)

Gender Mainstreaming

1948 | '65 | '70 | '75 | '79 | '94 | '95 | 2000 | '05 | '08 '09 '10 '11 | '13

1970s | Late '70s | 1980s | 1990s

Approaches | UN Declarations, Conventions, Security Council Resolutions | Summits | Aid-Effectiveness | Seminal Events

A snapshot of key developments in UNDP from 1975 through 2013

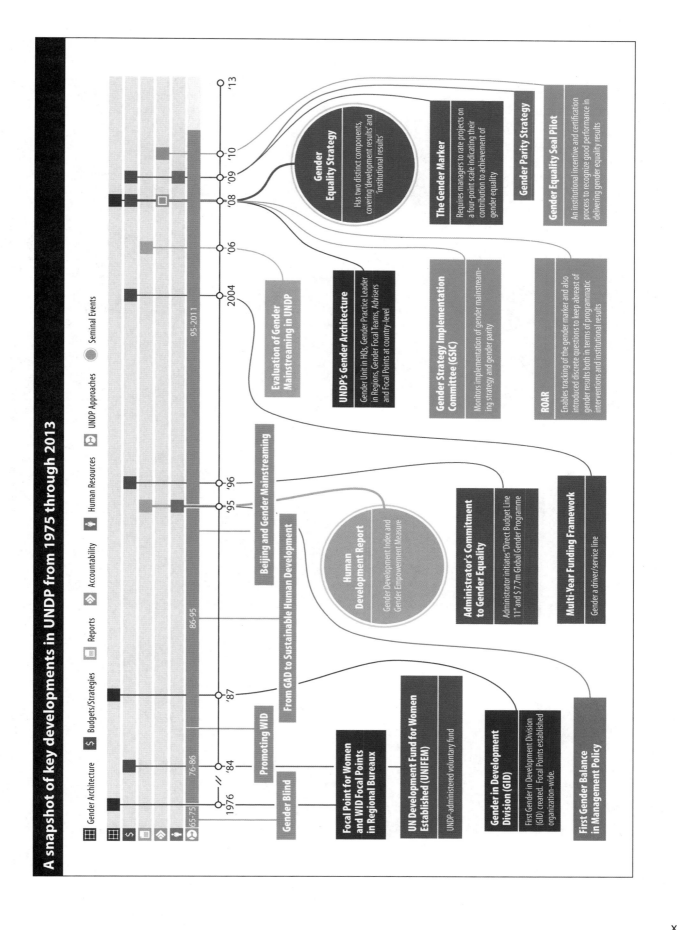

Gender Architecture | Budgets/Strategies | Reports | Accountability | Human Resources | UNDP Approaches | Seminal Events

Gender Equality Strategy
Has two distinct components, covering development results and institutional results

The Gender Marker
Requires managers to rate projects on a four-point scale indicating their contribution to achievement of gender equality

Gender Parity Strategy

Gender Equality Seal Pilot
An institutional incentive and certification process to recognize good performance in delivering gender equality results

Evaluation of Gender Mainstreaming in UNDP

UNDP's Gender Architecture
Gender Unit in HQs, Gender Practice Leader in Regions, Gender Focal Teams, Advisers and Focal Points at country-level

Gender Strategy Implementation Committee (GSIC)
Monitors implementation of gender mainstreaming strategy and gender parity

ROAR
Enables tracking of the gender marker and also introduced discrete questions to keep abreast of gender results both in terms of programmatic interventions and institutional results

Beijing and Gender Mainstreaming

Human Development Report
Gender Development Index and Gender Empowerment Measure

Administrator's Commitment to Gender Equality
Administrator initiates "Direct Budget Line 11" and $ 7.7m Global Gender Programme

Multi-Year Funding Framework
Gender a driver/service line

From GAD to Sustainable Human Development

Promoting WID

Focal Point for Women and WID Focal Points in Regional Bureaux

UN Development Fund for Women Established (UNIFEM)
UNDP-administered voluntary fund

Gender in Development Division (GID)
First Gender in Development Division (GID) created. Focal Points established organization-wide.

First Gender Balance in Management Policy

Gender Blind

1976 '84 '87 '95 '96 2004 '06 '08 '09 '10 '13

65-75 76-86 86-95 95-2011

Chapter 1

INTRODUCTION

1.1 BACKGROUND

Gender equality remains a crucial and unfulfilled human right. Together with the empowerment of women, it is a major theme in the global commitments emerging from the world conferences of the 1990s and the first decade of the twenty-first century, including the Millennium Declaration and Millennium Development Goals and their reviews; Security Council Resolution 1325; and the UN World Summit of 2005. Gender equality is recognized as integral to successful human development.

UNDP's response to the gender equality mandate was to adopt gender mainstreaming for all its activities across the board and develop a Gender Equality Strategy (GES) for the period 2008–2013. It aims to (a) develop capacities, in country and in house, to integrate gender concerns into all programmes and practice areas; (b) provide gender-responsive policy advisory services that promote gender equality and women's empowerment (GEWE) in all focus areas, including in-country programmes, planning instruments and sector-wide programmes; and (c) support specific interventions that benefit women and scale up innovative models.

In 2014 and early 2015, the Independent Evaluation Office (IEO) of the United Nations Development Programme (UNDP) conducted a thematic evaluation of the contribution of UNDP to GEWE. (It was the second IEO exercise dedicated to the theme; the first, an evaluation of gender mainstreaming, was in 2006). The evaluation took place at the request of the UNDP Executive Board at its annual session in June 2010.[1]

The frames of reference for the evaluation were the UNDP Strategic Plan 2008–2013 and the GES, which was "designed to complement and reinforce UNDP's Strategic Plan … by defining in more detail how attention to gender equality and women's empowerment will strengthen action in all areas of our work."[2] This evaluation assesses UNDP's overall performance in mainstreaming gender and the organization's contribution to development results and institutional change in terms of GEWE. The purposes of the evaluation are to:

- Provide substantive support to the Administrator's accountability function in reporting to the Executive Board

- Support greater UNDP accountability to stakeholders and partners

- Serve as a means of quality assurance for UNDP interventions

- Contribute to learning at corporate, regional and country levels.

1.2 OBJECTIVES AND SCOPE OF THE EVALUATION

The primary objectives of the evaluation were to:

- Assess UNDP's contributions to GEWE during the period 2008–2013

- Assess the extent to which the GES functioned as an integrating dimension in implementation of the Strategic Plan

- Provide actionable recommendations of relevance to implementation of UNDP's new

---

1   UNDP, Executive Board decision 2010/15 regarding proposed evaluation programme of work in DP/2010/19/.

2   UNDP, 'Empowered and Equal: Gender Equality Strategy 2008–2011', foreword.

Gender Equality Strategy, which covers 2014 to 2017.

The findings, conclusions and recommendations of the evaluation are also expected to inform the development of the next strategic plan and gender strategy.

The scope of the evaluation is aligned with the Strategic Plan's vision of mainstreaming gender throughout the four UNDP focus areas—poverty reduction, democratic governance, crisis prevention and recovery, and energy and environment—at the global, regional and country levels. The evaluation covers two distinct but linked results areas as framed in the GES: development results and institutional results. Specifically, the evaluation assesses the extent to which the GES functioned as "an integrating dimension of UNDP's work"[3] in implementing the Strategic Plan.

It is important to note that since the GES was framed as a source of guidance, the evaluation does not address the content of the GES as a stand-alone document. Instead, it serves as an inquiry of the extent to which the GES played a role in guiding the institutional and development contributions UNDP made to GEWE during the implementation of the 2008–2013 Strategic Plan.

The evaluation seeks to answer three broad evaluation questions:

1. **Has UNDP contributed to GEWE development results?**

   - How effective has UNDP been in contributing to development results being gender responsive?[4]

   - To what extent has UNDP contributed to development results being gender transformative?[5]

   - What is UNDP's value added in promoting GEWE results?

   - How has UNDP used partnerships to promote GEWE at global, regional and national level?

2. **Has UNDP integrated gender equality across the institution at the programme, policy, technical and cultural levels during the period 2008–2013?**

   - How effective has UNDP been in implementing gender mainstreaming and contributing to institutional change results?

   - How effective has UNDP been in building in-house gender equality capacity and accountability frameworks?

   - To what extent is gender equality a priority in the culture and leadership of the organization?

3. **Where have UNDP's institutional change results been the most and least successful in improving GEWE development results?**

   - To what extent has UNDP's gender mainstreaming strengthened the link between development results and institutional change?

   - What are the key factors contributing to successful GEWE results?

   - To what extent has UNDP learned from past evaluation findings to strengthen gender equality results at the programme and institutional levels?

Attention was placed on assessing UNDP's positioning and comparative advantage in the area of gender and women's empowerment in relation to other UN agencies, including the United Nations Entity for Gender Equality and the

---

3 UNDP, Ibid., p. 2.

4 Gender responsiveness implies consciously creating an environment that reflects an understanding of the realities of the lives of women or men within their social setting.

5 Making results gender transformative means considering not only symptoms of gender inequality but also how to produce results that address the social norms, behaviours and social systems that underlie them.

Empowerment of Women (UN-Women), and on how UNDP contributes to the UN's collective vision for advancing gender equality in the country context. Complementarities between agencies, efficient division of labour and strategic exchange of information were also assessed.

1.3 APPROACH AND METHODOLOGY

The theory of change or underlying assumption of the UNDP Gender Equality Strategy is that setting out a range of desired 'gender-responsive' results that are integral to UNDP programmes will help guide country offices and other units to pay appropriate attention to women's rights, women's empowerment and gender equality. This in turn will lead to development results that have a sound gender dimension. The GES lays out desired 'institutional results' with outputs and targets to build UNDP capacity to mainstream gender within the organization. Achieving these facilitates the achievement of gendered 'development results' at country, regional and global levels. 'Gender results' were defined for the purposes of this evaluation as outputs or outcomes that have been found to be contributing (positively or negatively) to GEWE in UNDP interventions.

Given the broad scope and cross-cutting nature of gender equality across all levels of UNDP programming, it was not possible to select a fully representative sample of all projects, programmes and countries to validate all relevant global and regional programmes. The evaluation therefore drew extensively on previous evaluations, publications and UNDP's own self-reporting as the primary data source for the analysis. Reports for public consumption and other forms of self-reporting were also used as sources of information, keeping in mind the inherent limitations that such reports do not generally offer critical analyses but tend to focus on successes and change stories.

Aggregate analyses are presented along with a deeper look at country-specific case examples and evaluation reports that validate self-reported results (or do not). It was possible to

validate some aspects of the global and regional programming during the country visits undertaken for this evaluation. This served to confirm and give context to some overall trends in UNDP's performance on gender equality globally. Accordingly, this report provides snapshots and high-level trends of UNDP's results in GEWE; it is not intended to comprehensively cover all of this work.

It is important to address the dimensions of context, backlash and accelerators of progress when assessing the results of work in GEWE. Progress in this area is complex and takes longer to achieve since it requires redistribution of power to shift unequal norms, relations and structures of discrimination and inequality. The issue of sustainability of results thus comes to the forefront in addressing gender equality results. Gender analysis and monitoring the evolution of gender results (including pushbacks and steps forward) within a context is crucial to learning and refining programming for greater effectiveness.

1.4 DATA COLLECTION AND ANALYSIS

The evaluation required mixed methods and a variety of data collection sources to validate, analyse and triangulate gender mainstreaming and GEWE results (Table 1).

Databases: The following databases were compiled to better understand gender mainstreaming processes and gender results across the institution:

- **Gender marker data** derived from the UNDP Atlas system helped give context to the coverage of gender in country office project outputs and estimated expenditures on gender.

- **The Results-oriented Annual Report (ROAR)** database covering all 136 country offices was prepared to track gender results reported on from 2011 to 2013. This corporate database focused on global trends of gender results in each focus area over time in relation to areas of work, as well as their alignment to corporate Strategic Plan

Table 1. Data collection methods and sources		
Method	**Sources**	**Total**
Country office visits	Africa: 2 countries Asia Pacific: 4 countries Arab States: 2 countries Europe & CIS: 2 countries Latin America & Caribbean: 3 countries	13
Regional centre visits	3 regional centres: Istanbul, Cairo, Bangkok	3
Evaluation reports: ADRs	Africa: 20 countries Asia Pacific: 16 countries Arab States: 6 countries Europe & CIS: 8 countries Latin America & Caribbean: 12 countries	62
Evaluation reports: regional and global programmes	Regional: 9 evaluation reports Global: 2 evaluation reports	11
Evaluation reports: thematic	Evaluation of UNDP Support to Conflict-affected Countries in the Context of UN Peace Operations Evaluation of UNDP Contribution to Strengthening Electoral System and Processes Evaluation of UNDP Contribution to Poverty Reduction Evaluation of UNDP Partnership with Global Funds and Philanthropic Foundations	4
ROAR 2011-2013	All UNDP country offices	136
Gender staff survey	250 UNDP gender staff members in 136 country offices	250
Cybermetrics 2008-2013 (Key word analysis)	20 global and regional UNDP publications 15 UNDP and benchmarking websites (Teamworks, iKnowPolitics, UNDP America Latina Genera) Social Media – Twitter	—

outcomes. Gender information was available mainly in narrative form from 2008 to 2010. In 2010 the ROAR interface was changed to be more data driven, and the evaluation drew on this material for the analysis.

■ **Human Resource Office data** provided gender parity statistics at global and regional levels for different professional grades, as well as data highlighting resource allocations for gender-related work at global level over the evaluation time period.

■ **Global staff survey data** from annual surveys from 2010 to 2013 were used to explore whether there were any gender-related differences in office culture.

■ A **gender staff survey** was developed by the IEO core team to gain staff insight into gen-

der mainstreaming processes in offices. It consisted of an online survey of 53 questions administered to individuals who worked on gender in country offices. Its object was to obtain their views on key aspects of UNDP's performance in support of GEWE with respect to gender architecture/institutional arrangements; the enabling environment for gender mainstreaming; gender mainstreaming tools; and links between gender mainstreaming and results. A total of 250 responses were received from 136 country offices and regional bureaux.

Key documents: The following documentation was reviewed as part of the analysis:

■ Country programme documents, financial and gender marker data, the UNDP Strategic

Plan 2008–2013, the GES for 2008–2013, annual reports to the Executive Board on implementing the GES for 2009–2013, relevant IEO thematic evaluation reports, and associated policies, country and regional programme documents, assessments, and evaluations in the four Strategic Plan areas, along with secondary research and global, regional and country level evaluations of gender-related work where relevant.

- Meta-analysis of 62 assessment of development results (ADR) reports over the evaluation time period (2008–2014).[6] Gender results (outputs and outcomes) were extracted from ADRs to create a database. The results were then categorized according to the thematic areas (institutional; poverty reduction and Millennium Development Goals [MDGs]; democratic governance; energy and environment; and conflict prevention and recovery); depth of coverage of the gender result (quality of reporting indicator); level of effectiveness (e.g., gender responsive or transformative); and type of change by the Gender@Work framework quadrant (see Chapter 5 and Annex 5 for more details).

- Global and regional IEO evaluations. Nine regional evaluations were used to create a database, and all results that addressed gender issues were categorized by thematic area. Results drawn from these sources were used to complement and triangulate results reported in the institutional change and focus area chapters.

Country visits and interviews: The following data were collected in country visits and other interviews:

- Country visits were undertaken by the IEO core team and development results team between October 2014 and January 2015 in 13 UNDP country offices (Argentina, Bangladesh, Bhutan, Brazil, Cambodia, Democratic Republic of the Congo, Egypt, Haiti, Kenya, Kyrgyzstan, Nepal, Tunisia and Turkey), 3 regional centres (Thailand, Egypt and Istanbul) and UNDP headquarters. The IEO core team produced country information briefs for use by the teams visiting countries and regional centres. These included information on the gender mainstreaming profile in the country together with a compilation of country-specific ROAR gender results. Summaries of country notes were then prepared by team members and shared with all involved in the evaluation. More information on the sample selection and country visit data collection process can be found in Annex 4.

- Focus groups were conducted in each country to gather the most significant outcomes over the evaluation period. The focus group meetings were held at the beginning of the country visits, involving individuals from each thematic area and management for an 'outcome-gathering' exercise. The exercise blended the 'outcome harvesting' and 'most significant change' approaches.[7] At the beginning of each session staff were asked to reflect on what was the most significant change in their thematic area over the 2008–2013 period. Follow-up questions then addressed UNDP's role in that change process; other actors or factors that contributed to that change; any evidence that supported these changes; and whether any unexpected changes had occurred.

- Semi-structured interviews were conducted with key UNDP staff in country and regional offices and at headquarters. The focus was on senior leadership and management, e.g., Resident Coordinators, Deputy Resident

---

6   One 2014 report was included as it covered results in the evaluation time period 2008–2013.

7   'Outcome harvesting' is a method for systematically gathering outcomes and validating them. (See Ricardo Wilson-Grau and Heather Britt, 'Outcome Harvesting', Ford Foundation, 2012.) 'Most significant change' is a method for gathering stories of most significant change from stakeholders to analyse illustrative trends and changes stemming from the programming. (See Rick Davies and Jess Dart, "The 'Most Significant Change' Technique", 2005.)

Representatives and thematic team leaders as well as the gender focal points and/or members of the gender focal team, in addition to monitoring and evaluation staff. Interviews were also conducted with a selection of government counterparts and partners, including UN agencies, such as UN-Women, the United Nations Population Fund (UNFPA), United Nations Children's Fund (UNICEF), donors and civil society organizations, including women's organizations. Their purpose was to assess UNDP's added value, partnership strategies and relevance of approach.

These also were useful in documenting and/or validating the main results reported in the ROARs or stated in staff interviews. In each country visited, there was an effort to meet representatives from the UN country team (UNCT) and the Resident Coordinator. Beneficiaries were also interviewed. Data were collected on six cross-cutting questions[8] to assess nationally driven efforts to promote GEWE and whether/the extent to which the GES has provided guidance across the thematic area.

Commissioned reports: The following reports were commissioned to allow the evaluation to examine specific aspects of the UNDP gender profile:

■ Cybermetric analysis[9] assessed the reach and content of UNDP gender-related knowledge.

The analysis supplemented triangulation by providing a stream of evidence and mapping large-scale trends to augment traditional programme evaluation work. The data analysed included a range of UNDP knowledge products, key publications, knowledge-sharing platforms and social media, such as Twitter accounts.

■ UN-SWAP analysis reviewed UNDP performance in 2010–2012 on the UN System-wide Action Plan on Gender Mainstreaming (UN-SWAP) platform. An independent consultant was commissioned to assess UNDP's performance in response to the plan, which included a meta-evaluation of 30 evaluation reports produced in 2014.[10] The meta-evaluation was conducted using the UN Evaluation Group Technical Note guidance for reporting on evaluation.

All of the various data and analysis streams were synthesized by the IEO core team to produce this report. The Gender Equality Strategy contains references to 'gender explicit' and 'gender responsive' outcomes. However, it does not contain a framework to determine the degree of effectiveness or the change in gender results. Therefore, the evaluation used two analytical frameworks for this purpose: the Gender Results Effectiveness Scale (GRES) and the Gender@ Work Framework. Both are described in further detail in Chapter 5.

---

8   The evaluation team developed the questions to explore six assumptions (some not necessarily true) shaping UNDP's gender mainstreaming implementation. The assumptions are: (1) UNDP staff understand the concept of gender and the different ways that gender matters to development results and institutional work. (2) Gender is a shared priority in UNDP. (3) If you have gender parity, then you have achieved gender equality, and equal power is shared by men/women in the institution. (4) Committed leadership that prioritizes gender equality makes a difference to achieving gender development results. (5) Gender mainstreaming is the responsibility of gender focal points and gender experts. Gender expertise (plus evidence) is needed to do good gender mainstreaming and challenge resistance. (6) UNDP can transform power imbalances and gender norms in the office and in the field through gender mainstreaming mechanisms.

9   Cybermetric methods provide insight into activity happening anywhere on the public web, drawing on data from any public website. This provides insight into larger online trends, such as what types of organizations are citing documents, their geographic distribution and, most importantly, how and why they are referencing publications.

10 The UN-SWAP was introduced in 2011 as the accountability framework for gender mainstreaming in the UN system. It consists of 15 system-wide performance indicators, clustered around 6 broad functional areas: accountability, results-based management, oversight, human and financial resources, capacity and coherence, knowledge and information management.

1.5 EVALUATION MANAGEMENT, PROCESS AND LIMITATIONS

One IEO staff member functioned as evaluation manager and another as associate manager. They were supported by a methodologist with expertise in gender and feminist approaches to evaluation, who was responsible for guiding the data collection and synthesis aspects of the evaluation and for their quality assurance. A team of five development results experts familiar with gender issues covered the focus areas of poverty, democratic governance, crisis prevention and recovery, energy and environment, and institutional assessment. Each was responsible for producing thematic contributions for use in the synthesis report. An evaluation consultant supported the process by providing research, data collection and analysis, and synthesis of the report, and a part-time consultant assisted in data analysis.

The analysis began with a review of data from the ROAR platform and from the various evaluations and assessments to formulate an aggregate, high-level picture of self-reported data on country-level outcomes that contributed to gender equality results.[11] To delve deeper into these changes and gain clarity on the quality of gender results achieved, results were traced using two strategies: gathering outcomes at the country level and engaging in meta-analysis of gender results as reported in 62 ADRs and 5 regional programme evaluations conducted during the evaluation period. These data gathering and analysis strategies are described in more detail in Annex 5.

Deeper analysis of the effectiveness of gender results[12] and the type of gender change was limited. This is because no common framework was developed to measure gender results as such, despite the fact that the GES contains examples of gender-explicit indicators and highlights the objective of UNDP contributions to gender-responsive results. The evaluation was also limited by the lack of UNDP's systematic collection of sex-disaggregated data and specific indicators for GEWE that are collected in the same way over time. This made it problematic to obtain a picture of overarching trends across all UNDP country offices, from which sampling and validation could take place.

To address this shortcoming, the evaluation team created its own framework, the Gender Results Effectiveness Scale, to capture the type and quality of gender results that UNDP achieved at an aggregate level. It consists of a five-point scale showing different levels of effectiveness, both positive and negative, moving towards transformation. The team also used the Gender@Work framework to categorize the type and areas of work to which UNDP contributed over the evaluation time period.[13] The evaluation team categorized results from the database created, consisting of ADR and country visit outcomes. The team experimented with this approach to establish meaningful aggregate-level trends of UNDP's contributions to GEWE results. Together with the other data sources, this helped provide broad-based illustrations of UNDP's contributions to GEWE and its role in the change process.

A group composed of representatives from UNDP headquarters and regional bureaux representing each level of UNDP's gender

---

11   Country-specific ROAR results were compiled for the use of evaluators undertaking each country visit.

12   Gender results are defined as outputs or outcomes that have been assessed to be contributing (positively or negatively) in UNDP interventions aimed at gender equality and women's empowerment.

13   The GRES consists of a five-point scale that measures results as gender blind, gender negative, gender targeted, gender responsive or gender transformative. The Gender@Work framework (developed by an international collaborative that helps organizations to build cultures of equality and justice) looks at change in terms of consciousness and awareness, access to resources and opportunities, formal policies, laws and institutional arrangements, and informal cultural change and deep structure. Qualitative thematic coding techniques were applied to categorize these gender results (see Chapter 5 for details).

architecture (e.g. Resident Representatives, Gender Team leaders, gender focal points) was consulted during the pre-scoping and design phase of the evaluation. Members of this group also commented on the draft report, with a focus on identifying errors of fact, interpretation or omission. Further, two high-level development experts, Michael Bamberger and Jayati Ghosh, members of the IEO Evaluation Advisory Panel, served as external advisors, reporting directly to the IEO Director on the quality of the evaluation. They provided substantive review of the terms of reference, the methodology manual and the draft evaluation report.

1.6 STRUCTURE OF THE REPORT

In Chapter 2, the report presents a summary of gender equality and gender mainstreaming in the context of international development. Chapter 3 provides an overview of UNDP's initiatives to promote gender equality and gender mainstreaming within the agency and in its programming at national, regional and global levels, following the underlying theory of change of the GES. Chapter 4 presents an assessment of UNDP's initiatives to promote institutional change. Chapter 5 provides an assessment of UNDP's contribution to development results in the four focus areas of poverty reduction and MDG achievement, democratic governance, crisis prevention and recovery, and energy and environment. Chapter 6 provides conclusions and recommendations.

Chapter 2

GENDER AND GENDER MAINSTREAMING IN INTERNATIONAL DEVELOPMENT

Globally, gender inequality is one of the most pervasive forms of human rights violations. It affects more than half of the global population and touches the lives of every person. Inequalities are manifested in terms of unequal economic status; low political representation and power; unequal access to health care and other services; high levels of maternal mortality; high rates of violence and sexual harassment; unequal education; low social status; and subtle forms of discrimination—all of which are fuelled by gender stereotypes, roles and norms, as well as discriminatory institutions and legal frameworks.

Gender also interacts with other aspects of identity—including race, class, caste, ethnicity, sexual orientation, religion, health and ability status—to further marginalize individuals. In many cases control over women and their bodies is woven into the cultural fabric of communities through traditional practices, such as early marriage, female genital cutting and virginity pledges. It is less blatantly maintained through gender segregation of roles and activities. Justifications for this discrimination are sometimes explicitly tied to religious or cultural mores to add social legitimacy. Sometimes they are framed as being 'natural' given a particular gender's disposition. But when stripped down to their roots, they are merely aims to prevent women from obtaining power, resources and control. Though some inequalities run deeper and are more present in some contexts globally than others, gender inequality is a long-standing, persistent and virtually universal phenomenon.

Both men and women have roles in maintaining and reproducing gender norms and discrimination. Gender roles and stereotypes of what it means to be masculine or feminine or a 'true man or woman' often pervade social interactions. Subtle social control mechanisms can often limit the expression and full potential of people's social and emotional development.

As the Executive Director of UN-Women recently highlighted, "Patriarchy is bestowed on men at birth. Whether you want it or not, you have privilege as a man, and you either fight against it and reject it by becoming a feminist man, or you enjoy the privileges that come with it."[14] Men who do not fit the hegemonic masculine mold often face bullying, physical threats and sexual violation. Moreover, the notion that gender is binary—man and woman—restricts every person's freedom, regardless of their gender identity, to enjoy fully and equally the privileges guaranteed by international human rights norms. Cutting off the development of an individual's full potential as a human being, whether man, woman or transgender, is also a rights violation.

The need to include men as more active agents in changing gender discrimination has been highlighted in studies dating back more than a decade.[15] The overwhelming majority of decision-makers and government civil servants are men in many countries around the world. Therefore addressing the issue of how to engage with men on changing their attitudes towards more gender equality is necessary

---

14 P. Mlambo-Ngcuka, Undersecretary-General and Executive Director, UN-Women, World Economic Forum session on 'Ending poverty through parity', 24 January 2015.

15 See e.g. F. Cleaver, *Masculinities matter! Men, Gender and Development*, Zedbooks, 2002.

for transformational change that reaches to the roots of this inequality and discrimination.

Given these realities, the global women's and feminist movements and the international development community have taken notice of the need to address these challenges from different perspectives. The following sections explore the global landscape and international development interventions in more depth. Section 2.1 highlights data on gender equality and inequality. Section 2.2 explores the normative underpinnings that pledge protection of women's rights and gender equality globally. Section 2.3 describes the major international development approaches to addressing these challenges in the past decade, from 'women in development' to 'gender and development' to 'gender mainstreaming', as set out in the Beijing Platform for Action. Section 2.4 highlights the post-2000 environment covering the MDGs, the emerging aid effectiveness frameworks and the politics of gender in international development.

2.1 THE GLOBAL STATE OF GENDER INEQUALITY

The global scope and depth of gender inequality are a strong reminder that, despite years of development investment and indeed progress, achievement of gender equality globally still has a long way to go and requires attention. Nearly half of the world's population, 3 billion people, lives in poverty, on less than $2.50 a day. Of these, nearly 1.3 billion people live in extreme poverty, subsisting on less than $1.25 a day. Poverty affects women more severely, and globally they earn on average 24 percent less than men (with variations across regions).[16] Women make up just 40 percent of the global workforce, with significant regional disparities.

Informal employment is an important source of employment for both men and women in developing countries.[17] Poor women working in the informal sector generally face greater constraints than men in accessing markets, credit, infrastructure and equipment, as well as business management skills. They also face social or economic discrimination. The global financial crisis of 2008 exacerbated the employment challenges facing both men and women. Women continue to face a greater degree of poverty, under-employment and unemployment.

Gender stereotypes often segregate women in 'feminized' professions that typically pay lower wages, and this gender-based occupational segregation is pervasive across all regions. Globally women are overrepresented in clerical and support positions (holding 63 percent of these jobs) compared to managerial positions (33 percent).[18] Women are prevented from entering the labour market in many conservative and traditional societies, decreasing their economic productivity. This results in the loss of the potential of a significant percentage of the population.[19] The glass ceiling consistently keeps women from reaching parity in executive and leadership positions. The burden of unpaid care activities, including care of children and elderly and sick people, falls heavily on women, limiting their participation in labour markets. Gender discrimination, sexual harassment and rights violations all affect women's

---

16 UN-Women, 'Progress of the World's Women 2015-2016: Transforming Economies, Realizing Rights', Summary, p. 12.

17 Data from 2014 from the International Labour Organization (ILO) indicated that a greater proportion of women in sub-Saharan Africa were informally employed than men; in Latin America the trend was reversed, with more men working in the informal sector and more women outside the informal sector, such as in domestic work. In Asia the proportion of women and men in informal employment was roughly equal. In the Middle East and North Africa, more men were informally employed than women, which is partially related to low female labour participation rates overall. See *Women and Men in the Informal Economy. A Statistical Picture*, ILO, 2014.

18 UN-Women op. cit.

19 For example in Turkey economic participation by women is among the lowest in the European region. The female labour participation rate as of 2014 (ages 15 and older) is 29.4%, compared to the male participation rate of 70.8%. Source: UNDP Country Overview, www.tr.undp.org/content/turkey/en/home/countryinfo/.

access to equitable incomes, fair and safe working conditions, and parity at the highest levels, across all industrialized and developing nations.

Multiple factors increase the risk of living in poverty for individuals and groups. These include lack of access to work, high unemployment rates, hunger and malnutrition, illiteracy and lack of access to education, low access to social networks (social capital) and safety nets, increased morbidity and mortality, homelessness and inadequate housing, lack of access to safe drinking water and sanitation, unsafe and insecure living environments, social discrimination, rights abuses and exclusion, and the inability to participate in decision-making at household and national levels and in civil, social and cultural life.[20,21]

Poverty is interlinked with other socio-political trends, such as political repression, conflict and disasters, and marginalized status, that deepen deprivation. For example, research has shown that "persistent levels of poverty, particularly when associated with profound deprivation (also referred to as "resource deprivation") and perceived injustices, are likely to create the grounds for increased social discontent. This may create the conditions for the onset of violent forms of conflict."[22]

One certainty is that chronically poor people, especially women and children, suffer disproportionately from violent conflict, due to their inability to cope with its negative effects. The people most affected by disasters and conflicts are those who are more vulnerable in general, living in the least developed parts of the world and in poverty. Women are also more likely than men to die in natural and climate-related

disasters. Changes to the environment as a result of climate change are likely to result in unique risks for women and girls in other ways as well. Disasters typically magnify existing patterns of inequality, including gender inequality. Violence against women and girls can occur, for example, because scarce resources result in lack of street lighting at night in areas where women are obliged to collect fuel or water from remote and isolated areas.

Women, elderly people and children are also known to be most vulnerable to the effects of natural disasters, such as earthquakes, floods and hurricanes, due to physiological or social factors. Women run more slowly than men, for instance, and face greater difficulties in climbing rescue points such as trees and posts. They often cannot swim and may be prohibited from leaving their homes. Thus climate change will have broad impacts not only on the environment but also on economic and social development.

In conflict settings, women are disproportionally targeted in campaigns designed to fracture the human spirit and social cohesion, such as through rape and other forms of violence. The many impacts of sexual violence include high rates of trauma and reproductive health issues, such as internal bleeding, gynaecologic fistula,[23] sexually transmitted diseases such as HIV/AIDS (some rape campaigns have the explicit purpose of infecting people), unwanted pregnancies and post-traumatic stress syndrome. UN-Women notes that tens of thousands of women are estimated to have suffered from sexual violence in the Democratic Republic of the Congo since the beginning of the conflict.[24] Perpetrators of

---

20 United Nations, World Summit on Social Development, Copenhagen Programme of Action, 1995.

21 Some indicators have been recently developed to try to capture the multidimensional nature of poverty. For example since income poverty does not sufficiently reflect overall deprivation, the Oxford Poverty and Human Development initiative developed a new measure, the Multidimensional Poverty Index, in 2010. It reflects multiple deprivations faced by poor people in education, health and living standards. The index for each country indicates the percentage of the population that is multidimensionally poor adjusted by the intensity of the deprivation. Populations with a score of 50% or more are designated as suffering severe multidimensional poverty.

22 Brian J. Atwood, 'The link between poverty and violent conflict', *New England Journal of Public Policy*, 2003.

23 An injury that results in incontinence due to severe vaginal tearing.

24 UN-Women, 'Unite to End Violence against Women' fact sheet, www.un.org/en/women/endviolence/pdf/VAW.pdf.

gender-based violence, which is common in conflict settings, are rarely held accountable, and this normalizes and reinforces it.[25] Conflicts and disasters upend development progress, deepen poverty and exacerbate inequalities and human rights violations.

Community acceptance of certain norms of masculine behaviour and men's use of power over women promotes inequality between the sexes. It can also lead to violence when accepted roles or norms are threatened. Gender-based violence (physical, sexual, psychological and economic) has also been identified as a significant driver of HIV infection among women and girls.

In peacekeeping efforts in both formal and informal settings women are rarely included in negotiations and decision-making processes. Globally, women are significantly underrepresented in all levels of governance relative to men. Worldwide just 22 percent of parliamentarians are women. In 38 States women account for less than 10 percent of parliamentarians in single or lower houses, and in five chambers there are no women at all.[26] Ten women serve as heads of state and 14 as heads of government.[27] The highest share of women in parliament is in the Americas and the lowest is in the Pacific. Yet women's representation in parliament has increased. In sub-Saharan Africa it more than doubled, from 10.6 percent to 22.6 percent, in the lower house of parliament from 1996 to 2014, and it grew almost fivefold in the Arab States, from 3.6 percent to 17.8 percent.[28]

In many countries legal frameworks discriminate based on gender—despite the fact that 186 countries are signatories to the Convention on the Elimination of All Forms of Discrimination against Women (CEDAW), which forbids such discrimination. In addition to laws that are explicitly discriminatory, numerous countries have laws that have a discriminatory impact or implementation. Others lack laws to prevent discrimination, such as against gender-based violence, and rights abuses.[29]

Amending or repealing discriminatory laws may not immediately end discrimination, but it creates a legal framework and norms that send a strong message on what social norms are acceptable and important to uphold. It also gives recourse to women whose rights are not respected.[30] This is particularly important since customary and/or religious laws that discriminate against women often co-exist with the formal legal framework, and sometimes prevail over it. The Committee on the Elimination of Discrimination against Women has urged States to harmonize civil, customary and/or religious law with the provisions of CEDAW.

Even once such laws are in place, State impunity can impede their implementation. Despite institutional advancements, many governments still have not put in place a binding representative social contract with the people it is supposed to represent. In particular, refugees and displaced populations often find themselves in a precarious middle zone with no state protection.

---

25   Rashida Manjoo and Calleigh McRaith, 'Gender-Based Violence and Justice in Conflict and Post-Conflict Areas', *Cornell International Law Journal*, vol. 44, 2011.

26   Ibid.

27   Inter-Parliamentary Union and UN-Women, Women in Politics: 2015.

28   L. Svågsand, 'International Party Assistance: What Do We Know about the Effects?', University of Bergen. Expertgruppen för Biståndsanalys, 2014:03, Sweden, February 2015.

29   Equality Now, 'Discrimination against Women in Law: A Report Drawing from the Concluding Observations of the Committee on the Elimination of Discrimination against Women', New York, May 2011.

30   Equality Now, 'The impact of discrimination in law and legal processes on women and girls – some case examples, Submission to the Working Group on the issue of discrimination against women in law and practice', New York, October 2012.

2.2 NORMATIVE UNDERPINNINGS AND EVOLUTION OF THE APPROACH TO GENDER EQUALITY AND WOMEN'S EMPOWERMENT[31]

In 1948, the Universal Declaration of Human Rights set out the fundamental basis of universal freedoms, equality and rights. Article 2 of the Declaration forbids discrimination based on sex (meaning the biological and physiological characteristics defining males and females, not gender[32]), race, language, politics, religion and other social categories. Although the Declaration is not binding, it is referenced as the foundation document establishing a global normative framework and enshrining the protection and promotion of universal human rights. Legally binding treaties and optional protocols[33] further delineate specific human rights protections, creating a comprehensive normative human rights legal framework.

Throughout the 1970s and 1980s, discussions in civil society, governments and UN agencies focused on developing protection mechanisms and raising resources to advance women's equity[34] and social justice. This came to the fore during the first World Conference on Women (1975, Mexico City), the United Nations Decade on Women (1976–1985) and debates on international norms, such as CEDAW.[35] The 1979 adoption of CEDAW established a critical reference point underscoring the importance of gender equality[36] in development with an explicit focus on reducing discrimination against women. CEDAW provided a definition of discrimination against women[37] and called for States to protect against gender discrimination and rights violations.

The attention to women as a particular target group emerged because international development aid directed at women was not having its expected positive impact, and in some cases progress in women's status and income reversed.[38] Figure 1 presents a timeline of key international developments related to gender.

---

31 This section is reproduced from the occasional paper entitled, 'Fast Forwarding Gender Equality and Women's Empowerment?', which was commissioned by UNDP's IEO and prepared by Alexandra Pittman for a scoping workshop.

32 Current definitions of sex focus on biological and physiological differences, distinguishing males, females and intersex. Gender, on the other hand, focuses on socially constructed roles, behaviours, activities and attributes that a given society considers appropriate for men or women. Gender identity is the internal sense of being a woman or man, or some other category (transgender).

33 The nine treaties are: International Convention on the Elimination of All Forms of Racial Discrimination (1965); International Covenant on Civil and Political Rights (1966); International Covenant on Economic, Social and Cultural Rights (1966); CEDAW (1979); Convention against Torture and Other Cruel, Inhuman or Degrading Treatment or Punishment (1984); Convention on the Rights of the Child (1989); International Convention on the Protection of the Rights of All Migrant Workers and Members of their Families (1990); International Convention for the Protection of All Persons from Enforced Disappearance (2006); and Convention on the Rights of Persons with Disabilities (2006).

34 Equity involves the reduction of inequalities between men and women, focusing on equal access, not necessarily equality in opportunities and participation.

35 Razavi and Miller, 'From WID to GAD: Conceptual Shifts in the Women and Development Discourse', Fourth World Conference on Women, Occasional Paper No. 1, United Nations Research Institute for Social Development, 1995.

36 The Office of the Special Adviser to the Secretary-General on Gender Issues and Advancement of Women notes, "Gender equality refers to the equal rights, responsibilities and opportunities of women and men and girls and boys... Gender equality implies that the interests, needs and priorities of both women and men are taken into consideration, recognizing the diversity of different groups of women and men. Gender equality is not a women's issue but should concern and fully engage men as well as women. Equality between women and men is seen both as a human rights issue and as a precondition for, and indicator of, sustainable people-centred development."

37 CEDAW defines discrimination of women as "...any distinction, exclusion or restriction made on the basis of sex which has the effect or purpose of impairing or nullifying the recognition, enjoyment or exercise by women, irrespective of their marital status, on a basis of equality of men and women, of human rights and fundamental freedoms in the political, economic, social, cultural, civil or any other field."

38 Razavi and Miller, op. cit.

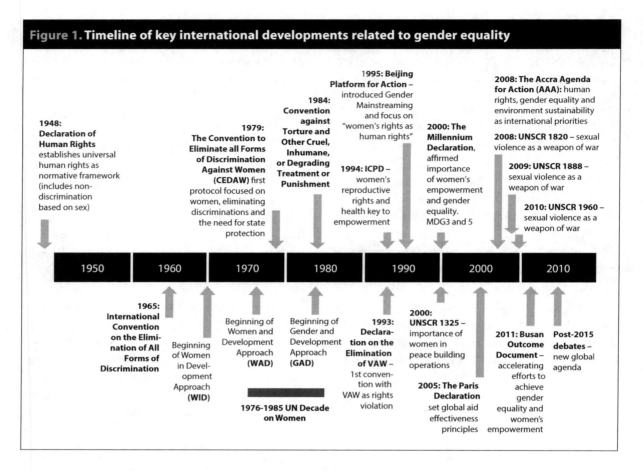

Figure 1. Timeline of key international developments related to gender equality

Since the 1970s, efforts have been made to transform normative gains into concrete action to eliminate discrimination. Key phases of this process are summarized below.

Women in development: The 'women in development' (WID) approach arose in the 1970s, drawing on Western, liberal feminist theory. The aim of this discourse and policy approach was to influence the agendas of international donor agencies and increase development resources directed to women. Advocates of WID promoted equity and economic efficiency arguments, aiming to show the value of investing in women. The approach analysed the contributions of women, particularly poor women, to formal and productive economic development spheres, and their status in them. Policy solutions and interventions focused on strategies to increase women's access to employment, markets, education and other material resources.

The assumption was that if women's economic inequalities were eliminated, their status and power would increase in other spheres.[39] This approach was criticized by many feminists, in both the global North and South, for 'instrumentalizing' women and making invisible the structural factors that created the inequalities the interventions were trying to address. This included issues such as limiting social norms around men's and women's work and gender roles or community expectations of 'appropriate' behaviour and roles; discrimination and rights violations, often codified in law; differential access to power and influence, and unequal

---

39 Various iterations of WID emerged and had different emphases over time. WID approaches moved from equity and access to development, to poverty alleviation, and then to economic efficiency models. See Caroline O.N. Moser, *Gender Planning and Development: Theory, Practice and Training*, London and New York: Routledge, 1993.

participation; inequities in accessing and controlling resources, both material and non-material; and the devaluation of women's labour in the marketplace, along with labour discrimination. The WID approach also faced resistance in the development community, although for reasons other than feminist concerns. In particular, many officials did not consider it necessary to redistribute power and to channel relatively scarce resources to women.[40]

Women and development: Moving on from economic efficiency arguments, the 'women and development' approach emerged in the late 1970s, emphasizing equitable participation. It analysed the structure of public and private participation in developing countries and how that structure marginalized women and maintained existing inequalities. The approach broadened analysis to men, recognizing some intersections of gender, privilege, race, class and social location, such as the fact that men in developing countries who do not enjoy privileged status also experience the negative impacts of social inequalities. In this way, development interventions focused largely on getting more women to participate and be represented in social, economic, political and legal structures.

However, the women and development approach did not focus on shifting underlying gender roles or the norms that sustain inequalities and discrimination.[41] Research has shown that the approach

"... offers a more critical view of women's position than does WID, but it fails to undertake a full-scale analysis of the relationship between patriarchy, differing modes of production and women's subordination and oppression."[42]

Gender and development: The 'gender and development' approach marked a distinct leap forward. It arose from calls from women's rights scholars and activists, as well as the women's and feminist movements, to address the power and patriarchy that lie at the root of discrimination and inequality. This introduced a need to broaden and deepen the development focus beyond women, to address gender roles and relations, differential access to resources and control of them, and ultimately the power imbalance between men and women.

This approach gave attention to gender, and to the socially constructed roles, behaviours, activities and attributes that a given society considers appropriate for men and women. In doing so it opened an opportunity to question how traditional social roles, norms and expectations formed the basis for inequality in the private and public spheres, as ensconced in unequal institutions—whether in families, communities, schools, the professional sphere, politics or beyond. It introduced ideas such as women's triple roles (productive, reproductive and community),[43] the double burden (of paid and unpaid work), and power and empowerment.[44, 45] These were important advances in development

---

40   Moser, op. cit. and Razavi and Miller, op. cit.

41   E. Rathgeber, 1990, 'WID, WAD, GAD: Trends in Research and Practice', *The Journal of Developing Areas* 24, pp. 498-502.

42   Ibid.

43   Productive roles are those that are monetarily reimbursed. Reproductive roles are those associated with child rearing/raising and caretaking of the home (i.e., cooking and cleaning). Community involvement highlights those tasks related to collective support and community gain. (From Moser, op. cit.)

44   According to UNFPA, women's empowerment has five components: "Women's sense of self-worth; their right to have and to determine choices; their right to have access to opportunities and resources; their right to have the power to control their own lives, both within and outside the home; and their ability to influence the direction of social change to create a more just social and economic order, nationally and internationally." Feminists have also highlighted the importance of the collective dimensions of empowerment and power, in addition to individual empowerment. For example, see Srilatha Batliwala, 'The Meaning of Women's Empowerment: New Concepts from Action', in G. Sen, A. Germain and L. C. Chen (eds.), *Population Policies Reconsidered: Health, Empowerment and Rights*, pp. 127-138, Boston: Harvard University Press, 1994.

45   Moser, op. cit. and Nick Pialek, 'Gender Mainstreaming from Theory to Praxis' (PowerPoint presentation).

thinking and practice in the promotion of gender equality and women's rights.

In the early to mid-1990s, a number of international commitments were made that further advanced the women's human rights agenda. Women's rights and feminist activists were central to the development of these international agreements and the promotion of new norms for equality and women's rights globally. In 1993, the Declaration on the Elimination of Violence against Women became the first global declaration to address violence against women explicitly and highlight it as a violation of human rights. In the following year, the International Conference on Population and Development further contributed to the women's rights agenda when delegates affirmed that women's equality and empowerment was a global priority and critical to eradicating poverty and curbing population growth. Importantly, women's reproductive rights and health were seen as a key component of women's empowerment.

In 1995, governments took the important step of promoting an agenda for women's empowerment by signing the Beijing Platform for Action. It provides concrete areas of action for governments, the United Nations system, civil society and the private sector to promote the women's empowerment, rights and equality agenda. The Platform for Action frames the advancement of women and gender equality as a human rights issue and a necessary condition for social justice. It affirms that, "…empowerment of women and equality between women and men are prerequisites for achieving political, social, economic, cultural and environmental security among all peoples." It also promotes the principle of gender mainstreaming, which prioritizes women's empowerment and gender equality as a cross-cutting development objective. In 1997, a concrete definition of gender mainstreaming was adopted, building on the Platform for Action:

"Mainstreaming a gender perspective is the process of assessing the implications for women and men of any planned action, including legislation, policies or programmes, in all areas and at all levels. It is a strategy for making women's as well as men's concerns and experiences an integral dimension of the design, implementation, monitoring and evaluation of policies and programmes in all political, economic and societal spheres so that women and men benefit equally and inequality is not perpetuated. The ultimate goal is to achieve gender equality."[46]

Global women's movements lobbied extensively to ensure recognition and prioritization of women's rights and to ensure that the 'women's rights as human rights' frame was integrated into the Platform for Action. This culminated over 20 years of activism to end discriminatory treatment of women.[47] The frame has become a major tool for feminist and women's rights activists arguing for changes in transnational policy and practice across the globe.

2.3 GENDER, THE MDGS AND BEYOND

Since the start of this millennium, international development discourse and formal agreements have increasingly emphasized the importance of gender equality. The Millennium Declaration in 2000, supported by governments across the world, affirmed that women's empowerment and gender equality is one of the most useful mechanisms to "combat poverty, hunger and disease and to stimulate development that is truly

---

46 Report of the Fourth World Conference on Women, Beijing, 4–15 September 1997 (United Nations publication, Sales No. E.96.IV.13), chap. I, resolution 1, annex II.

47 See Meillon and Bunch, Eds., 'Holding on to the Promise: Women's Human Rights and the Beijing + 5 Review', Centre for Women's Global Leadership, 2001.

sustainable." Specifically, MDG 3 and MDG 5 integrated women's empowerment,[48] reduction of maternal mortality and women's reproductive health.[49] At the United Nations World Summit in 2005, gender equality was reaffirmed as a development goal in itself, in MDG 3. It was also highlighted as a means to fast-forward achievement of all the other MDGs.

Other international resolutions and commitments were established in the first decade of the 2000s, including United Nations Security Council Resolution 1325 (2000) and Resolution 1889 (2009), both of which underscored the importance of women's representation and voices in peacebuilding processes; Resolution 1820 (2008), which states that sexual violence is an explicit weapon of war and a war crime and requires immediate protection and disciplinary mechanisms; and Resolutions 1888 (2009) and 1960 (2010), both of which served to further strengthen the women, peace and security agendas.

Debates on the global aid effectiveness architecture, from the Paris Declaration (2005) to the Busan Outcome Document (2011), focused increasingly on gender equality as an important dimension for achieving sustainable development. Aid effectiveness debates were critical, as the outcome documents set the overarching framework and principles through which international aid is to be delivered and established global priorities and standards with which to assess progress.

Many women's rights advocates criticized the Paris Declaration as gender blind.[50] Advocates demanded that greater attention be given to gender and women's rights at the Third High Level Forum on Aid Effectiveness (Accra, 2008). The Accra Agenda for Action significantly raised the focus on gender. However, many of the demands of the women's rights advocates remained unmet, particularly those calling for ensuring that gender equality and women's rights were a priority through dedicated resources, strong accountability and results-based tracking mechanisms.

There has also been increasing influence of conservatism (often religious) and the presence of the private sector in high-level policy spaces, such as the United Nations Conference on Sustainable Development (2012, Rio de Janeiro), the Fourth High-Level Forum on Aid Effectiveness (Busan, 2011) and the debate on the post-2015 development agenda. To some extent, this has resulted in backtracking on existing development agreements. The outcome of these debates has been mixed. Some advances have been held, but there has also been some degradation of previous women's rights commitments.

The gender equality focus as set out in the 1995 Beijing Platform for Action has been mostly integrated into the language of high-level aid and development effectiveness architectures and agreements. Much of this is connected to the concentrated advocacy efforts of feminist and

---

48 MDG 3 aimed to eliminate gender disparity in primary and secondary education, preferably by 2005, and in all levels of education no later than 2015. While globally there has been progress in eliminating gender disparity at the primary education level, in 2013 only 2 of 130 countries had achieved gender equality at every education level. In particular, increased rates of poverty, high levels of gender-based violence, economic inequalities, unequal and fragile employment opportunities, significant wage gaps, low rates of political participation and of formal and informal leadership, differential legal frameworks that marginalize women as landowners and unequal inheritance and marriage rights are but a few of the diverse realities that threaten the global achievement of women's empowerment and gender equality and fulfilment of their rights. See UN-Women, 'The Gender Dimension of the Millennium Development Goals Report', 1 July 2013.

49 MDG 5 targets aimed to reduce by three quarters, between 1990 and 2015, the maternal mortality ratio and achieve, by 2015, universal access to reproductive health. There has been progress on the achievement of these goals. Globally the rate of maternal deaths has been cut by nearly half (47%), and in Eastern Asia, Northern Africa and Southern Asia by nearly two thirds. However, mortality rates could be further reduced through proper nutrition, skilled birth attendance and proper antenatal and postnatal care. In terms of access to reproductive health, data show that much progress remains to be achieved—over 140 million married women say they would delay or avoid childbearing if they had access to family planning resources. See UN, 'Goal 5. Improve Maternal Health' fact sheet.

50 See Association for Women's Rights in Development, 'Primer #8: Development Cooperation and Women's Rights series. The Accra Agenda for Action: A brief review from a women's rights perspective', 2010.

women's rights advocates and work with key allies, such as the Organisation for Economic Co-operation and Development (OECD), United Nations agencies and civil society actors.[51] While these high-level commitments clearly prioritize a mainstreamed and dedicated focus on gender equality, the extent to which they led to more resources and concrete results remains an open question.

The data from the gender equality policy marker of the OECD's Development Assistance Committee (DAC), based on the 2011–2012 average, show only $3.5 billion of screened aid (4 percent of total aid) was allocated to GEWE projects as a principal objective.[52] Given growing recognition of and interest in the catalytic role that gender equality can play, questions remain as to why development investments, commitments and action have remained modest. There is also deep interest in the quality, merit and worth of interventions undertaken using gender mainstreaming as an approach to address GEWE. It is with this background in mind that the evaluation approached the assessment of UNDP's own experience in gender mainstreaming, particularly during the period 2008–2013.

---

51 For more on the advocacy wins and losses of feminist groups at and on the road to Busan, see Alexandra Pittman, 'Learning Assessment for the Mobilization of Women's Rights Organizations and Networks on the Road to Busan and Beyond Project', internal report, Alexandra Pittman, 2012.

52 OECD DAC, 'Aid in Support of Gender Equality and Women's Empowerment: Donor Charts', 2014. Statistics based on DAC Members' reporting on the Gender Equality Policy Marker, 2011–2012.

Chapter 3

GENDER EQUALITY AND WOMEN'S EMPOWERMENT IN UNDP

This chapter presents a summary of how UNDP's approach to gender programming has evolved from its response to the first World Conference on Women to the present. It analyses UNDP's response to the international developments summarized in Chapter 2 and traces the policy priorities and institutional activities that characterized UNDP efforts between 1975 and 2005 (covered in the previous evaluation of gender programming). It demonstrates the organization's efforts to respond to external developments in the international arena as well as to directions from its governing body.[53] The chapter also summarizes salient features of the 2008–2013 Gender Equality Strategy, which was prepared in parallel to the Strategic Plan to guide gender programming. It concludes with a brief overview of development results and institutional results addressing GEWE initiatives.

1965–1975: The 'gender blind' period. During the 10 years from its establishment in 1965 until 1975, UNDP could be classified, along with other development agencies, as 'gender blind' in its programming. Women were generally targets of population policies and programmes, while productive sectors of the economy were generally associated with men.

1976–1986: Promoting the WID paradigm. Pressure from the international women's movement led to the first World Conference on Women,

at which the following decade (1976–1985) was established as the UN Decade for Women. In response, UNDP "became an early leader amongst the international organizations in the incorporation of a gender component into their organizational structure."[54] 'Women in development' became official UNDP policy, and a focal point for women was appointed in 1976. Early initiatives involved the development of WID guidelines, which were incorporated into the UNDP Programme Manual as an additional section on 'special considerations'. WID focal points were established in the regional bureaux but received no resources to support their activities.

Also during this period, in 1984, the United Nations Development Fund for Women was established as a UNDP-administered voluntary fund with the mandate to finance and implement projects of its own. Nevertheless, gains were modest. A 1985 report estimated that "fewer than 16 percent of development projects affecting women actually incorporated women into the process of implementation".[55] These projects were generally in the traditionally 'female' sectors of education, health and handicrafts. Commentators have also noted that these early efforts were typical of an "integrationist approach" in which UNDP grafted consideration of women and gender issues onto existing policy, "rather than rethinking the fundamental aims of the organization from a gender perspective".[56]

---

53 In this connection, a 1995 report by the United Nations Research Institute for Social Development observed that "UNDP is funded entirely through voluntary contributions, with the Nordic countries providing a significant proportion of resources, which effectively gives them greater 'voice' … the extent to which UNDP has taken up the WID/gender mandate has depended to a large degree on the support of committed donors, especially from the Nordic countries, the Netherlands and Canada." (Razavi and Miller, op. cit.)

54 E. Hafner-Burton and Mark A. Pollock, 'Mainstreaming Gender in Global Governance', 2000, p. 15.

55 Hafner-Burton and Pollock, Ibid., p. 12.

56 Hafner-Burton and Pollock, Ibid., p. 10.

1986–1995: From gender and development to sustainable human development. The second phase began with the third World Conference on Women in Nairobi (1985) and ended with the fourth in Beijing (1995). It was marked by efforts to address the concern that "WID efforts in the UN Decade had created ghettos in the name of integration".[57] The concept of 'gender and development' gained currency, and it was adopted as part of the proposed new strategy. In 1987, UNDP established a new Division of Women, with three professional staff, in the Bureau for Programme Policy and Evaluation. The staff worked as gender 'advocates' whose role was to promote through persuasion. Attention was placed on consideration of gender issues at the country programming rather than project level. Training was revamped and an organization-wide gender focal point system was established in 1987.

Significantly, during this period UNDP's policy lens also was sharpened to cover the concepts of human development and sustainable human development. These served as organizing principles that explicitly acknowledged the central role of women in development and "built the bridge between "development and 'human rights' … and decisively shifted 'development' from being more than an issue of the empowerment and equality of nations. It also became an issue of empowerment and equality of individuals."[58] The first Human Development Report was published in 1990, and the 1995 report, subtitled 'Gender and Human Development', was considered "bold and innovative, quantifying the value of non-monetized production by women (and men) in economic and household activities".[59] It also introduced two special indicators: the Gender-Related Development Index and the Gender Empowerment Measure.

1995 to 2005: Beijing and gender mainstreaming. The 1995 Beijing Platform for Action formally introduced the term 'gender mainstreaming' into the policy vocabulary. In 1992, the Gender Division had been transformed into the Gender in Development Programme as part of the Social Development and Poverty Alleviation division within the Bureau for Policy and Programme Support (BPPS). While this change integrated gender as a UNDP key priority by making it a cross-cutting issue, it also decreased the influence of the entity by adding a layer between the division and the bureau director.[60]

In November 1996 the UNDP Administrator issued a memorandum to all Resident Representatives and Resident Coordinators reiterating UNDP's commitment to gender equality. It noted that "Gender equality is an intrinsic dimension of equitable and sustained human development." A direct line was introduced in the budget to promote gender, and a global gender programme of $7.7 million was set up for the period 1976–2000.

The 2006 evaluation of gender mainstreaming described the period 1996–2005 as a time of "good starts and lost momentum, intermittent declarations and mixed signals."[61] It concluded that gender mainstreaming had not been visible and explicit and that implementation had suffered from confusion about what gender mainstreaming means and how to apply it. The evaluation found that "while there are many committed individuals and some 'islands of success', the organization lacks a systematic approach to gender mainstreaming. UNDP has not adopted clearly defined goals, nor dedicated the resources necessary to set and achieve them. There is a lack of systemic approaches, leadership and commitment at the highest levels and of capacity at all levels."[62]

---

57 Razavi and Miller, op. cit., p. 1, quoting Jahan, 1995.

58 Craig N. Murphy, *The United Nations Development Programme: A better way?,*' p. 206, UNDP, 2006.

59 United Nations, 'UN Ideas that Changed the World', pp. 77-78, 2009.

60 Razavi and Miller, op. cit., p. 19.

61 EO UNDP, 'Evaluation of Gender Mainstreaming', January 2006, page vi.

62 UNDP Ibid., p. iii.

Inadequacies in leadership, commitment and financial resources had limited UNDP's ability to fully integrate gender equality considerations at all levels of the organization and in all activities. Gender mainstreaming had been overshadowed by the larger effort to restructure the organization, and the Global Gender Programme was reduced to one fifth of its earlier budget. The programme's location under one of the five thematic areas (poverty) meant that it did not have oversight over gender aspects of the other thematic areas or any UNDP-wide authority.

The multi-year funding framework for 2004–2007 (predecessor to strategic plans) had promoted gender equality as a driver for development effectiveness, but country offices had demonstrated little awareness of what this required. In short, as noted by the 2006 evaluation, "Gender mainstreaming became less visible within the organization than it was five years ago." Furthermore, there was "…no accountability for gender mainstreaming. Gender mainstreaming is not included in assessments of senior staff performance. There are no rewards and incentives for good performance. In addition, there has been little proactive leadership and guidance from top management."

3.1 THE GENDER EQUALITY STRATEGY

UNDP responded swiftly to the 2006 evaluation, adopting an interim Gender Action Plan 2006–2007. This was meant to fill the gap until the complete Gender Equality Strategy was finalized for 2008–2013. In 2007, UNDP released a document titled 'Empowered and Equal', which contains a fully articulated GES for 2008–2011. It is important to note that this policy was not presented formally to the Executive Board but was launched as a parallel document to the Strategic Plan. The aim of the GES was to provide guidance on how and where to integrate a gender perspective across operations.

The GES has two distinct components, covering 'development results' and 'institutional results' (Figure 2). The development results framework addresses both Strategic Plan outcomes and GES outcomes in four focus areas: Achieving

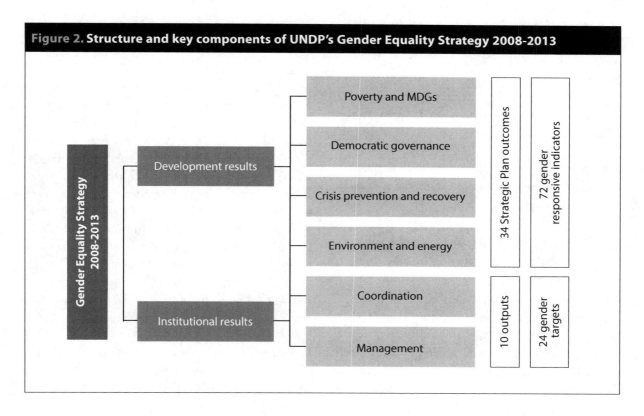

Figure 2. Structure and key components of UNDP's Gender Equality Strategy 2008-2013

the MDGs and reducing human poverty; fostering democratic governance; supporting crisis prevention and recovery; and managing energy and the environment for sustainable development. A detailed results matrix was also developed, denoting those Strategic Plan outcomes that were 'gender explicit' and providing 'gender responsive' outcome indicators for each Strategic Plan outcome. The 'institutional results' section similarly presents outputs, indicators and targets for two areas, namely 'coordination results', which focus on collaboration with UN agencies, joint programmes and within country teams, and 'management results', which focus on internal aspects such as organizational culture, knowledge management, communication, human resources, capacity building and financial resources.

At a simple level, there were two underlying assumptions (a theory of change) implicit in the GES. The first was that by fully integrating the GES into the UNDP Strategic Plan and implementing the two in conjunction, UNDP could contribute more substantially to gender equality as part of longer term development processes in the four focus areas of the plan. The second was that attention to internal institutional results (within the arena of UNDP control) that focused on strengthening staff capacity and accountability would be critical to delivering better external development results at global, regional and country levels.

The following paragraphs summarize the key features that were implemented in the two areas of the GES during the period 2008–2013.

3.1.1 INSTITUTIONAL PROCESSES FOR GENDER EQUALITY AND WOMEN'S EMPOWERMENT

During the 2008–2013 period and in keeping with the areas outlined in the GES, UNDP introduced a series of institutional gender mainstreaming mechanisms designed to strengthen internal accountability for its GEWE results. Prominent among these were the following:

The Gender Steering Implementation Committee (GSIC): Acting as a senior management peer review committee, the GSIC has a mandate to set policy on gender mainstreaming and gender parity within the organization; hold senior managers accountable for achieving GEWE results; and monitor organizational investments in the GES. Each regional bureau reports annually to the GSIC on programme and institutional results, and the Office for Human Resources reports on implementation of UNDP's Gender Parity Strategy and Action Plan.

Gender marker and revisions to annual ROAR reporting: The gender marker, introduced as a two-year pilot in 2008, requires managers to rate projects on a four-point scale indicating their contribution to achievement of gender equality. This accountability tool was introduced to allow UNDP to track allocations and expenditures for GEWE results through the Atlas financial management system.

The ROAR performance reporting tool was revised to enable tracking of the gender marker and also introduced discrete questions to keep abreast of gender results both in terms of programmatic interventions and institutional results.

Gender Parity Strategy: The underlying premises of UNDP's Gender Parity Strategy and Action Plan are that gender parity in staffing, particularly at the management level, is needed to ensure that (a) UNDP is a fair organization that puts into practice the rights-based approaches to which the UN system is committed; (b) diversity in management will lead to greater institutional effectiveness and efficiency; and (c) increased input from female staff and managers will lead to improved GEWE inputs in programming. Each senior manager is responsible for working to help UNDP reach its gender parity targets. Unlike the institutional processes described above, UNDP's gender parity strategies pre-date the 2008–2013 GES.

Gender Equality Seal Initiative: In 2011, UNDP initiated development of an institutional incentive and certification process known as the

Gender Equality Seal. It is adapted from a similar process developed for the private sector through UNDP's programming in Latin America. The UNDP seal was envisaged as a corporate certification process to recognize good performance of offices/units in delivering gender equality results. The aim was also to provide incentives for country offices to engage in more substantive work on GEWE in programming as well as to help improve organizational efficiency to deliver results and improve consistency of performance across the organization. The seal draws its conceptual framework from UNDP's global GES.

Certification is a four-stage process: (1) Online self-assessment to identify gender gaps of the office/unit; (2) design and implementation of an action plan; (3) final assessment to identify level of certification; and (4) certification.[63] The online assessment tool is a benchmarking matrix that provides a snapshot of the 'state of play' of gender mainstreaming in the country office. The tool scores the office against 44 benchmarks organized in seven sections, corresponding to the elements identified by UNDP as essential for gender mainstreaming.[64]

UNDP's gender architecture: While UNDP has assigned staff with specific responsibility for gender issues since the 1970s, there was more attention to developing a dedicated staff cadre to support and deepen gender programming under the GES (from 2008 to 2013). Country offices and regional bureaux and service centres developed diverse models and structures for staffing and reporting lines for gender personnel. The evaluation has reviewed these structures and the ways in which their resources have changed during the evaluation period.

Gender equality and women's empowerment in knowledge management: UNDP's Gender Team, regional centres and BPPS all contributed knowledge products and services related to GEWE during the evaluation period. These include thematic resource guides, briefing notes and peer networks. The evaluation reviewed these materials and instruments to determine which have had the most effect and reach and the sustainability of the GEWE knowledge management system.

Each of these initiatives is discussed in the next chapter, which assesses institutional results in promoting GEWE in UNDP programming.

3.1.2 DEVELOPMENT TRENDS AND CORPORATE REPORTING ON GENDER QUALITY AND WOMEN'S EMPOWERMENT

During the period 2008–2013, UNDP country offices provided annual reports on various dimensions of gender results. For an overview of trends in UNDP corporate reporting, the evaluation examined gender marker data and ROAR data. Two dimensions were reviewed: the number of gender results reported by region; and the depth of gender reporting by gender marker criteria.

---

63 Applying for certification is voluntary. Country offices aiming for the gold level must have an assessment by a team of experts who work with country office managers and the gender focal team to collect and verify data on the status of key indicators and match them against the 92 Seal benchmarks. Scores are determined based on data from three sources: primary actors, internal records and reports, and external sources. During the assessment mission information is triangulated; each benchmark is assessed against evidence from a minimum of three sources, and scored positively only if all three are consistent. Data sources and data collection options for each of the benchmarks are included in the matrix. Key sources used to verify evidence are (1) self-reporting by the country office (corporate reports and reporting tools such as the gender marker and the results-based management reports); (2) one-on-one interviews with key informants inside and outside the organization; (3) focus group discussions, workshops and participatory exercises with selected groups of informants; and (d) questionnaires and surveys.

64 The seven sections are (1) strong management systems and accountability mechanisms; (2) systematic investment in building in-house capacities; (3) an enabling internal environment; (4) effective systems for knowledge management and communication; (5) effective integration of gender concerns into the programme/project cycle; (6) partnerships with other actors for gender equality inside and outside the UN system; and (7) achievement of sustainable gender equality results.

Poverty & MDGs — Democratic governance — Crisis prevention & recovery — Environment & energy

Legend:
- Average number of ROAR outcomes where gender results were reported
- Percentage of ROAR outcomes on crisis prevention and recovery where gender results were reported

Source: ROAR

Gender results: Number and proportion by focus area and region

Figure 3 provides comparative information on the number and proportion of gender-related ROAR outcomes by region in the four focus areas.

The **poverty reduction and MDG** focus area averaged 232 gender results per year (696 total ROAR outcomes for all three years) across UNDP's country operations. This represented an average of 75 percent of the total number of country outcomes reported over the period. The highest proportion of gender results was reported in the Africa region (78 percent) and the lowest in the Asia Pacific region (69 percent).

In the **democratic governance** focus area, an average of 210 gender outcomes were reported annually (631 ROAR outcomes for all three years) across UNDP's country operations for the period. This represented 72 percent of the total number of outcomes reported.[65] On average, the Asia Pacific region reported the most gendered results (77 percent) and the Arab States the least (66 percent).

In **crisis prevention and recovery** an average of 76 gender results a year (229 total ROAR outcomes across the three years) were reported from UNDP's country operations. This represented 71 percent of the total number of results reported for

---

65 For 2011, 2012 and 2013, a total of 877 outcomes were reported, of which 628 reported gender results.

the period. While this is the third largest area of programme intervention by expenditure, it had the smallest number of gender results reported. The highest proportion was reported in the Africa region (80 percent) and the lowest in the European region (58 percent).

The **energy and environment** portfolio averaged 101 gender results per year (304 total ROAR outcomes for all three years) across UNDP's country operations. This represented an average of 58 percent of the total number of country outcomes reported for the portfolio over the period. This was the least amount of progress on gender results compared to other thematic areas. The highest proportion of gender results was reported in the Africa region (69 percent) and the lowest in the Arab States region (45 percent).

Depth of gender content

ROAR reporting during the period 2011–2013[66] provides an overview of UNDP's broad contributions to gender results. Reported outcomes totalled 877 for the three years, of which 628 were gender results. Figure 4 shows the depth of gender content, or the extent to which each focus area contributed to GEWE, using the four gender marker criteria. Three of the four thematic areas are succeeding in mainstreaming gender, with 'significant gender content' in terms of contributions to development results. The exception is energy and environment, which has the largest proportion of outcomes with no gender content or some gender content.[67] Poverty and MDGs has the highest proportion of country outcomes with gender as the main objective, closely followed by democratic governance.

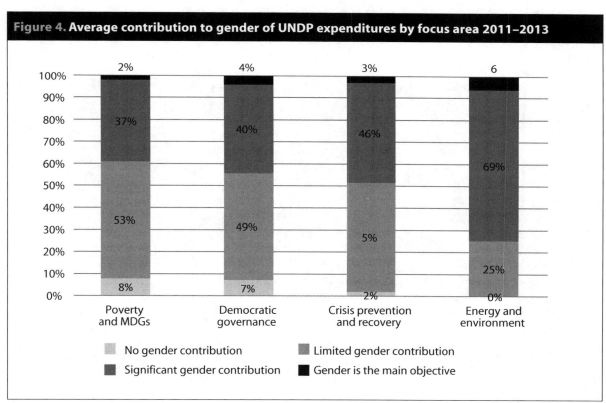

Figure 4. Average contribution to gender of UNDP expenditures by focus area 2011–2013

Legend:
- No gender contribution
- Limited gender contribution
- Significant gender contribution
- Gender is the main objective

Source: Averages of gender marker rating from UNDP ROAR / gender marker classification

---

66   There was a change in ROAR reporting from 2011 onwards that enabled more data-driven rather than narrative-based reporting.

67   The poverty and MDGs area had the greatest number of results (888), followed closely by democratic governance (855). Next was energy and environment (518) and finally crisis prevention and recovery (312).

Chapter 4

ASSESSMENT OF INSTITUTIONAL CHANGE RESULTS IN UNDP

The Gender Equality Strategy contains a section covering institutional results that details outputs, indicators and targets. This chapter assesses the initiatives developed by UNDP during the period 2008–2013 to promote gender mainstreaming efforts within the organization.

As noted in section 1.3, the theory of change of the GES builds on the basic assumption that implementing a series of institutional measures will bolster and enhance UNDP's contribution to development results in the four focus areas. The assumed pathway of results moves from internal change (institutional changes), in which UNDP has more control and influence over what is implemented, to the arena of development results, in which UNDP only contributes to gender results. This is seen in changes in policies, laws, attitudes and behaviours. UNDP has less influence and/or direct control in this area because it works with national and regional partners and stakeholders. In line with this theory of change, this chapter seeks to answer the following evaluation question: *Did UNDP integrate gender equality across the institution at the programme, policy, technical and cultural levels during the period 2008–2013?*

The chapter assesses institutional change results through UNDP's contributions in these areas:

- Planning and resources

- Innovations to promote gender mainstreaming

- Mechanisms for tracking gender investments and reporting on results

- Gender parity and organizational culture

- Accountability and oversight

- Knowledge management and communication

- UN system collaboration on gender.

4.1 PLANNING AND RESOURCES

This section evaluates UNDP progress in terms of planning, strategy and allocation of human and financial resources to promote GEWE.

4.1.1 GENDER EQUALITY STRATEGY (2008–2013)

Finding 1: UNDP's first Gender Equality Strategy was a significant step forward with regard to providing guidance on gender mainstreaming and programming. The GES included programmatic and institutional guidance and a results framework, which are essential ingredients for strong gender mainstreaming. However, it was not endorsed by the Executive Board, which made its guidance voluntary. This weakened its potential impact and integration. In a context of multiple competing priorities, staff reported that they do not prioritize an area unless a guidance document has been endorsed by the Executive Board, the area is considered mandatory or an urgent directive has been issued by the Administrator.

The Gender Equality Strategy, which is comprehensive and thorough, was developed as a guidance document to accompany UNDP's Strategic Plan 2008–2013. It presents outcomes related to GEWE at the programmatic level together with institutional change indicators for better mainstreaming. The majority of senior managers interviewed saw the GES as a useful framework that helped guide action covering core UNDP priorities at different institutional levels.[68] Nevertheless, the evaluation found that a variety of issues constrained the full integration of gender mainstreaming principles and structures as set forth in the GES, including its 'optional' nature, uneven communication about it and competing corporate priorities. A comparative assessment of gender evaluations in 18 agencies found similarly that "… staff at all levels feel a sense of policy and procedures overload [which] results in a focus on 'essential' priorities….Gender is rarely seen as a top priority – and even if it is, then not for long."[69]

4.1.2 HUMAN AND FINANCIAL RESOURCES FOR GENDER

This section assesses the financial allocations and gender architecture (human resources) available to UNDP at global, regional and country office levels during the evaluation period. It also assesses the extent to which UNDP has responded to the Strategic Plan indicators in this area.

Finding 2: UNDP did not establish clear, steady financial benchmarks and mechanisms in support of core Global Gender Team activities during 2008–2013. There was a promising increase in resources from $4.20 million in 2008 to an average of $6.13 million in 2012, but in 2013 expenditures fell significantly, to $4.16 million.[70] In 2014 they were further reduced to $3.37 million. In addition the share of non-core resources in Gender Team expenditures grew from 23 percent in 2008 to 39 percent in 2013.

Financial resources: Gender Team activities are financed by both core and non-core funding. Core funds, derived from the organization's regular budget, provide stability, predictability and sustainability of unit activities. Non-core funds are generally of limited duration and tied to specific activities. Figure 5 illustrates the proportion of core to non-core funds during the evaluation period. A basic and often powerful means of prioritizing an issue is establishing financial benchmarks, and it is evident that UNDP did not establish such benchmarks for its core activities to promote GEWE during this period.[71]

Human resources: The Global Gender Team, based at headquarters, underwent several changes between 2008 and 2014. The 2006 evaluation found "…the Global Gender [Team] is seriously understaffed and underresourced", with just four professional posts. By 2010, this team had grown to 23 posts but by 2014 it had been reduced to just 8 posts.

In terms of functions, the Gender Team's role has become increasingly central and strategic, particularly when compared to the profile accorded this team in previous years. It has an internal corporate responsibility to provide policy advice and an external representational function in the UN system. It also serves as secretariat of the Gender Strategy Implementation Committee, set up after the launch of the GES, which was chaired in the early years by the Administrator and later by the Associate Administrator. The Gender Team for-

---

68 With regard to the GES and its effect on promoting gender mainstreaming in their country offices, 46% of the 175 respondents to the gender staff survey indicated that the GES was "helpful". Another 39% indicated it was "somewhat helpful" and 10% indicated it was "very helpful". Only 5% of respondents indicated the GES was "not helpful at all". In addition, 46% of respondents indicated that their office created its own gender equality strategy and action plan to guide its work.

69 African Development Bank, 'Mainstreaming Gender Equality: A Road to Results or a Road to Nowhere?', 2012.

70 It should be noted that during this period there was an overall reduction in UNDP expenditures.

71 The instability of resources for gender has been a recurring issue in UNDP. The 2006 evaluation found that "much of the information about UNDP resource allocation to gender is missing, incomplete or inconsistent. There is no accurate way to estimate exact expenditures on programmes which pay attention to gender mainstreaming". In 2011, the midterm review also concluded that "UNDP should demonstrate its commitment through allocation of adequate resources from its core budget and better track resources for gender mainstreaming." In the same year, UNDP's Executive Board reported that "…since 2008, UNDP has invested great efforts in strengthening capacity for gender mainstreaming, and requests UNDP both to continue to maintain and to increase its investments to accelerate the strengthening of capacity and the delivery of programming for gender equality and the empowerment of women in line with the Gender Equality Strategy."

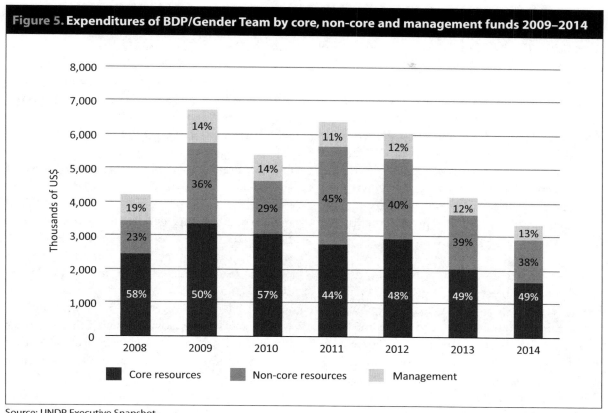

Figure 5. Expenditures of BDP/Gender Team by core, non-core and management funds 2009–2014

Source: UNDP Executive Snapshot

mulates the annual reports on GEWE presented to the Executive Board. It also co-chairs the United Nations Development Group subgroup on accounting for resources and will serve on the UN-SWAP Gender Marker Help Desk in 2015. The Global Gender Team also provides technical support to the World Food Programme in its development of a certificate of excellence similar to the Gender Equality Seal and has advised on its gender policy.

Thirty-eight percent of respondents to the gender staff survey administered as part of the evaluation reported they had received support from the Global Gender Team during the period 2008–2013. The vast majority of this support was policy advice and advice on piloting new approaches and tools. Around half of the staff

members had received support in advocacy initiatives and development of knowledge products and around a third indicated they had received support in developing partnerships. Regarding effectiveness, the bulk of the survey respondents indicated that the Global Gender Team was very effective/effective in carrying out its functions.[72] Nevertheless, given the increase in duties and reduction of posts, it is unclear whether the team has the capacity to fully carry out its functions.

Finding 3: At the regional level, gender practice leaders consistently had a position of seniority (P5 level). Evidence suggests that the majority of country offices have received support from gender practice leaders and that this guidance was valued.

---

72 Almost three quarters (70%) of gender staff survey respondents indicated that the Gender Team was "very effective"/"effective" in their support policy advice. More than half of respondents (53%, 25 of 47) indicated the Gender Team was "effective" in providing policy advice with another 17% (8 of 47) indicating it was "very effective". In terms of piloting new approaches and tools, 72% of respondents indicated the Gender Team was "very effective/effective" in their support.

During the evaluation period, there were gender practice leaders at the P5 level, funded through the Global Gender Programme, in six regional centres (Bangkok, Bratislava, Cairo, Dakar, Panama City and Pretoria). In 2010, each region except the Arab States had a regional senior gender advisor who serviced the country offices.[73] The gender staff survey found that 74 percent of respondents received support from the regional gender practice leader between 2008 and 2013. Respondents reported that most support was provided in the form of technical advice on gender mainstreaming during programme/project formulation.

Gender advisers also worked to build capacity among country office staff and national partners (44 percent of respondents). The organization of annual or bi-annual gender focal point meetings at regional level was valued by 38 percent of respondents. Country offices also received budgetary inputs from regional gender programmes (15 percent of respondents) or periodic missions to monitor progress (19 percent). In terms of effectiveness, 78 percent of respondents found the support either somewhat effective (38 percent) or effective (40 percent), 20 percent indicated the support was very effective and 2 percent found it not effective at all.

Finding 4: Country offices had insufficient gender staff throughout the evaluation period. Only 45 percent of country offices had gender focal team structures in place in 2013, indicating a relatively weak response to the indicators established in the Strategic Plan and GES.[74]

Previous evaluations and reports suggested the optimal arrangement is a cross-unit gender focal team led by a senior gender adviser. The evaluation found that gender focal points covered gender issues in 80 percent of country offices, and only 20 percent of them worked full time on the issue. Moreover, these staff were at junior levels with little specialized gender training.

Gender focal teams led by senior managers: At the country level, the Strategic Plan and GES established indicators that required establishment of cross-unit gender focal teams under the leadership of a senior manager (Figure 6). In 2010, just over a third of country offices (38 percent) had complied with this requirement. By 2013, 45 percent of country offices had such teams in place. However, only 30 percent of these were led by senior advisors, and this figure has remained unchanged. Evidence suggests that country offices that had established a gender focal team had a stronger approach to gender mainstreaming in their policy and programming, administrative and operational efforts, and reporting functions.[75] Country visits undertaken under this evaluation reconfirmed the finding of the midterm review of the GES that a cross-unit gender team, supported by a senior advisor, was the optimal arrangement.

Gender focal points: The main responsibility for gender mainstreaming in country offices is often assigned to gender focal points, and 80 percent of country offices have them. They tend to have broad job descriptions, most often without specific terms of reference. Frequently only 20

---

73 This structure changed in 2014 when the two regional centres in Africa were consolidated into one and relocated to Addis Ababa. The gender practice leaders were then organized into a cluster system based on focus areas. At present, the title of 'gender practice leader' has evolved to 'team leader' (Bangkok, Istanbul and Cairo), 'head of cluster' (Panama) and 'programme gender adviser' (Addis Ababa). The need to maintain the seniority of these regional advisers has been recognized and their funding now comes from the BPPS's core resources instead of the Global Gender Programme, making them more sustainable.

74 Indicator: Percentage of country offices that have established a gender focal team led by a senior manager. Target: 25% improvement per year.

75 Twelve percent of respondents to the gender staff survey indicated that the gender focal team in their offices has been "very effective", 27% indicated it was "effective" and 32% said it was "somewhat effective" in executing its functions. Nine percent of respondents felt the gender focal team was not effective at all (and 21% had no gender focal team).

(UNDP, 'Mid Term Review: UNDP Gender Equality Strategy (2008–2013)', February 2011 (draft): "In 2010, 30 percent of Country Offices had appointed a Senior Gender Advisor/Specialist.")

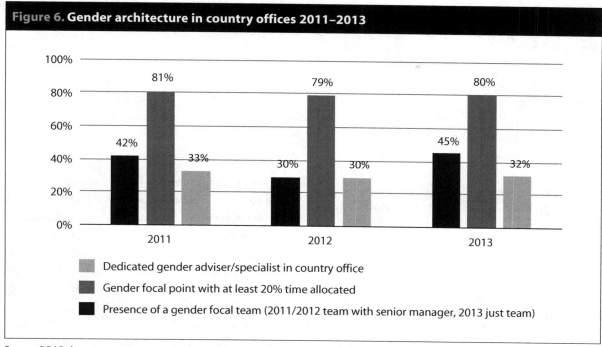

Figure 6. Gender architecture in country offices 2011–2013

Legend:
- Dedicated gender adviser/specialist in country office
- Gender focal point with at least 20% time allocated
- Presence of a gender focal team (2011/2012 team with senior manager, 2013 just team)

Source: ROAR data

percent of their time is allocated to the gender focal point role. Only 20 percent of survey respondents confirmed that their gender focal point was a full-time position. The survey data also reveal that many focal points have limited background in gender (the gender staff survey found that 44 percent had two years of gender experience or less) or are junior staff without a direct reporting relationship with senior management.[76]

4.2 INNOVATIONS TO PROMOTE GENDER MAINSTREAMING

This section assesses two innovations introduced as part of the GES, the GSIC and the Gender Equality Seal. The GSIC was designed to ensure systematic monitoring of implementation of the GES by senior management and to facilitate coherent annual reporting to the Executive Board. The Gender Seal was a certification initiative to motivate country offices and reward strong performance on gender mainstreaming.

4.2.1 GENDER STEERING AND IMPLEMENTATION COMMITTEE

Finding 5: The GSIC mechanism has evolved from a pro forma exercise to a key instrument for reporting on accountability for promoting gender equality by senior managers at headquarters level. It has functioned mainly as a forum for sharing cross-bureau experience. Regional GSICs, which were an explicit target in the GES, have yet to become a uniform feature.

UNDP established the GSIC in 2010 to enable effective monitoring of implementation of the GES and to maintain the organization's strategic focus on gender mainstreaming. The first year each bureau prepared a basic narrative report for GSIC review. Since 2011, the reports have evolved to include more information and analysis of weaknesses, areas of action and responses to previous GSIC recommendations. The reports are now comprehensive, using a common format in line with GES priorities.

---

76 According to the gender staff survey, 7% of respondents were the senior gender advisor and 15% indicated their office had a senior gender advisor, but the remainder (78%) indicated they did not have such a role in their office during the period 2008–2013.

They include sections on programme management, highlighting regional challenges and responses, progress in achieving gender equality development results for each of the four focus areas of the Strategic Plan, knowledge management activities, human resources, accountability efforts, inter-agency collaboration, financial resources, response to recommendations and suggestions for support.

The reports serve the twin purposes of reporting on progress and furnishing the Gender Team with material for the annual report to the Executive Board. Topics of concern that surface regularly include gender parity and measures to develop talent; establishment of mentoring programmes targeting women in junior and middle management; improvement in the use of the gender marker for planning and monitoring; and reporting and resource mobilization.

In some bureaux, the GSIC has provided a forum for reviewing regional results of gender mainstreaming accountability tools and taking stock of and evaluating actions across the regions. In its more robust form, the GSIC is now seen by senior management as a serious peer review process. Some interviewees noted that it should perhaps have a higher profile and report directly to the Administrator's Executive Group, particularly on matters such as strategic collaboration with UN-Women, resource constraints affecting programming, and gender parity issues.

The evaluation found five key issues for refinement that aligned with perceptions expressed in the GSIC reports: (a) The reporting burden, which needs to be streamlined; (b) the concentration on gender parity issues at meetings,

rather than on programming results (or the lack thereof); (c) the low frequency of GSIC meetings, which impedes oversight; (d) the need for regional and practice bureau-level GSICs; and (e) the need to make gender a mandatory standing item at regional bureau cluster meetings and to require all participants to contribute.

4.2.2 GENDER EQUALITY SEAL PILOT

Finding 6: The Gender Equality Seal pilot is a unique initiative developed by UNDP's Global Gender Team and applied in around 30 country offices since 2010. The certification process has motivated country offices and tapped a competitive vein among those volunteering to be part of the pilot process. While it is too soon to conduct a comprehensive assessment of the seal's impact on results in GEWE, it clearly is motivating change and promoting appreciation that gender mainstreaming is tangible and achievable.

The Gender Seal was adapted from UNDP's certification programme for private and public organizations to promote gender equality in Latin America. It was initially piloted in three countries, Argentina, Bhutan and Kyrgyzstan, and all three received gold level certification. When a second, extended pilot was launched, 41 offices volunteered, of which 29[77] completed the process by the end of 2014.

The evaluation found that the success of the Gender Seal derives from a sound methodology and highly participatory approach. Its comprehensive framework links institutional gender mainstreaming efforts and development results.[78] It is flexible and can be adjusted to country contexts to serve as a benchmarking process, a

---

77   Ten offices in RBA (Democratic Republic of the Congo, Ethiopia, Guinea, Lesotho, Madagascar, Mozambique, Niger, Nigeria, Rwanda and Zambia); four in RBEC (Belarus, Kosovo, Moldova and Montenegro); six in RBAS (Bahrain, Egypt, Morocco, State of Palestine, Somalia and Sudan); four in RBAP (Afghanistan, Cambodia, Fiji/multi-country and Nepal; and five in RBLAC (Cuba, El Salvador, Jamaica, Nicaragua and Peru). Argentina re-certified at gold level.

78   It includes human resource indicators derived from senior manager performance goals, gender parity targets, sexual harassment policies and gender equality in recruitment and promotion, including the results of capacity-building efforts, such as the ability of staff to explain how gender mainstreaming is relevant to their work. There are 44 performance benchmarks, overall.

capacity-building opportunity or a transformative experience. As one Resident Coordinator described it, "The Gender Seal finally helps create the 'aha' or the 'click' moment to identify the connectors with gender mainstreaming and the technical programme portfolio."

The evaluation found that the voluntary nature of the Gender Seal may have raised its appeal. Several senior managers and regional staff noted that UNDP does not generally give incentives; rather it is more prone to setting up mandatory accountability mechanisms. There has also been some debate as to whether the Gender Seal exercise should become mandatory. In this connection, 57 per cent of respondents to the gender staff survey indicated that the voluntary nature of the Gender Seal was an important feature.

In terms of gender results, the evaluation found that the Gender Seal process has promoted positive contributions to GEWE.[79] Data from interviews, further triangulated by the gender staff survey, indicate that the Gender Seal has increased integration of GEWE in programming; use of gender analysis to inform project/programme design; funding for GEWE components in projects/programmes; and awareness and engagement among country office staff.

Staff interviewed in the Regional Bureau for Africa (RBA) and Regional Bureau for the Arab States (RBAS) see the Gender Equality Seal as an opportunity to help country offices implement gender mainstreaming processes, and they are encouraging all country offices in their regions to apply. The seal has been used by the Africa Bureau as a diagnostic tool to assess weaknesses and strengths in country offices and establish a baseline for gender mainstreaming efforts. The regional centre, based in Cairo, has observed a visible difference in performance in the participating countries, particularly as the process requires the formation of gender focal teams.

In the Latin America and Caribbean region, in addition to the six countries that have taken part in the seal process, regional staff are supporting two other country offices (Colombia and Panama) with their gender mainstreaming processes. They are using the Gender Seal standard as a guide, rather than applying for a full-blown certification exercise. Similarly, the Armenia country office has decided to use the seal methodology to help identify gaps and strengths without applying to take part in the formal certification process.

The process has also reinforced the message that country offices that elect to be certified need to make it a central office priority and not an exercise that is done 'in addition' to the daily work. The evaluation found that the success of the Gender Seal in Egypt was partly due to the fact that the country office incorporated it as part of a restructuring exercise. This facilitated a shift from a structural approach that revolved around self-contained focal areas to an issue-based approach that allowed for easier horizontal collaboration[80] and strong attention to GEWE. The process also enhanced team building and created a more gender-equal working environment.[81]

However, sustaining the momentum generated by the Gender Seal process could be problematic in situations with high staff turnover and in offices where staff involved in the annual recertification were not participants in the original exercise. Moreover, uptake of the Gender Seal is partly dependent on external factors such as the country office and country context.[82]

---

79 The team observed the Gender Seal assessment process in a country seeking the gold rating.

80 C. Bugnion, 'Evaluation Country Mission Brief – Egypt', 2014.

81 Interview with three UNDP consultants/personnel, January 2015.

82 For example, in Argentina and Kyrgyzstan, the external environment was relatively supportive of gender mainstreaming among government partners. Similarly in Malaysia the process of discussing the Gender Seal in the context of the ADR sparked interest within the Government.

4.3 MECHANISMS FOR TRACKING GENDER INVESTMENTS AND REPORTING ON RESULTS

This section focuses on the assessment of gender equality and tracking mechanisms as seen in the gender marker and the ROAR.

4.3.1 GENDER MARKER

Finding 7: Making the gender marker mandatory during budget submission has served to heighten awareness of the need to consider gender during budget allocation. Nevertheless, evidence suggests that it is not being used effectively as a planning tool and is disconnected from the workflow of the programme cycle, particularly during the appraisal, approval, monitoring and closure stages. Furthermore, there are variations in the way the gender marker codes are awarded, which has compromised the accuracy of the information being produced by this tool.

In 2010, UNDP rolled out the gender marker for tracking expenditures made to support GEWE. The gender marker system requires coding of every output of projects against a four-point scale: GEN 0 (not expected to contribute to gender equality), GEN 1 (contributes to gender equality in a limited way), GEN 2 (gender equality is a significant objective) and GEN 3 (gender equality is a principle objective).

Despite the development of gender marker guidelines and briefings by the Global Gender Team, there has been some misunderstanding about its purpose, with some staff believing that it is a ranking rather than a means of classification. For example, some staff were reluctant to assign GEN 0 or GEN 1 because they deemed them as low scores, while others perceived GEN 3 as better than GEN 2.[83]

With respect to application of the gender marker, a 2012 review concluded there "was no standardized and institutionalized quality control in place to monitor implementation of the gender marker".[84] Country visits for this evaluation validated this finding. Evaluation team members discovered that different staff members or gender focal points used different processes in applying the rating. Similarly, responses to the gender staff survey indicated there was no clear designation of who was responsible to apply it.[85] Furthermore, close to 40 percent of survey respondents indicated there was no clear understanding of how to apply the ratings.

Evidence suggests that uneven understanding and inconsistent practices in country offices may have limited the accuracy of the tool. The 2012 review concluded that "approximately one third of all projects/outputs that were assessed were incorrectly scored, meaning that more than $264 million dollars in planned budgets reported with an erroneous score". In the gender staff survey, 71 percent of respondents felt the gender marker provided only a "somewhat accurate" picture of gender mainstreaming activity. Only 19 percent rated it as an "accurate" representation.

Overall, there were mixed views on the current usefulness of the gender marker and concerns about the subjectivity and "arbitrary" nature of the exercise. As one former Country Director succinctly put it, "We never integrated the logic of the marker at the programme design and appraisal stage." The gender marker appeared to be implemented most effectively in country offices that had invested in tailor-made training and where there was also a gender advisor who was able to train people on how to use this new system. At best, it was seen as a useful reminder to be gender sensitive. At worst it was seen as a headquarters

---

83 UNFPA has changed the rankings in its gender marker system to 2a and 2b instead of GEN 2 and GEN 3 to help clarify this distinction. UNDP may want to investigate how well this change worked for UNFPA and consider applying the same shift in categorization.

84 UNDP, 'Assessment of the UNDP Gender Marker: Successes, Challenges and the Way Forward', December 2012.

85 In 12% of cases a senior manager assigned the gender marker rating while 42% of responses indicated individual project staff were responsible.

imposition without relevance to country office planning and monitoring needs and that it was an "added burden, with no incentive".[86]

4.3.2 RESULTS-BASED REPORTING: RESULTS-ORIENTED ANNUAL REPORTING

Finding 8: The ROAR, an annual requirement, has become an important driver of reporting on GEWE. However, this corporate reporting does not systematically track the quality or type of gender results and has not explored trends in how change happens in GEWE work.

In 2008, UNDP incorporated gender equality considerations in its ROAR process based on the gender outcomes and indicators in the 2008–2013 Strategic Plan and the GES. The ROAR process requires programme managers to specify gender-related outcomes and indicators and tracks these by focus area, country and region. Seventy six percent of respondents to the gender staff survey said that reporting mechanisms, such as the ROAR, were one of the most effective tools to increase attention to gender equality.

The effectiveness of ROAR reporting appears to depend upon staff access to internal gender expertise as well as monitoring and evaluation expertise.[87] In Kyrgyzstan, for example, the office has a gender focal team, the M&E officer is the gender focal point and gender specialists have been on staff for close to 10 years. It was therefore not surprising that the ROAR reported change in GEWE at the outcome level, which could then be triangulated through interviews with UNDP partners and relevant evaluations.

At the headquarters level, ROAR gender results are a key source for reporting to UNDP's Executive Board. Headquarters staff have generally found ROAR results a useful source of self-reported data, providing a good summary of the gender profile at the country level. Headquarters staff responsible for the ROAR indicate that it has become increasingly possible to track the link between better GEWE outcomes (resulting from more attention to gender planning) and better development results overall. Regional staff indicated that responding to the annual ROAR questionnaire has helped stimulate internal discussions about gender. At the country level, ROAR results are used in Gender Seal discussions, in discussions of results with development partners and in independent evaluations.

Efforts have been made to deepen the inquiry in terms of annual reporting on gender in the ROAR exercise. The current template requires reporting on gender marker expenditures, provides a drop-down menu for specifying areas of work and provides a 3,000-character text box for a description of key gender results. It also includes a number of questions that require reporting on institutional results in gender, such as the proportion of the budget devoted to gender learning and collaboration with UN-Women. However, as ROAR reporting is increasingly used for GSIC discussions and in evaluation, this form of self-reporting does not produce information on the type and quality of gender results and progress over time. Nor does it cover unintended effects such as backlash or other contextualized issues that would help enrich understanding of key issues.

4.4 GENDER PARITY AND ORGANIZATONAL CULTURE

The evaluation focused on assessing the gender parity profile as well as key messages from the global staff survey, which has been an annual exercise since 1999.

---

86 The most positive feedback came from staff who had received this type of training (Argentina, Kyrgyzstan and Egypt). The Panama Regional Centre has found it to be a very powerful tool and uses it in all training exercises to stimulate discussion. Other country office staff involved in environment projects indicated there were complications in reconciling the gender marker with the social and environmental screening process. Argentina's country office was a pilot for implementation and assessment of the gender marker tool, and the Gender Unit provided tailored training for the office.

87 Interviews with five country office personnel and three consultants in November and December 2014 and January 2015.

4.4.1 GENDER PARITY

Finding 9: UNDP has been working on gender parity internally since 1995 and has achieved it at the aggregate level. However, the organization lags behind in parity at the senior (D1/D2) and middle (P4/P5) management levels, which is a serious concern. The institutionalization of policies intended to promote more female candidates has not yielded tangible results. Furthermore, no explicit steps are being taken to address male employees' concerns about the effects of pro-female policies on men's career prospects.

UNDP's Gender Action Plan 2009 and Gender Parity Strategy 2013–2017 address the gender parity targets mandated by the General Assembly and the UNDP Executive Board. These call for achievement of 50/50 gender parity at all levels of appointments and a 55/45 distribution for senior management by 2011. This was to be irrespective of the type or duration of staff appointment, the series of the Staff Rules under which the appointment was made or the source of funding, as per UN Secretariat ST/AI/1999/9.

Data provided by the Office of Human Resources (OHR) based on Atlas reports showed that gender balance remained equitable between 2008 and 2013 and that the proportion of female employees increased by 2 percentage points, from 49 to 51 percent. By 2015, parity figures stood equal, with 50 percent men and women. Around 74 percent of country offices reported taking some gender parity actions between 2011 and 2013. However, as shown in Figure 7, disaggregating parity figures by professional grade reveals a much less equitable picture.

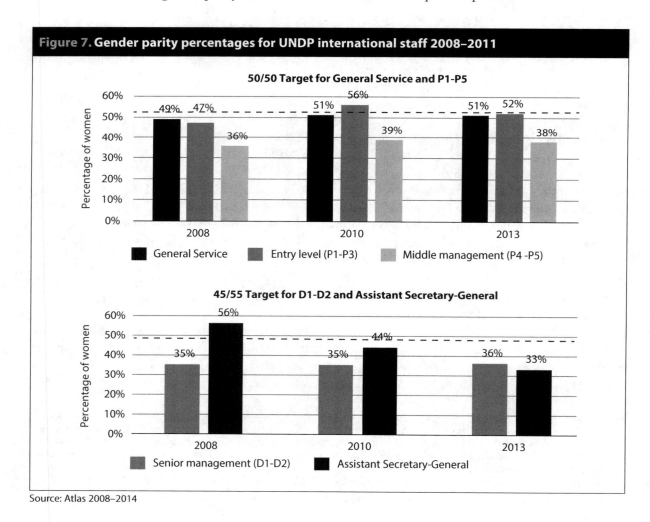

Figure 7. Gender parity percentages for UNDP international staff 2008–2011

50/50 Target for General Service and P1-P5

General Service — Entry level (P1-P3) — Middle management (P4 -P5)

45/55 Target for D1-D2 and Assistant Secretary-General

Senior management (D1-D2) — Assistant Secretary-General

Source: Atlas 2008–2014

UNDP's parity performance ranks tenth out of 15 field-based UN agencies (Figure 8).

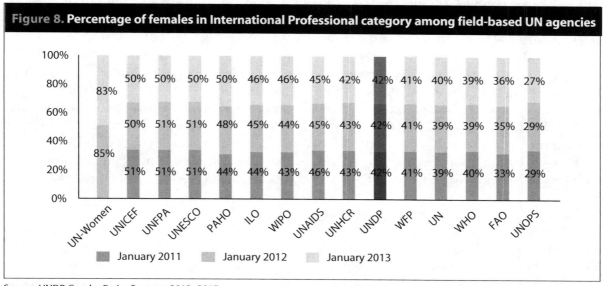

Figure 8. Percentage of females in International Professional category among field-based UN agencies

Source: UNDP Gender Parity Strategy 2013–2017

Compared to 25 UN organizations, UNDP sinks to sixteenth place (Figure 9).

Figure 9. Percentage of females in International Professional category in UN system 2013

Source: UNDP Gender Parity Strategy 2013-2017

Since 2008, there has been little fluctuation in overall percentages by grade. UNDP has almost met its gender parity targets of 55/45 at the Assistant Secretary-General level and has met the 50/50 target at entry-level Professionals (P1-P3) and at all General Service levels. It is clear, however, that UNDP has yet to meet parity targets at the P4/P5 and D1/D2 levels. The Gender Parity Strategy indicates that men enter the organization at a higher level and thus advance quickly. It is estimated that men take an average of 7.1 years to be promoted to P5, while women take 10 years. The strategy postulates that "institutional structures may restrict and impede or hinder women's process", but it does not elaborate on what these may be.

At the senior management level, UNDP consistently puts forward more women candidates for positions than other UN agencies, and accountability mechanisms are in place to facilitate this. These include (a) the use of a 'balanced scorecard' (up until 2013) that included female/male balance as part of the workforce indicator for which Heads of Office were accountable and (b) a GSIC review of corporate performance in gender parity by individual bureaux and offices. All bureau directors interviewed noted this and the fact that progress (or not) on gender parity targets is included in reports to the GSIC. Furthermore, two bureaux reported having taken specific measures to mentor and support female staff so they could take on more senior responsibilities, and that these measures had yielded success. The point was also made that appointments at the Resident Coordinator level are outside the control of the regional bureaux.

UNDP's Gender Parity Strategy 2013–2017 provides information on additional measures taken to redress this situation. It introduces new recruitment policies requiring all interview panels to be gender balanced, gives preference for qualified women candidates, includes gender considerations in recruitment shortlists and provides opportunities for accelerated promotions for women in P4/P5 posts. Where women should be hired to establish parity but suitable female candidates cannot be found, a waiver can be approved by the Executive Director's office.[88]

Even with these policies in place, uptake is uneven. Some staff attribute this to the nature of the work and others to the nature of the organization. Data from the Gender Parity Strategy suggest that women with families may find hardship or non-family postings a challenge unless they are willing to separate from their families for several years. In 2013, women made up 38 percent of managers in country offices. However, that number dropped to 35 percent in hardship stations and to 31 percent in non-family duty stations. Interviews with headquarters and regional office staff suggest that the rotational nature of UNDP's posts presents a greater challenge for female candidates in some cultural contexts, such as when male are reluctant or unwilling to follow their spouses to a new posting.[89]

Interviews with UNDP staff at all levels suggested that in some ways UNDP has a rather 'masculine' organizational culture[90] that does not favour or support management styles perceived as female.[91] This may be one factor contributing to the slower rate of promotion among female International Professional staff.[92]

Feedback from country visits and regional staff interviews indicated some resentment among male staff and concern among female staff due to the perception that women are promoted because of gender rather than competence. Moreover, some men perceived that the policy explicitly limited their promotion possibilities. The evaluation did not find that OHR or senior management had taken any significant measures to address this view. This issue merits deeper scrutiny.

4.4.2 ORGANIZATIONAL CULTURE

Finding 10: While UNDP has instituted policies and mandatory mechanisms to promote GEWE and to sensitize staff on gender issues,

---

88 OHR reported receiving several requests for waivers due to a lack of qualified female candidates for specific positions, but precise data on this dimension were not available for the evaluation.

89 Interviews with headquarters and regional staff in January 2015.

90 UN-SWAP defines organizational culture as a shared set of beliefs, attitudes, behaviours, values and norms in force within an institution that are materialized through informal and formal rules through which the institution conducts its business, treats its employees and partners, involves workers in decision-making, distributes power and information, and supports workers towards collective objectives.

91 Two interviews with UNDP senior managers, two with regional staff and three with country office staff in November and December 2014 and January 2015.

92 UNDP, 'Gender Parity Strategy 2013–2017', 2013.

its organizational culture in this regard remains weak. Trends from the annual global staff survey indicate consistent differences in how female and male staff members score issues dealing with empowerment, professional growth, fairness/respect, work-life balance and conflict management. Women generally score UNDP less favourably on these aspects than do men.

As noted in the previous section, UNDP's policies promoting gender parity and women in leadership positions have yet to yield tangible results. Similarly, although UNDP has made a concerted effort to promote work-life balance and family-friendly policies (such as through provision of child care, flexible hours, parental leave and spousal employment), the uptake of such polices is uneven. The evaluation found that where senior management is supportive of these policies, staff reported it was easier to take advantage of them. However, the manner in which family-friendly policies are implemented and accepted culturally varies among country offices. Some country office staff felt pressure not to take advantage of particular policies, such as the breastfeeding leave

policy. In some duty stations, such as in conflict zones or humanitarian assistance locations, implementation of policies such as work/life balance is not entirely feasible.

To enhance gender awareness and capacity among staff, UNDP introduced mandatory online basic gender courses for all staff in 2008. OHR data indicate that 3,807 staff have taken the Gender Journey course and 2,680 staff have completed the Sexual Harassment course. The evaluation did not undertake a detailed inquiry on the merits of this form of capacity building. A brief analysis of the content revealed that while Gender Journey provides an introduction to gender equality concepts, it is not specific enough to support staff in day-to-day, specialized work on GEWE.[93]

The annual global staff survey gathers data from staff members with respect to various aspects of organizational culture, including how UNDP rates as a place to work, opportunities for professional growth and development, engagement, accountability and empowerment. The data have been disaggregated by sex since the survey's

Table 2. Trends from UNDP global staff survey (2010, 2013)

Annual global staff survey question	Percent favourable Women / Men	
	2010	2013
Empowerment		
Job provides a chance to have your ideas adopted and put into use	44/55	45/57
Job provides an opportunity to do challenging and interesting work	56/66	55/67
Job provides authority to make decisions about how to do your job	41/52	44/52
Professional growth		
How would you rate UNDP on your opportunity for advancement	43/51	42/50
Openness, fairness and respect		
UNDP employees are treated without regard to race, ethnicity, religion, gender identity, sexual orientation, age, nationality, disability or language	72/78	71/74
Work/life balance		
My management team is sensitive to the relationship between my work life and my personal life	58/64	63/66
Office management		
My management team effectively manages conflict and grievances in my office	50/61	50/64

Source: UNDP global staff survey

---

93   Gabriela Byron, 'Study to Assess UNDP's Performance in the SWAP, Final Report', March 2015, p. 21.

inception in 1999 (and now includes an 'other' category in addition to male/female). Based on results from 2010 to 2013 (except 2011, when no survey was administered), there have been consistent differences in the responses of women versus men. Generally speaking, men have tended to report more favourable experiences than women with respect to empowerment, professional growth, openness, fairness and respect, work-life balance and office management (Table 2).

OHR does not provide comprehensive information on the reasons for these gaps, and the evaluation did not investigate this dimension deeply. However, there appears to be notable consistency in the gender gap over the years, pointing to the need for further analysis.

4.5 ACCOUNTABILITY AND OVERSIGHT

This section assesses the extent to which UNDP's evaluation and audit functions have approached evaluation and auditing of UNDP's GEWE initiative, programming and institutional change efforts.

4.5.1 EVALUATION

Finding 11: The UNDP handbook on planning, monitoring and evaluating for results (published in 2009 and updated in 2011) does not provide adequate guidance on how to undertake gender-related evaluations. It is limited to highlighting the need for gender targeting inputs, such as sex-disaggregated data. Furthermore, decentralized evaluations have not paid sufficient attention to ensuring that the GEWE dimensions of UNDP programmes are consistently covered in depth.

An external consultant conducted a meta-evaluation of 30 gender-related reports from 2014, consisting of four ADRs conducted by IEO and 26 evaluations conducted at country, regional or headquarters levels. The composite score for the 30 reports was "Approaches requirements", which represented a downgrading from the previous year. (The four ADR reports were rated "Exceeds requirements" [11/12] and the 26 decentralized evaluation reports were rated "Approaches requirements" [5/12].) This rating should be seen in the context of overall UNDP monitoring and evaluation capacity. In 2012, only 23 percent of country offices had a dedicated monitoring and evaluation person, down from 29 percent the previous year. This left the 12 regional specialists to cover the gaps.[94]

Several factors were noted as contributing to high ratings of gender-related evaluation reports: (a) application of a gender perspective in the contextual analysis; (b) data collection and analysis that was consistently disaggregated by gender; (c) inclusion of women and/or people with knowledge of gender theory on the evaluation team; and (d) sufficient resources and time to fully incorporate gender in the methodology. The meta-evaluation also concluded that "There are still a number of essentially gender-blind evaluations"[95] (meaning they did not address gender).

4.5.2 GENDER-RESPONSIVE AUDITING

Finding 12: Office of Audits and Investigations practice conforms to international standards based on risk assessment. The focus has been limited to assessing gender-parity levels in country offices, and audits have not generally addressed GEWE. Moreover, there has been no systematic practice of undertaking gender audits.

---

94 UNDP, 'Annual Report on Evaluation, 2012', pp. 11–12.

95 An evaluation of a community forest management programme, for example, gave a fairly detailed description of timber and non-timber forestry uses by "the community", their labour intensity and the risks and benefits under the programme, but it provided no disaggregation below "community". It is most likely there are gendered roles. However, without knowing the specific roles of women and men, it is impossible to know if the "20-40%" participation rate of women is a positive or negative change in gender relations.

The UN-SWAP reporting on gender mainstreaming requires specific responses on the extent to which UNDP audit practices are gender sensitive. For 2012–2014, this aspect was rated as "approaches requirements". According to staff interviews, the main reason for this tepid assessment is that the Office of Audits and Investigations conforms to the strict International Standards for the Professional Practice of Internal Auditing, which limits the audit to assessing how the risks are managed in relation to the achievement of GEWE, particularly in terms of gender parity policies.

UN-SWAP recognizes two agencies (the International Labour Organization [ILO] and the Food and Agriculture Organization of the United Nations [FAO]) as having good practices in undertaking gender audits. According to ILO, a gender audit is not a traditional financial audit but a 'social audit' that monitors and assesses relative progress in gender mainstreaming. It is meant to look at internal practices and related support systems for gender mainstreaming to determine if they are effective and reinforce each other and whether they are being followed.[96] In its 2013 UN-SWAP report, UNDP reported that the Office of Audit and Investigations would consider expanding its approach in 2014 to provide its auditors with tools to carry out audits focused on the efficiency, effectiveness and economy of operations, not just on compliance and financial information. The office's proposal to expand the scope of its audits could provide a framework for undertaking gender audits in UNDP.

To date, there is no systematic practice or common framework for gender audits. Between 2010 and 2013, the Regional Service Centre for Africa supported some UNDP country offices (e.g Burkina Faso and Cameroon) to conduct gender audits using ILO methodology. Other country offices (e.g. Rwanda and Uganda) conducted gender audits in the framework of UNCTs with support from UN-Women. To aggregate and compare data among the country offices requires a common framework of analysis. During country visits, the evaluators noted that some country offices expressed an interest in undertaking gender audits as a complement to the work being done through the Gender Seal. Given the nature of both exercises, undertaking them in parallel may yield better results in terms of data collection and reporting, as well as cost sharing.

4.6 KNOWLEDGE MANAGEMENT AND COMMUNICATION

Finding 13: UNDP developed a set of global and regional knowledge platforms and communities of practice on gender during the evaluation period, but by and large these have not been sustained. The use of knowledge products was not systematically tracked or monitored. Cybermetric analysis also revealed that the UNDP network of websites is highly complex and potentially difficult to navigate. Interviews at regional and country level revealed that the lack of gender materials in languages other than English also posed a problem.

UNDP has established diverse knowledge management processes that were operating during the evaluation period at both global and regional levels. Gender Net, a peer information-sharing and problem-solving network for UNDP staff, was initially set up as an email-based platform, later becoming an active network. In addition, communities of practice were established by each regional centre, curated by regional gender advisors/practice leaders, and these were subsequently transferred to the Teamworks platform. UNDP's 2010 switch to the Teamworks system led to a steep decline in queries and participation,[97] and activity has not returned to previous levels.

---

96 ILO Participatory Gender Audit, www.ilo.org/wcmsp5/groups/public/---dgreports/---gender/documents/publication/wcms_101030.pdf.

97 Interview with UNDP headquarters staff, January 2015. Participation dropped 30% to 40% from one year to the next according to statistics maintained by the knowledge management staff. This was attributed to bandwidth issues, a lack of understanding of the business case for Team Works, confusion on how to contribute and a change of tone to a more formal exchange within Gender Net.

Country and regional staff indicated that the materials they found most useful were resources in the main regional languages. Scarcity of materials in languages other than English, particularly Arabic and Russian, was a problem. UNDP staff also observed that dissemination of knowledge products is often easier for regional centres than for headquarters, as regional centres can promote them through country offices as well as other national and regional networks.

The most successful online platform for gender resources is the America Latina Genera website, which was set up as a regional project to provide gender resources and services for all the Latin America and Caribbean country offices and their stakeholders (www.americalatinagenera.org). The other global resource widely cited as useful by country and regional staff is the website of the International Knowledge Network of Women in Politics, known as iKNOW Politics (www.iknow-politics.org). This portal is designed to serve the needs of elected officials, candidates, political party leaders, researchers and other practitioners interested in advancing women in politics. It links women from around the world with online expertise provided by more than 70 political experts.

Cybermetric analysis also revealed sizable numbers of unique web domains pointing to these two websites, indicating that they are relatively well known and well regarded online. Both the UNDP America Latina Genera website and the iKNOW Politics website were mentioned by over 1,000 other web domains (which are roughly equivalent to websites). To put this in perspective, the number of links (1,199 for America Latina Genera and 1,019 for iKNOW Politics) is just slightly lower than the domain links to the website of the Association for Women's Rights in Development (1,416), a reputable women's rights organization; roughly half the number of links to the Gender

Inequality Index (2,317); and a quarter of the links to the UN-Women website (4,204).

During the evaluation time frame, 87 gender-related UNDP publications were identified, primarily at global and regional levels, and 20 were subjected to Cybermetrics analysis. The top three publications in terms of 'positivity'[98] and 'contribution'[99] were 'Women's Green Initiative', 'The Gender Equality Strategy 2008–2013' and 'From Transition to Transformation: Sustainable and inclusive development in Europe and Central Asia'. Also positively rated in terms of contribution were 'Policy Briefing Paper: Gender-sensitive Police Reform in Post-conflict Societies', 'Integrating Gender in Disaster Management in Small Island Developing States: A Guide', 'Grassroots Women's Perspectives on Corruption and Anti-corruption' and 'Making the MDGs Work Better for Women: Implementing Gender-responsive National Development Plans and Programmes'.

Interviews indicated that in some cases the process for disseminating knowledge products was an afterthought, not part of the planning for promoting specific products. Furthermore, the different units working on gender-related knowledge products did not necessarily coordinate their efforts.[100] The evaluation found a lack of capacity in the use of tools for analytics and for tracking the response to and effect of knowledge products overall.[101] In this respect, UNDP was not able to leverage online analytics tools to run adaptive digital campaigns based on rapid cycles of user insight and adaptation.

4.7 UN SYSTEM COLLABORATION ON GENDER

Finding 14: UNDP country offices are members of UN country gender theme groups and participate in joint gender programmes. How-

---

98   The percentage of web documents mentioning a UNDP publication that expressed a positive sentiment.

99   The percentage of web documents that contained evidence that they were making a contribution to programmes, mainstreaming and policy.

100   Interview with regional staff and headquarters staff, January 2015.

101   Interview with UNDP headquarters staff, January 2015.

ever, the evaluative evidence indicates that joint programming with UN-Women is still at a nascent stage,[102] and UNDP's relationships with UN-Women are central to such coordination. As UN-Women establishes a firmer global footprint, the partnership between the two agencies is maturing, reflecting comparative advantages that address country-specific contexts and needs.

The gender staff survey indicated that 80 percent of UNDP country offices participate in gender theme groups set up by Resident Coordinators. It also indicated that around 70 percent of offices have participated in gender-related inter-agency joint programming. This has been done in some countries through joint programmes, such as the Joint Programme on Fostering an Enabling Environment for Gender Equality in Turkey. Nevertheless, a joint evaluation of joint programmes on gender equality conducted in 2013 found that "Many joint programmes... showed a misplaced confidence in the capability of the national operating architecture and partners, and the capacity of the United Nations itself, to absorb a joint modality. The challenges for implementation were therefore demanding from the outset, and the learning curve for partners both sharp and steep."[103]

UN-Women sees UNDP as a UN leader with regard to its institutional gender mainstreaming processes, particularly the gender marker and Gender Seal.[104] At the country level, UNDP generally has well-established relationships with government institutions, which increases its influence in policy dialogue and programming negotiations. This comparative advantage places an even greater onus on UNDP to collaborate closely with UN-Women and other UN agencies on gender mainstreaming and women's empowerment initiatives and issues, yet there is still a need for clarity on how to do this.

In countries where both UN-Women and UNDP have offices, it is generally accepted that the UN-Women country director should play a full role in the UNCT. In this context, UN-Women often serves as the chair of the UN gender theme group and helps to coordinate gender inputs in the UN Development Assistance Framework planning process. Where UN-Women is not present there is no standardized approach for filling this role. In some countries, for example, UNFPA may take a stronger lead on gender while in others it may be UNDP or UNICEF.

Regional gender personnel and senior managers interviewed at UNDP headquarters did not think there was a great need to standardize this role, feeling that it should be based on the country context and the individuals. However, where UNDP provides the Resident Coordinator, UNDP staff thought it was logical for UNDP to play this coordinating role with regard to gender for the UNCT. This was particularly the case in countries where UNDP had full-time gender personnel on staff. UN-Women's partners and relationships are generally with national government gender mechanisms and women's organizations, although in some countries UNDP also works closely with women's organizations. In general, however, UNDP's primary relationships are with the line and executive ministries (Finance, Planning, Development Cooperation, etc.).

Thus both UN-Women and UNDP have a role to play in promoting a mainstreamed approach to GEWE within the government, and in ideal circumstances they should coordinate a common approach. As one UNDP senior country manager stated, "Given that UNDP has bigger budgets, works with core governmental institutions and has an organic link with UN-Women, it has a responsibility to work alongside the agency and not step aside when dealing with matters of gender."

---

102 UNDP, UNFPA, UNICEF and UN-Women, 'Joint Evaluation of Joint Programmes on Gender Equality in the United Nations System', November 2013.

103 Ibid., p. 7.

104 Interviews with UN-Women staff, December 2014 and January 2015.

Finding 15: The UN-SWAP reporting platform represents an advance in terms of system-wide accountability and coherence for gender mainstreaming. While the framework relies on self-reported data and is susceptible to 'over-rating', the SWAP still provides a means for systematic data collection on common performance indicators within UNDP and across the UN system. UNDP has been recognized by UN-Women as "spearheading initiatives that propel progress on gender mainstreaming and gender equality".[105]

The UN-SWAP is a relatively new accountability process, and currently 62 UN entities participate. UNDP started submitting annual SWAP reports in 2012. They cover 15 indicators under 6 areas: accountability, results, oversight, human and financial resources, knowledge management, and coherence. Since the UN-SWAP requires UNDP to review its progress in gender mainstreaming against a set of standard indicators, this mechanism has been helping UNDP take annual stock of its progress.

As with the ROAR, data in the UN-SWAP are self-reported. A review of the ratings UNDP has allocated itself for the 15 indicators shows that in some categories the organization has assessed itself at a higher level of progress than is merited based on the evidence presented on the SWAP platform.[106] While this is understandable given that reporting has taken place for just three years, it would be prudent for UNDP to set up quality assurance systems, as the SWAP process is expected to be reviewed by an external body (such as the Joint Inspection Unit) once every five years.[107] In the other performance indicators, UNDP has surpassed the requirements. UNDP has been commended by UN-Women on such initiatives for documentation of best practices.[108]

For the coherence indicator, peer reviews must be undertaken by entities seeking to be ranked as having exceeded the requirements. A peer review involves two entities visiting each other and reviewing their respective SWAP reporting procedures and results. This promotes cross-agency learning and sharing of experiences while also ensuring accuracy of results. The Rome-based entities (International Fund for Agricultural Development, World Food Programme and FAO) partake in a review annually. Peer reviews are planned in 2015 by the Economic and Social Commission for Western Asia, Economic and Social Commission for Asia and the Pacific, United Nations Human Settlements Programme and United Nations Environment Programme (UNEP). UNDP should consider the merits of involvement in this form of assessment in the future.

---

105 Communication from Phumzile Mlamabo-Nguka to Helen Clark, 2 September 2014.

106 'Study to Assess UNDP's performance in the UN System-wide Action Plan for Gender Mainstreaming', commissioned by IEO in 2015. The study referenced six performance indicators that had insufficient or incomplete evidence supporting the rating providing by UNDP. These included accountability, results-based management, evaluation, financial resource tracking, gender architecture and capacity development.

107 'UN System-Wide Action Plan for Implementation of the UN Chief Executives Board's Policy on Gender Equality and the Empowerment of Women' (2011), p. 15; also referenced in the inter-agency network report 'Women and Gender Equality' of the 12th annual session, 2013.

108 UN System-wide Action Plan op. cit., Performance Indicators Technical Notes, December 2014.

Chapter 5

ASSESSMENT OF UNDP'S CONTRIBUTION TO GENDER EQUITY AND WOMEN'S EMPOWERMENT DEVELOPMENT RESULTS

The Gender Equality Strategy contains a section covering development results that details outcomes and gender-explicit indicators that link to the Strategic Plan. This chapter assesses UNDP's contribution to results in GEWE in the four focus areas and seeks to answer the following evaluation question: *"Has UNDP contributed to development results in gender equality and women's empowerment?"*

Reliable GEWE data for all 136 country offices were limited due to lack of sex-disaggregated data and consistent indicators, so the evaluation team created a dataset consisting of data from the ADRs and gender results collected in the country visits. As such, the evaluation assessed UNDP's contribution to development results by creating a database of 260 gender results from 62 ADR reports and 13 country visits, and then by assessing these results based on two scales or frameworks:[109]

- Level of effectiveness of gender results, using the Gender Results Effectiveness Scale

- Type of change in gender results, using the Gender@Work Framework

In this evaluation, 'gender results' are defined as outputs or outcomes that have been found to be contributing (positively or negatively) to GEWE in UNDP interventions. Qualitative thematic coding techniques were applied to gender results according to the two frameworks identified above,[110] which were used to show UNDP's progress in moving towards gender-responsive and transformative results.

The GRES provides a five-point scale showing different levels of effectiveness, both positive and negative, moving towards transformation, and the Gender@Work framework identifies the areas of change that must occur to achieve transformative change. Taken together, the results produced by the two frameworks helped create a more comprehensive perspective on the quality of gender results, their level of effectiveness and the type of change to which UNDP contributed.[111] The team experimented with this approach to establish meaningful aggregate-level trends of UNDP's contributions to GEWE results.

The frameworks have been used in this evaluation to provide an analytical framework to assess the gender results in the four development focus areas. They reflect the fact that working towards GEWE requires more than simply targeting women (or men) or ensuring that a certain number of women benefit from a programme. The frameworks aim at making visible the quality and content issues that are too often absent in accountability and reporting systems and also to capture the level of effectiveness of gender results as well as the type of gender change.

---

109 The team extracted and analysed 178 gender results in the four focus areas from 62 ADR reports and 82 validated results from country visits, for a total of 260 results. These were taken from 64 of 136 countries, so the analysis represents results from 47% of UNDP country offices.

110 These categories and quadrants are not mutually exclusive, and there may be some blurring between them, but in most cases one prominent theme emerged and was coded for. Results were only coded once in the GRES and once with the Gender@Work framework.

111 These frameworks were developed in a context-neutral way, but it is possible to add in the context for the analysis and description of specific results.

In terms of the level of effectiveness of gender results, GRES rates results as gender negative, gender blind, gender targeted, gender responsive or gender transformative (Table 3).[112] (To see how the GRES interacts with political contexts and approaches, see the text box in Annex 5, which presents five different results from a political participation programme.)

Results may evolve over time. Gender-targeted or gender-responsive results have the potential to become transformative and induce transformative shifts. Because underlying power structures are being tackled, there is also the possibility of reversal or backlash.[113] (Instances of backlash were coded from the ADR gender results, and that analysis appears below.)

In terms of the type of gender change, the Gender@Work framework[114] enables a deeper analysis of the types of changes that occur when trying to achieve gender awareness and transformation. It was originally developed for programming and planning purposes based on the premise that effective GEWE programming requires four types of change: individual change, formal change, systemic change and informal change (Table 4).[115] For this evaluation, each result was categorized

Table 3. Gender results effectiveness scale (GRES)

Gender negative	Result had a negative outcome that aggravated or reinforced existing gender inequalities and norms.
Gender blind	Result had no attention to gender, failed to acknowledge the different needs of men, women, girls and boys, or marginalized populations.
Gender targeted	Result focused on the number or equity (50/50) of women, men or marginalized populations that were targeted.
Gender responsive	Result addressed differential needs of men or women and addressed equitable distribution of benefits, resources, status, rights but did not address root causes of inequalities in their lives.
Gender transformative	Result contributed to changes in norms, cultural values, power structures and the roots of gender inequalities and discriminations. The aim was to redefine systems and institutions where inequalities are created and maintained.

Table 4. Gender@Work quadrants of change

Individual change	Consciousness and awareness	Changes that occur in women's and men's consciousness, capacities, and behaviour.
Formal change	Access to resources and opportunities	Changes that occur in terms of access to resources, services and opportunities.
Systemic change	Formal policies, laws, and institutional arrangements	Formal rules are adequate and gender-equitable policies and laws are in place to protect against gender discrimination.
Informal change	Informal cultural norms and deep structure	Changes that take place in deep structure and the implicit norms and social values that undergird the way institutions operate, often in invisible ways.

---

112   The gender-responsive category is as used in the GES 2008–2013 (p. 50).

113   Sheela Patel, co-founder of SPARC & Slum/Shack Dwellers International (1987), notes, "When you work for women's interests, it is two steps forward and at least one step back. And those steps back are… often evidence of your effectiveness; they represent the threat you have posed to the power structure, and its attempt to push you back. Sadly, even our 'success stories' are sometimes nothing more than ways the power structure is trying to accommodate and contain the threat of more fundamental change by making small concessions to us."

114   A. Rao and D. Kelleher, 'Is There Life after Gender Mainstreaming?', 2005, http://genderatwork.org/Portals/0/Uploads/Documents/Resources/Ispercent20therepercent20Lifepercent20Afterpercent20Mainstreaming.pdf.

115   This classification scheme has also been used in UNDP Executive Board reports, e.g., awareness, policy reform, implementation.

into one of these four areas of change. In terms of interpreting the results, the assumption is that if UNDP is conducting transformative GEWE programming, a similar number and concentration of changes would be present in each quadrant. This chapter contains text boxes that describe programmes with multiple dimensions of the Gender@Work change quadrants.

5.1 OVERVIEW ASSESSMENT OF UNDP'S CONTRIBUTION TO GENDER RESULTS

This section examines gender results in the focus areas of the 2008–2013 Strategic Plan, drawing on evidence collected during country visits and from ADRs and other independent regional, global and thematic evaluation reports. It is important to note that the focus area findings are illustrative of UNDP's gender results but do not represent a comprehensive assessment of all gender-oriented activities undertaken during the period, which is beyond the scope of this exercise.

5.1.1 EFFECTIVENESS AND TYPE OF GENDER RESULTS

Finding 16: Gender results from all focus areas except democratic governance were overwhelmingly 'gender targeted', meaning they were limited to counting the number of women and men involved. Democratic governance was the only area that consistently delivered on 'gender responsive' results (over 62 percent of its results), demonstrating more meaningful results by addressing the different needs and priorities of women and men.

Looking across the spectrum of results identified in Table 3, from gender blind through gender transformative, the vast majority of gender results reported in country visits and ADRs were *gender targeted*.[116] Examples of gender-targeted

results included counting the number of women and men or members of marginalized populations who participated in or benefited from programming, such as people living with HIV/AIDs who were reached through interventions, or quotas set for increased incomes of women and men. Poverty and the MDGs had the highest number of gender-targeted results, at 73 percent, followed by crisis prevention and recovery at 60 percent, energy and environment at 50 percent, and democratic governance at 27 percent. While gender targeting is a necessary first step in promoting results that address GEWE, UNDP has yet to deliver on its objective of achieving gender-responsive results across all thematic areas as called for in its GES strategy.

Democratic governance had the highest number of results categorized as *gender responsive*, at 62 percent, followed by energy and environment at 43 percent, crisis prevention and recovery at 37 percent, and poverty and the MDGs at 21 percent. Examples of gender-responsive results include increased women's participation in commissions and political parties; strengthened justice mechanisms for sexual violence in post-conflict situations; and increased economic empowerment of women through skills-building, trainings and network building.

Very few results, only five in total, were *gender transformative*. These results were related to shifts in power and changes in norms, often in relation to traditional practices. An example is the establishment of villages free of female genital mutilation. Transformative outcomes generally emerge from a change process that has several stages, moving from awareness raising, to attitude change, to change in behaviour and rules, often accompanied by institutionalization of a new norm (as described in the Gender@Work framework). This process was seen where transformative changes had taken place, such as in Tunisia's process of

---

116   Of the 260 total gender results, democratic governance had the highest number (129), followed by poverty and MDGs (73). The other focal areas had very low reported results levels—30 for crisis prevention and recovery and 28 for energy and environment.

constitutional reform. In such cases, UNDP was one actor among many that contributed to the end result. For example, in Tunisia UNDP's role typically involved providing legal expertise and financial resources and serving as a neutral actor supporting the platforms on which other actors could then mobilize necessary changes.

A number of results were classified as *gender negative,* meaning that negative outcomes or reversals in progress were seen. Sometimes the negative results followed earlier progress that could not be maintained due to backlash. At other times only the negative pushback was seen, with no signs of progress, due to strongly entrenched cultural and patriarchal norms.

A small number of results, 4 percent or 11 of the cases analysed, were *gender blind.* These failed to acknowledge the needs of men and women and other marginalized populations.

5.1.2 QUALITY OF GENDER RESULTS

To explore the type of gender results to which UNDP contributed, the ADRs and country visit results were combined and categorized according to the four Gender@Work categories (Figure 10).

Finding 17: With respect to outcomes, UNDP is contributing most in terms of improving access to resources and opportunities; changing policies, laws and institutional arrangements; and strengthening consciousness and awareness raising. A few results signal that UNDP has contributed to systemic changes in internal culture and deep structure, which are needed for transformative change.

The findings show what types of changes UNDP most often contributes to and how that varies across the different focus areas. Nearly half of all outcomes, 44 percent, were connected to

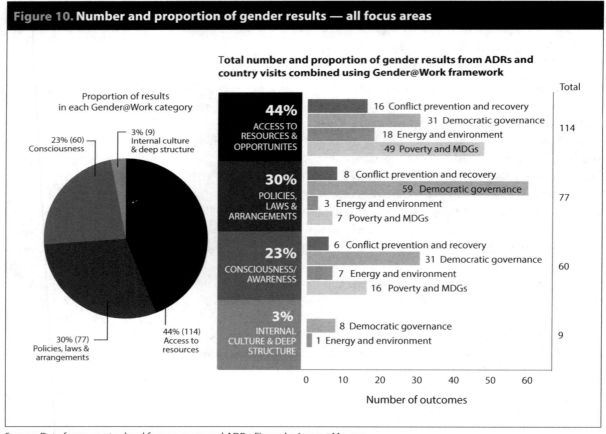

Figure 10. **Number and proportion of gender results — all focus areas**

Total number and proportion of gender results from ADRs and country visits combined using Gender@Work framework

Proportion of results in each Gender@Work category

23% (60) Consciousness

3% (9) Internal culture & deep structure

30% (77) Policies, laws & arrangements

44% (114) Access to resources

44% ACCESS TO RESOURCES & OPPORTUNITES

16 Conflict prevention and recovery
31 Democratic governance
18 Energy and environment
49 Poverty and MDGs

30% POLICIES, LAWS & ARRANGEMENTS

8 Conflict prevention and recovery
59 Democratic governance
3 Energy and environment
7 Poverty and MDGs

23% CONSCIOUSNESS/ AWARENESS

6 Conflict prevention and recovery
31 Democratic governance
7 Energy and environment
16 Poverty and MDGs

3% INTERNAL CULTURE & DEEP STRUCTURE

8 Democratic governance
1 Energy and environment

Total
114
77
60
9

Number of outcomes

Source: Data from country-level focus groups and ADRs. Figure by Impact Mapper

increasing access to resources and opportunities, while nearly a third, 30 percent, related to changed policies, laws and institutional arrangements. More than a fifth of results, 23 percent, were categorized as shifting consciousness and raising awareness. Just 3 percent of results were linked to changes in internal culture and deep structure.

In the two focus areas that reported the greatest number of gender results, the democratic governance area overwhelmingly drove the results in the law and policy reform outcome category[117] and the consciousness and awareness-raising category. Poverty and MDGs was an important driver of gender results for the access to resources

outcome. Both energy and environment and crisis prevention and recovery had the majority of results related to an increase in access to resources and opportunities. The following sections provide a more detailed breakdown of the types of results for each focus area.

Overall, figure 11 shows unbalanced progress in the four quadrants in each focus area. This variation shows gaps in addressing the four dimensions of change necessary for deeper structural transformation. This finding is not surprising given that the majority of results are gender targeted and that UNDP programming is rarely based on gender analysis or informed by communities or key stakeholders such as women's groups.

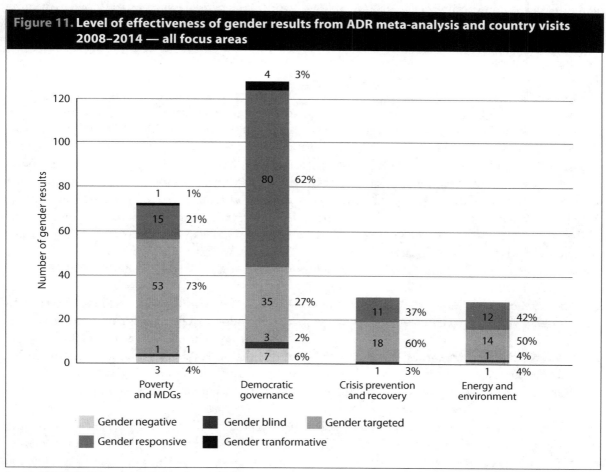

Figure 11. Level of effectiveness of gender results from ADR meta-analysis and country visits 2008–2014 — all focus areas

Source: UNDP IEO ADR meta-analysis and country visits

---

117 The ROAR analysis does not use the Gender@Work framework to analyse frameworks. A similar coding exercise has been used to categorize results into 'awareness', 'policy' or 'implementation'. This categorization may not appropriately capture key gender contributions, and the Gender@Work framework was selected as more appropriate to capture distinctions in quality of change.

Finding 18: UNDP faces many barriers to taking a strategic and longer term approach that would stimulate transformative change. Many project and programme cycles are short, lasting only two years. Furthermore, UNDP tends to engage in programming that addresses women's practical needs; it has not consistently leveraged the value addition of its long-term presence in-country to tackle deeper structural change. Uniform categorization to capture and document gender-responsive and gender-transformative change has also been challenging.

Genuine empowerment results from a long-term, transformative approach to gender equality. The evaluation found that, despite the introduction of multi-year funding frameworks, most gender budgets remain largely focused on short-term interventions, more in line with an approach focusing on equity (50/50) in access to income, public services and access to justice, for example. Even in the case of protracted or recurrent crises that extend for long periods, such as in the Democratic Republic of the Congo, the changing context does not enable UNDP to take a consistent line in support of GEWE. This is partly because the funding remains segmented for short-term interventions and partly because there is not enough interest in and understanding of the importance of long-term processes. This precludes UNDP from pursuing deeper and more sustainable changes in GEWE. Despite improved advocacy, donors have not yet made the commitment needed to ensure access to long-term strategic funding windows to achieve gender equality.

Though UNDP programmes have made substantial and meaningful contributions to addressing practical gender needs, strategic needs remain largely unaddressed. Reforms and changes at the practical level may pave the way for strategic changes, and encouraging this evolution calls for strong advocacy by UNDP. It is important for the organization to reflect on how to leverage its added value to enable interventions that promote deeper structural changes. Bangladesh, for example, has a strong patriarchal societal structure, and while appreciable gender mainstreaming has been achieved, the need remains to address both practical day-to-day gender concerns and the strategic, structural changes that will alter the socioeconomic and religious barriers to fundamental changes in women's lives. The Bangladesh ADR noted that UNDP can play a much more strategic role in advocacy for this deeper structural change, even in challenging contexts.

The evaluation found that capturing and documenting the continuum of gender-oriented change from 'targeted' through 'responsive' to 'transformative' results has been a challenge for UNDP. One reason for this is the lack of a uniform results framework at the corporate level (such as the GRES or Gender@Work framework) to provide guidance on how to capture such results. Another challenge is lack of a common understanding of what constitutes gender-transformative or gender-responsive results.

Additionally, because social and normative change can take years, gender-transformative results may only become visible after additional years of efforts, even after UNDP interventions have ended. Annual results-based management reporting has encouraged provision of system-wide data focused on numbers of men and women in projects and programmes. Yet numbers simply reconfirm a gender-targeting approach. They do not capture how change processes were initiated and if they were on track to achieve intended objectives.

Finding 19: Instances of backlash (barriers to or reversals of progress) were reported across all thematic areas. Backlash raises the issue of sustainability of results. Gender analysis and monitoring and evaluation of gender results have been inconsistent in tracking gender reversals.

Forty percent of the ADRs reviewed (25 of the 62 ADRs) described backlash against gender equality progress or efforts (Table 5). This effect, sometimes described as 'one step forward, two steps back', was mentioned most often in democratic governance results, followed by institutional gender mainstreaming and then the poverty and MDG area. However, ADR report writers were

Table 5. Evidence of backlash in gender results		
Backlash by focus areas	**Numbers of results**	**Percentage of total results**
Crisis prevention and recovery results	1	3%
Energy and Eenvironment results	1	3%
Institutional (gender mainstreaming) results	11	33%
Democratic governance results	16	48%
Poverty & MDGs	4	12%

Source: ADR meta-analysis

not told to systematically address backlash, so the finding that backlash occurs more in democratic governance work is merely suggestive of a trend. There are more such results in this area that have not been captured.

Backlash occurred most often in relation to the redistribution of power, status or resources. This was evident in the reactions of the public and political parties to the increase of women in parliaments and political posts, reactions of families and communities when women enjoyed financial gains, and in the level of implementation of gender parity measures and gender mainstreaming processes in UNDP offices. Resistance to progress often was described as linked to unequal and patriarchal gender roles that resulted in a range of negative consequences. The most prominent of these included increased violence in the home due to women's greater financial status, men's take-over of jobs for women that had been created by UNDP programming, and reported exploitation of women by lending institutions through high interest rates and threats related to nonrepayment of loans.

Backlash may also be sign of success. For example, in Nepal UNDP supported a cross-party women's caucus that successfully built power and a common agenda around women's rights in the Constituent Assembly from 2008 to 2013.[118] However, its success was not long lasting, and the second Constituent Assembly, elected in 2013, abolished the caucus. In the eyes of the women involved in the caucus, this was because they had built up a solid power base, solidarity and a strong voice across party lines that threatened the leadership and status quo. This group continues informally and voluntarily to lobby and advocate for the inclusion of a women's caucus in the new constitution.[119]

Significant backsliding in women's economic and political power has been observed in the past few decades in Central Asia. Under the Soviet Union, women's participation in labour markets and politics was equal to men's participation. Yet decades after the fall of the Soviet Union, significant backlashes to women's equality and power have occurred. Many countries have experienced a return to 'traditional values', which has increased various forms of discrimination, such as forced marriages (as high as 60 percent in Tajikistan) and pressure for women to stay in the home.[120] In general, the region has seen a reduction in women's participation in labour markets and politics, based on Global Gender Gap research.[121]

Finding 20: The lack of gender analysis as a central component of programme design was evident in all focus areas. Dedicated funds are not regularly set aside to perform gender assessment at the design stage or to monitor and evaluate outcomes. Despite efforts to institutionalize gender thinking and the perception that the organization is now 'gender aware', the

---

118   For an example of resources produced by the women's caucus, see www.ccd.org.np/publications/Women_Participating_IN_FDR_Nepal_ENG.pdf.

119   Source: Gender evaluation country visit focus group in Nepal.

120   Moreover, RBEC analyses find education systems weakening in many countries in Central Asia. In addition women are being slotted into gender-stereotypical and lower-paying career paths in universities and are leaving high-earning careers, such as engineering. This has the potential to increase the wage gap in the region, further deepening segmentation of an already gender-segmented labour market and decreasing women's economic productivity, financial sustainability and autonomy.

121   See World Economic Forum, 'Global Gender Gap Reports', 2006–2014.

evaluation found a lack of deeper understanding of what gender means in development programming. In practice, 'doing gender' in UNDP often comes down to a targeting perspective. Women are often framed in a context of vulnerability rather than as key actors in a process of transformative social and development change.

Evidence from the ADR analysis and country visits revealed connections between negative development results and lack of consistent gender analysis of the differential needs of men and women in communities. For example, the Maldives ADR mentioned the reinforcement of gender stereotypes in livelihood projects because they only addressed practical needs, such as income, not strategic gender needs. In northern Uganda, gender inequality was inadequately addressed because neither gender analyses nor market analyses were undertaken. While the projects aimed to ensure that a minimum of 30 percent of their beneficiaries were women, the programme lacked a systematic framework for carrying out gender analysis that guided programme design and implementation or for monitoring progress in gender relations.

Feedback from country visits confirmed that only in rare instances were staff experienced in programming with the aim of transformative change. Moreover, while some ADRs presented outcomes that addressed gender relations and shifts in men's and women's behaviour and norms, the overwhelming focus was on women. The role of men is especially important when addressing changes in distribution of resources or decision-making power. This is because negative social consequences—such as intimidation, harassment or violence—often erupt when the status quo concerning power or privilege is threatened.

Furthermore, as ADRs have also noted, gender stereotypes affect both women and men. As such, they must be addressed in change interventions if the change is to be lasting. In addition, transgender issues were missing from the vast majority of results. The one thematic area in which both men and women were consistently the focus (albeit in a gender-targeted manner) was HIV/AIDS programming. Men having sex with men, lesbians, gay men, bisexuals, transgender individuals and sex workers were consistently gender disaggregated. UNDP has not yet updated its definitions of gender beyond the binary of men and women.

In some UNDP interventions in democratic governance and crisis prevention and recovery, women were framed in a context of vulnerability rather than as key actors in a process of transformative social and development change. Most interventions focused on women as beneficiaries and victims of abuse and discrimination (e.g. survivors of sexual and gender-based violence) rather than as stakeholders at the centre of change and transformational processes (e.g. women entrepreneurs).

Finding 21: UNDP is recognized for its ground-breaking and innovative contribution to human development through its Human Development Report[122] and Gender Inequality Index. However, the evaluation found little evidence that UNDP has succeeded in integrating such thinking in programming at country and regional levels. UNDP is not recognized as a 'thought leader' in GEWE, and it is more commonly described as a facilitator, enabler and useful reference point on UN commitments.

Civil society groups, especially women's organizations, do not look to UNDP for cutting-edge thinking on GEWE, according to interviews in the 10 countries visited. It was found that while UNDP is a highly respected and relevant partner, particularly in key governance processes, it was rarely referred to or seen to play the role of a 'thought leader' on how to work strategically to drive change through gender equality. More common descriptions of UNDP were 'facilitator', 'adviser' or 'enabler', and UNDP was also described as a helpful reference point on international UN commitments.

---

122 Particularly the 1995 Human Development Report on gender and human development.

In crisis prevention and response, UNDP's work was based on its eight-point agenda for women's empowerment and gender equality in crisis prevention and recovery. This agenda involves stopping violence against women; providing justice and security for women; advancing women as decision-makers; involving women in all peace processes; valuing women's knowledge and expertise in disaster risk reduction; supporting women and men to build back better; including women's issues on the national agenda; and supporting working together to transform society. Though the agenda was recognized as an important effort and potential blueprint, an independent evaluation conducted in 2012 found that it had not been harnessed as the working gender strategy within integrated missions.[123]

5.2 GENDER RESULTS IN THE FOUR FOCUS AREAS

This section examines gender results in the focus areas of the 2008–2013 Strategic Plan. Each subsection has two parts. First is key data, which describes the resources allocated to gender, gender results reported and the areas of work that characterize UNDP's contribution to gender in that focus. Second is the focus area findings based on the Gender@Work analysis applied to the four quadrants of change. These are supplemented by additional findings illustrative of significant gender programming. As noted at the start of this chapter, these sections do not present a comprehensive accounting of gender results in the four areas.

5.2.1 POVERTY REDUCTION AND ACHIEVEMENT OF THE MDGS

Key data

Resources: Between 2008 and 2013, total UNDP expenditure for poverty reduction and achievement of the MDGs was approximately $7.667 billion, averaging $1.277 billion annually.[124] Since 2010, it has been consistently the largest area of programme intervention by expenditure,[125] distributing an average of 29 percent of total UNDP resources. In the period 2010–2013, roughly one half (49 percent, $2,549 billion) of these expenditures made 'significant' or greater contributions to GEWE, according to the gender marker tracking system.[126]

Gender results: According to the ROAR, the poverty reduction focus area averaged 232 self-reported gender results per year (696 outcomes through all three years) across UNDP's country operations. This represented an average of 75 percent of the total number of country outcomes reported over the period. The highest proportion of gender results was reported in the Africa region (78 percent) and the lowest in the Asia Pacific region (69 percent).

Areas of work: Overall, country offices reported that most of the gender results in the poverty reduction and MDG portfolio were related to promoting women's economic rights and opportunities, followed by designing public services that benefit poor women and men equitably, and addressing the gender dimensions of HIV/AIDS (Figure 12). [127]

---

123   IEO UNDP, 'Evaluation of UNDP Support to Conflict-affected Countries', 2013.

124   Source: UNDP Atlas data 2008–2013.

125   In 2008–2009, poverty and MDG achievement was the second largest area of programme expenditure, second to democratic governance.

126   Data reflect expenditure-rated gender marker 2 (significant objective) and gender marker 3 (principal objective) extracted from the online UNDP programme overview in August 2014.

127   Note: Evaluation sample results — The findings were derived from the sample of country visits and ADR results and were drawn from secondary research and reviews of global and regional evaluations. Results are illustrative but not representative of changes UNDP made in the area of poverty and MDGs. Figure 13 presents the gender results culled from ADRs and country visits as categorized by the four quadrants of the Gender@Work framework for the poverty and MDGs focus area.

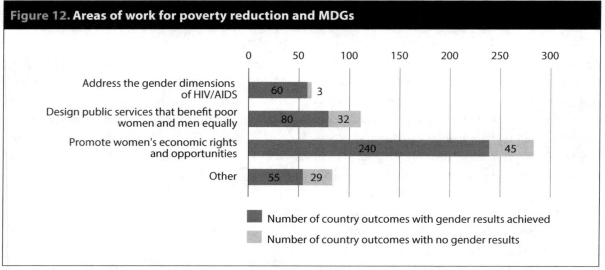

Figure 12. Areas of work for poverty reduction and MDGs

Address the gender dimensions of HIV/AIDS: 60, 3

Design public services that benefit poor women and men equally: 80, 32

Promote women's economic rights and opportunities: 240, 45

Other: 55, 29

■ Number of country outcomes with gender results achieved
■ Number of country outcomes with no gender results

Source: UNDP ROARs 2012 and 2013

Finding 22: The majority of changes in the poverty reduction and MDG portfolio occurred in 'increased access to resources and opportunities' (Figure 13). Targeting women as the main beneficiaries in poverty reduction, often through microcredit and inclusive growth programmes, has brought short-term results in GEWE. In many cases, UNDP's approach has lacked a comprehensive analysis incorporating attention to gender factors and dynamics that go beyond access to resources and opportunities. Success was more evident in programmes that had adopted a long-term perspective.

Most results were 'gender targeted' in nature, often merely mentioning the percentage of women receiving benefits, such as the number of women whose incomes and access to resources had increased or who were provided with jobs and skills for the labour market through UNDP programming. However, greater incomes did not necessarily translate into more power and control over their incomes. The ADRs reported that UNDP programming did not consistently use women's economic empowerment advances to create opportunities for articulating concerns specific to women and unequal gender relations. This had led to unsustainable results.

In Guyana, for example, where a poverty reduction effort provided microcredit to women, they were not able to access the funds available because they needed their husband's permission to do so. (Changes were made in the criteria for accessing the microcredit to resolve this situation.) In the Maldives, women were constrained from accessing employment in the tourist sector because of cultural expectations of gender roles and the premium attached to modesty. In Somalia, over 900 women learned employable skills and received microgrants and start-up kits. However, the grants were of short duration (six months or less) and there was little follow-up, so the programme has not been sustained. Moreover, there were reports of threats of violence from participants, who reported that microfinance staff visited their homes and "demand[ed] assets as payment, intimidating the women and sometimes using violence."[128]

More successful initiatives were characterized by comprehensive approaches and longer term programming. In Zambia a microcredit programme aimed at increasing women's income has been ongoing since 2004. Since the project addresses women only, the project staff have been attentive to negative impacts on family dynamics and used a women's group to mediate and defuse

---

128   G. Okonji, gender equality outcome paper for ADR, August 2014, p. 23.

CHAPTER 5. ASSESSMENT OF UNDP'S CONTRIBUTION TO GENDER EQUITY AND WOMEN'S EMPOWERMENT DEVELOPMENT RESULTS

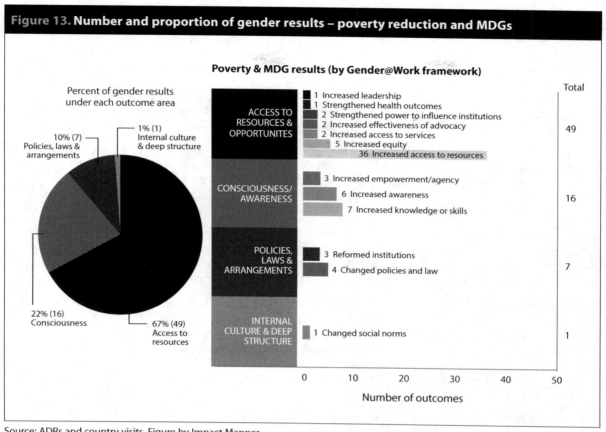

Figure 13. Number and proportion of gender results – poverty reduction and MDGs

Poverty & MDG results (by Gender@Work framework)

Percent of gender results under each outcome area

- 1% (1) Internal culture & deep structure
- 10% (7) Policies, laws & arrangements
- 22% (16) Consciousness
- 67% (49) Access to resources

ACCESS TO RESOURCES & OPPORTUNITES
- 1 Increased leadership
- 1 Strengthened health outcomes
- 2 Strengthened power to influence institutions
- 2 Increased effectiveness of advocacy
- 2 Increased access to services
- 5 Increased equity
- 36 Increased access to resources
- Total 49

CONSCIOUSNESS/ AWARENESS
- 3 Increased empowerment/agency
- 6 Increased awareness
- 7 Increased knowledge or skills
- Total 16

POLICIES, LAWS & ARRANGEMENTS
- 3 Reformed institutions
- 4 Changed policies and law
- Total 7

INTERNAL CULTURE & DEEP STRUCTURE
- 1 Changed social norms
- Total 1

Number of outcomes: 0 10 20 30 40 50

Source: ADRs and country visits. Figure by Impact Mapper

tensions. In Niger, a similar approach brought about the beginning of transformative shifts: women acquired some financial independence and control over income, gaining greater access to decision-makers and raising their status in the community. Men began to take on some of the tasks considered women's work, a significant relational achievement in this context.

Another example of UNDP's comprehensive approach assessed by this evaluation is the Urban Partnerships for Poverty Programme in Bangladesh, ongoing since 2007. The programme has a more targeted gender-awareness component, which has resulted in a drop in early marriage and a rise in adult literacy classes and training. Also notable is the implementation of regular couples training as a measure to minimize any backlash regarding women's control over their income. The Micro-Enterprise Development Programme (MEDEP) in Nepal is

another example demonstrating the importance of a comprehensive approach and long-term support (in this case 16 years) in producing sustainable development results (see Box 1).

Insufficient attention to selection of partners can have harmful consequences, as seen in Liberia. Beneficiaries interviewed by the Liberia ADR team were concerned about usurious interest rates in a microcredit programme implemented by UNDP projects and partners. This programme targeted at women was charging 30 percent over 3 months. The assessment suggests that programme resources should be given to women's groups and village savings and loan institutions (instead of individuals) to build their capacity to use credit. The approach of lending to individuals adopted by the programme was generally seen as inappropriate in the Liberian context. A similar issue was noted in a project targeting youth in Sierra Leone, with microfinance

Box 1. UNDP's multi-dimensional approach to transformative gender change in Nepal

Nepal's high rates of poverty and unemployment are deepened by caste, ethnic and gender inequalities. Poverty has been framed as one of the roots of civil conflict, and the Micro-Enterprise Development Programme (MEDEP) was developed to address the nexus of poverty, social exclusion and conflict. It was initiated in 1998 during a violent period of the civil war with Maoists, when political and caste tensions were running high. This UNDP-supported initiative, currently operational in 38 districts, targets 70 percent women. It works directly with District Development Committees under the Ministry of Industry.

MEDEP staff say that the programme was able to operate during a period of civil conflict because it was dealing with the very issues of poverty and exclusion that the Maoists were taking up. MEDEP targets people living below the poverty line, poor dalits, indigenous groups, people with disabilities and poor women. The aim is to create entrepreneurs and new businesses to raise the incomes of poor people, especially women. This underscores the relevance of the programme to the social issues of the time.

According to evaluation reports and the MEDEP team, 70,000 people have become micro-entrepreneurs (68 percent of them women), and most continue to operate. During a country visit, consultations with two women's micro-enterprise groups revealed evidence of concrete results in terms of improved economic empowerment and livelihoods. One member of a group had raised her monthly income from $50 to $175.

Women's economic status in the community has improved, increasing their access to and control of resources and power. This has enabled them to keep their children in school and to access health and agricultural services. The women volunteered that they had more confidence about speaking their opinions in public forums, showing evidence of increased empowerment and consciousness. Some women also shared examples of norm change, such as their increased ability to negotiate with their husbands. Some women had gone to work in the city or abroad—something they had never done before. This represented a major change in traditional norms.

The MEDEP programme started out as a targeted effort, but over the years it has been refined based on an empowerment model. Since then it has been yielding gender-responsive and to some extent gender-transformative results. It shows that sustainable results are possible with a comprehensive approach and longer term support—in this case 16 years. UNDP's role has been to provide technical advice to develop the initiative and resources to support its implementation throughout the 16 years, along with other donors, such as AusAid, and the Nepali government. Now in its fourth phase, MEDEP represents a long-term investment in lifting people out of poverty. Ownership is being transferred to the Government, with hopes for sustainability.

institutions providing loans at interest rates fluctuating between 5 and 25 percent.

Finding 23: In terms of 'increased knowledge and skills,' UNDP's Global Gender and Economic Policy Management Initiative (GEPMI) has provided capacity development and advisory services to planning and policy experts in governments. Data suggest that the GEPMI approach is relevant and potentially sustainable. However, further evidence is needed to assess its overall effectiveness and longer term impacts.

The GEPMI capacity development programme was designed in 2010 with three components: a short-term course; tailored country-level advisory services and capacity development workshops; and a master of arts degree in gender-aware economics, offered by Makerere University in Uganda. GEPMI has reached 1,165 policymakers, economists, statisticians and gender equality experts in 81 countries.[129] Moreover, 173 experts are members of the Global GEPMI Community of Practice, providing a discussion forum for trainers and experts. Close to 60 percent of GEPMI participants were women at the time of the evaluation.

---

129 UNDP, 'Monitoring Report, Gender and Economic Policy Management Initiative 2010–2013'. In total 1,165 participants were trained, 891 in Africa, 239 in Asia and the Pacific, and 35 in Latin America.

An independent evaluation of the UNDP regional programme was favourable about GEPMI, and confirmed the programme's relevance and sustainability. However, it also noted the importance of future reviews to fully assess the effectiveness and efficiency of the programme.[130] The implementation of GEPMI has also led to collaboration with partners, including economic and academic institutions and other UN entities, such as UN-Women.[131]

Finding 24: In terms of 'policy advice', UNDP developed and is currently implementing the MDG Acceleration Framework (MAF). This global initiative aims to help countries overcome slow and uneven progress towards achievement of the MDGs, including MDG 3 on GEWE and MDG 5 on maternal health. The MAF is present in over 50 countries, promoting gender equality not only in national action plans but also in MAF planning processes.

Launched in 2010, the MAF supports countries to develop nationally owned, multi-stakeholder action plans for improving their rate of progress on off-track MDGs within the context of their planning cycle and processes. Although each action plan aims at one specific lagging MDG, mutual synergies across goals generate positive spillover effects on others.[132] In this regard, the evaluation found advances towards achievement of MDG 3 through MAF action plans focused on other goals.

UNDP developed a toolkit in 2011 to integrate a gender component in each step of the MAF process. It includes ensuring that at least one of the MAF facilitators is gender sensitive. The kit also incorporates gender-sensitive and role-playing exercises, together with gender-relevant examples of suggested interventions. This has helped in promoting a gender-responsive MAF process and integrating gender dimensions in MAF action plans. However, the availability and quality of sex-disaggregated data are still challenges in many countries, limiting the ability to assess progress from a gender perspective.[133]

A global approach in the MAF action plans applied in 52 countries aided gender-oriented programming in Bangladesh, Kyrgyzstan and Nepal. The highest number of MAF action plans addressed MDG 5; only two countries reported they used MAFs with MDG 3.[134]

It is notable that the majority of MAF action plans focused on gender-targeted service delivery. The high focus on maternal mortality was also likely due to the fact that MDG 5 had the slowest progress. Through the MAF, UNDP has contributed to embedding poverty reduction and MDG achievement in national development agendas, but weaknesses remain in the availability of sex-disaggregated data. In Kyrgyzstan, the MAF action plan developed a 'beyond the health sector' approach to serving women who had moved to the capital city, providing an integrated package of social and medical support regardless of registration/permanent address. It provided counselling and support through village health committees and local authorities.[135]

Nepal also used the MAF on MDG 7 (water and sanitation and environmental sustainability) to address the lack of separate toilet facilities for girls in 35 percent of community schools, which had increased absenteeism among girls. A MAF steering committee under the leadership of the National Planning Commission brought

---

130   IEO UNDP, 'Evaluation of the Regional Programme for Africa', 2013.

131   UNDP, 'Light Assessment Gender and Economic Policy Management Initiative', 2013, p. 2.

132   UNDP, 'Accelerating Progress, Sustaining Results, the MDGs to 2015 and Beyond', September 2013.

133   Ibid.

134   UNDP IEO, 'Evaluation of the Role of UNDP in Supporting National Achievement of the Millennium Development Goals', 2014, p. 83.

135   Ibid.

together stakeholders, including the Ministry of Women and Children's Affairs, to participate in the process. By November 2012, 40 strategic solutions had been prioritized, validated and incorporated into an action plan prepared for potential funders. The goal was to persuade them to finance implementation of the action plan in partnership with the Government.

In Bangladesh the MAF process was implemented in the Chittagong Hill Tracts Development Facility. It resulted in mainstreaming women's needs, concerns and priorities in a multidimensional, multisectoral area-based programme. Some local government institutions became more aware of MDG issues and were keen to allocate their own resources to activities identified through the MAF process, which speaks to sustainability. Some unions (the smallest unit of local government) allocated nearly 15 percent of the total planned budget from their own sources. These funds were used to support the provision of agricultural equipment and of sewing machines for poor women and widows.

Finding 25: UNDP programming in HIV and AIDS has consistently advocated for a human development and human rights approach, which strives to address 'deep change' in cultural values and norms. It has also helped move the HIV and AIDS paradigm away from a biomedical focus to a broader development focus.

The UNDP Global Programme supported regional and country offices and brought attention to global norms, standards and practices related to HIV and AIDS. It also provided limited funding for specific activities that regional centres and country offices might not be able to fund, such as global knowledge products (interregional comparative studies on HIV and AIDS), good practice approaches and training on gender mainstreaming in HIV and AIDS programmes. UNDP's contribution was evident in a few

examples in terms of support to MDGs, promotion of transgender issues, and HIV and AIDS advocacy and support. UNDP supported the government in Bangladesh with analysis of gender in five of its MDG areas.

In Brazil the effectiveness of HIV and AIDS advocacy efforts was increased. Country visit interviews indicated that UNDP played a role in advocating for the rights of the lesbian, gay, bisexual and transgender population and raising awareness about homophobia and HIV.[136] At the regional level in Eastern Europe and the Central Asian countries, the UNDP HIV, Health and Development programme contributed to regional advocacy to increase sex workers' ability to access consultative processes related to the new funding process of the Global Fund to Fight AIDS, Tuberculosis and Malaria. This increased awareness about the purpose of the Global Fund and supported strategic discussions on integrating the needs of this key high-risk population.

The Global Fund is increasing access to HIV and AIDS services, and in Zimbabwe more women (59 percent) than men (41 percent) with advanced HIV received antiretroviral treatment in 2013.[137] The HIV epidemic remains a challenge to the country's government. Currently, 890,000 people (approximately 66 percent female) should be on treatment, but only 725,000 are receiving it, leaving 19 percent without access. The ADR assessment notes further that although access to antiretroviral treatment in Zimbabwe is laudable, greater attention needs to be paid to addressing the links between HIV and gender.

5.2.2 DEMOCRATIC GOVERNANCE
Key data

Resources: During the evaluation period, total UNDP expenditure for democratic governance was approximately $7.407 billion, averaging

---

136   One interviewee said, "When the government couldn't promote the debates, UNDP could, and did it in a way that was valued by society and Government."

137   UNDP, 'Towards Universal Access in HIV Prevention, Care and Support in Zimbabwe', end-of-project report, 2014.

$1.234 billion annually.[138] Democratic governance was the second largest area of programme intervention by expenditure across the four focus areas, distributing nearly a third of total UNDP resources. In the period 2010–2013, just over a quarter of these expenditures (28 percent) were categorized in the gender marker tracking system as making a 'significant' contribution to GEWE.[139]

Gender results: An average of 210 gender outcomes were reported annually in democratic governance across UNDP's country operations for the period, a total of 631 ROAR outcomes for the three years. This represented 72 percent of the total number of outcomes reported for the period.[140] On average, the Asia Pacific region reported the highest proportion of gender results (77 percent) and the Arab States region the lowest (66 percent).

Areas of work: Results focused mostly on promotion of women's political participation in governance institutions, followed by integration of gender equality in national development policies and budget frameworks (Figure 14).[141]

Finding 26: The most change occurred in the outcome areas of 'policies and laws and arrangements', in which UNDP helped strength-

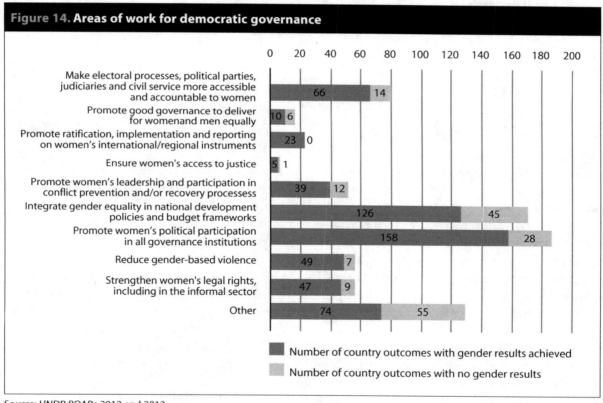

Figure 14. Areas of work for democratic governance

Make electoral processes, political parties, judiciaries and civil service more accessible and accountable to women: 66, 14
Promote good governance to deliver for women and men equally: 10, 6
Promote ratification, implementation and reporting on women's international/regional instruments: 23, 0
Ensure women's access to justice: 5, 1
Promote women's leadership and participation in conflict prevention and/or recovery processess: 39, 12
Integrate gender equality in national development policies and budget frameworks: 126, 45
Promote women's political participation in all governance institutions: 158, 28
Reduce gender-based violence: 49, 7
Strengthen women's legal rights, including in the informal sector: 47, 9
Other: 74, 55

◼ Number of country outcomes with gender results achieved
◻ Number of country outcomes with no gender results

Source: UNDP ROARs 2012 and 2013

138   Source: UNDP Atlas data, 2008–2013.

139   Data reflect expenditure-rated gender marker 2 (significant objective) and gender marker 3 (principal objective) extracted from the programme overview in December 2014.

140   For 2011, 2012 and 2013 the total number of reported outcomes was 877, of which 628 reported gender results.

141   Evaluation sample results: The findings were derived from country visits and ADR results, as well as secondary research and reviews of global and regional evaluations. Results are illustrative but not representative of changes UNDP made in the area of democratic governance.

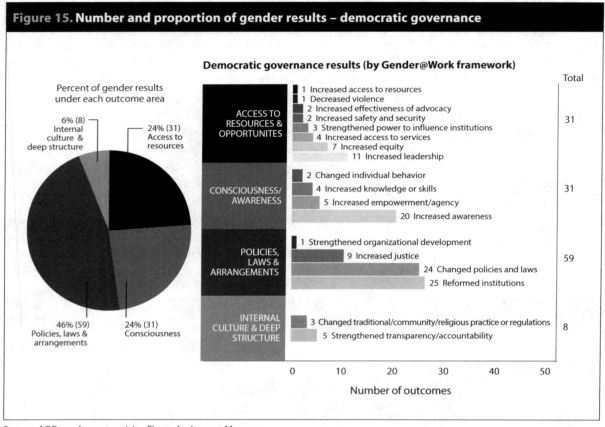

Figure 15. Number and proportion of gender results – democratic governance

Percent of gender results under each outcome area

- 6% (8) Internal culture & deep structure
- 24% (31) Access to resources
- 46% (59) Policies, laws & arrangements
- 24% (31) Consciousness

Democratic governance results (by Gender@Work framework)

ACCESS TO RESOURCES & OPPORTUNITES — Total 31
- 1 Increased access to resources
- 1 Decreased violence
- 2 Increased effectiveness of advocacy
- 2 Increased safety and security
- 3 Strengthened power to influence institutions
- 4 Increased access to services
- 7 Increased equity
- 11 Increased leadership

CONSCIOUSNESS/ AWARENESS — Total 31
- 2 Changed individual behavior
- 4 Increased knowledge or skills
- 5 Increased empowerment/agency
- 20 Increased awareness

POLICIES, LAWS & ARRANGEMENTS — Total 59
- 1 Strengthened organizational development
- 9 Increased justice
- 24 Changed policies and laws
- 25 Reformed institutions

INTERNAL CULTURE & DEEP STRUCTURE — Total 8
- 3 Changed traditional/community/religious practice or regulations
- 5 Strengthened transparency/accountability

Number of outcomes

Source: ADRs and country visits. Figure by Impact Mapper

en national legal and institutional frameworks to advance women's rights, placing women and men on a more even footing (Figure 15). Compared to other focus areas, democratic governance had the most coverage in the four Gender@Work categories, supporting the potential for more gender-transformative results. Results in this area were also more often gender responsive.

UNDP has provided technical and legal expertise to support the development and adoption of laws promoting women's rights and mainstreaming gender into national institutions. For example in Nepal, UNDP contributed to passage of several pieces of legislation, including a law against gender-based violence, amendment of a civil law to ensure inheritance rights for women, and a policy ensuring representation of women in the Constituent Assembly. UNDP also worked to align legal frameworks with international norms and standards on promoting GEWE.

To help address the deterioration of human rights and high rates of gender-based violence in Bangladesh, UNDP provided technical support to the National Human Rights Commission. This allowed it to link up with NGOs and establish a team of 204 investigators to address rights violations. To address the country's high rates of violence, UNDP also supported the Brave Man's Campaign, a school-based programme targeting boys and men. It challenges their perceptions of gender roles and encourages them to break their silence about violence against women.

Examples of UNDP support to reforming government institutions were found in Argentina and Brazil, where gender mainstreaming policies that helped reduce gender stereotypes were promoted by the Cabinet Secretariat. In Argentina, policies were also introduced to promote gender parity to improve governance in local institutions. Kyrgyzstan improved gender-responsive regulatory frameworks, mechanisms and systems of data collection and statistics used by government, civil society and other partners to inform policy and programme development.

Finding 27: Shifts in rates of 'consciousness and awareness of rights' were also a common result across UNDP programming. A significant number of changes were recorded with respect to 'changes in consciousness'.

Changes in consciousness were seen in several countries. One example concerned impunity for crimes involving sexual and gender-based violence in the Democratic Republic of the Congo. In Egypt an awareness campaign on citizenship rights lasting from 2012 to 2014 supported the registration of over 300,000 women. More than half (158,686) received their ID cards during the period, allowing them to realize their citizenship rights and fully participate in public life. Another innovation, in citizen awareness raising and planning for security, was the Women's Situation Room model (described under Finding 28), which was tested in Liberia and then applied in Kenya and Sierra Leone during the 2012 and 2013 election cycles.

A few shifts in 'internal culture and deep structure' were also seen, reflecting changes in traditional practices and customary law, which are gender transformative in nature. Specifically, men and women supported through the UNDP programme to fight female genital mutilation have changed their attitude and practice of it at village levels in Egypt (the practice has been illegal since 2008). Another example of movement towards transformative results was seen in the Democratic Republic of the Congo, where a woman associated with the UNDP-supported 'gender club' programme obtained land in her name in a chief-ruled traditional system, setting a precedent for women's land ownership. The gender clubs were the foundation for a variety of changes leading to substantive changes in people's lives. UNDP's role (in an initiative involving numerous other actors) was supporting a platform from which people could communicate on gender issues.

Finding 28: Gender results were prominent in the outcome area of 'access to resources and opportunities'. By supporting women in political caucuses, providing access to civic education and establishing safe and secure electoral spaces, UNDP helped open doors for women in the political realm. However, deeper shifts in attitudes and norms are needed to institutionalize women's participation in the political process and achieve equitable power distribution at a transformative level.

The Global Programme for Electoral Cycle Support (GPECS) has built up a high level of expertise and response capacity in providing gender support to electoral and parliamentary processes at global, regional and national levels. This programme promotes civic education and gender-inclusive national consultations and dialogue on governance issues. It has been independently evaluated and is seen as an important mechanism for increasing women's political participation as voters and candidates. Launched in 2009 as a three-year, $35 million initiative, it is now considered a model for UNDP programming.

In Kenya the Women's Situation Room, with contributions from UNDP's Quick Intervention Fund under GPECS, sought to promote a peaceful election. The extensive peace architecture it put in place from national to county and village levels, as well as extensive civic education and training of journalists on balanced election coverage, likely contributed, along with other factors, to peaceful elections in 2013. The effort was led by a group of eminent women from across the continent and also involved 500 local observers. This was a gender-responsive action to safeguard women's interests across ethnic and political lines. It could be transformative in terms of crossing ethnic barriers, although it was not possible to triangulate the transformative dimension.

In Bhutan, recent initiatives to promote women's participation in local governance combined traditional skills-building training with televised debates on key issues facing the country. Based on initial evidence, women felt more empowered, independent and fulfilled due to their new knowledge.[142] Of course, it cannot be assumed that just because women are elected to political office that they will necessarily represent women's right issues.[143] The issue is not just the number of women (or men for that matter) who are elected, but rather the quality of their leadership—and their ability to make sure that both female and male politicians help advance gender-equitable agendas and policies. This was clearly demonstrated in both the Haiti and Tunisia case country studies conducted for this evaluation.

In Tunisia, Haiti and Kenya, elections programmes were using GPECS knowledge products and approaches, including training for electoral management personnel.[144] In Tunisia, a programme budget of $1 million was invested to establish and build the capacity of an electoral management board and to promote gender equality throughout the 2011–2012 electoral cycle. In Nepal, support went to developing a national action plan to increase women's political participation, building on previous support to the establishment of a women's caucus in the Constituent Assembly.

Finding 29: One of UNDP's success factors has been its ability to promote gender equality through the neutrality of its mandate and its role as convener, knowledge broker, advisor and enabler supporting civil society, civic oversight actors and political parties as well as governments. It has done this in situations where the stakes are high and many actors have vested interests.

In Tunisia, for example, where the newly elected National Constituent Assembly began drafting a new constitution in 2012, UNDP successfully used the momentum for change to advance democratic governance. This included safeguarding women's rights and inclusive political participation through support to political parties and political dialogue. During the drafting of the constitution, UNDP provided training for women delegates and young female candidates from a wide range of political parties. Hands-on technical advice was also provided through feedback on the various drafts of the constitution, which reflected the perspective of Tunisia's international human rights commitments, including women's rights.

Although many actors were involved and many external factors were at play, it is possible to conclude (based on feedback from independent informants, political party candidates and civil society representatives) that UNDP played a positive role in providing expertise and supporting increased participation of women in the political arena and through political parties. UNDP used its mandate to bridge gaps and help align opinion, while some international non-governmental organizations supported their ideological allies, which was seen as divisive. (For more information see Box 2.)

Finding 30: Not all results were positive. Some well-intended programmes had negative consequences because of failure to analyse gender roles and power relations, precluding full and equal participation by women. In other cases, despite UNDP's contribution to creating an enabling environment, cultural norms and historical legacies of discrimination precluded good outcomes.

---

142   See 'UN in Bhutan', www.unct.org.bt/female-local-leaders-build-their-confidence-through-training-and-television-debates/.

143   In 2013, in the second democratic elections, only 3 women were elected out of 47 seats (compared to 4 women in 2008). In 2013, no women were elected to the National Council (compared to 3 in 2008). In both 2008 and 2013, His Majesty the King appointed two women (out of five positions) as eminent members in the National Council.

144   'Gender Mainstreaming in Electoral Assistance' and 'Gender Mainstreaming in Electoral Management Bodies' were being referred to.

Box 2. Finding common ground across religious divides in Tunisia

In October 2011, the newly elected National Constituent Assembly in Tunisia began drafting a new constitution. From the beginning, UNDP supported deputies through the Constitutional Support Project (2012–2015), providing special training for women delegates and young female candidates from a wide range of political parties. Hands-on technical advice in constitutional drafting was also provided, which included detailed feedback on the various drafts from the perspective of Tunisia's international human rights commitments, including women's rights.

The opportunity for women to voice their concerns increased consensus among different groups, according to female deputies of the assembly. This consciousness-raising process and sharing of views opened opportunities for collaboration and shifted norms and stereotypes related to religious affiliation. The women were able to unite around certain constitutional provisions partly as a result of having attended the same trainings.

Another advantage was the multi-party inclusive space that UNDP helped to open by facilitating broad consultations. Greater participation and access to this space provided the platform for deputies to agree on law and policy reforms for gender-related provisions in the constitution. Women deputies of the Constituent Assembly said that the UNDP multi-party approach was particularly useful in this regard. Other players (particularly international NGOs) provided support only to selected parties or candidates, often those sympathetic to their own ideological beliefs. This was found to reinforce divides rather than bridge them and was met with scepticism.

During a focus group meeting, women from political parties stressed the importance of women's active participation regardless of their views. However, they noted, "Not all women will be gender champions. We need more men as well." According to the UNDP gender advisers, there was little time and limited means to identify male gender champions in political parties at the time. One said, "Gender equality is such a personally driven matter. We had to take the calculated risk that women would be able unite across the religious divide to push agendas forward."

In Bangladesh, gender quotas were established in the National Area-Based Development Programme, requiring equal numbers of men and women in district development assemblies (DDAs). However, as the ADR reports, "Formal participation does not necessarily translate into increased substantive female participation in decision-making. Interviewed female DDA members often contended that although they were grateful to have the opportunity to be on a DDA, given that *shuras* are traditionally only male, they did not participate actively in their DDA, either because they are not invited to DDA meetings or they cannot physically attend the meetings."

Women also reported receiving less information about administration, finances and project management, which hampered their participation. In Côte d'Ivoire the ADR noted, "Despite the presence of UNDP making contributions to important laws being passed to protect women's rights and promote greater women's participation at the national level, structures of inequality remain untouched (because of) cultural resistance, inadequate education and inequitable gender norms (which) limit women's advancement, access to and participation."

5.2.3 CRISIS PREVENTION AND RECOVERY

Key data

Resources: During the evaluation period, total UNDP expenditure for crisis prevention and recovery was approximately $5.4 billion, averaging $900 million annually. It is consistently the third largest area of programme intervention by expenditure, accounting for an average of 20 percent of total UNDP resources. In the period 2010–2013, approximately one third (32 percent, totalling $1.321 billion) of these expenditures made 'significant' or greater contributions to

GEWE according to the gender marker tracking system.[145]

Gender results: There was an average of 76 gender results a year (a total of 229 ROAR outcomes across the three years) reported from UNDP's country offices over the 2011–2013 period. This represented 71 percent of the total number of results reported for the period. Crisis prevention and recovery had the lowest reported number of gender results of all the thematic areas. The highest proportion of gender results was reported in the Africa region (80 percent) and the lowest in the European region (58 percent).

Areas of work: Country programme data show that most of the gender results in the crisis prevention and recovery portfolio were related to ensuring that disaster risk reduction programmes benefit women and men equally (Figure 16).[146]

Finding 31: Results from the Gender@Work framework found that overall conflict prevention and recovery made the most contribution in the area of 'access to resources and opportunities' in the field of gender-targeted economic recovery (Figure 17). Furthermore, results in 'consciousness' and 'policies' related to the role UNDP has played in raising sustainable development concerns as well as promoting income-generation activities that increased the productive role of women in sustainable development.

In crisis situations where the cluster system is applied, UNDP is also the Early Recovery Cluster lead. This is a challenging role, requiring the flexibility to operate in a humanitarian context while pursuing a development agenda. In these situations, UNDP has been called upon to be the voice of sustainable development concerns. While humanitarian actors normally target women as a vulnerable group, the role of women as agents of change is rarely addressed. In these contexts, UNDP has been able to develop initiatives that allow women to benefit from income-generating interventions.

During the early post-earthquake recovery in Haiti, due to quotas established in manual labour and cash-for-work programmes, women were

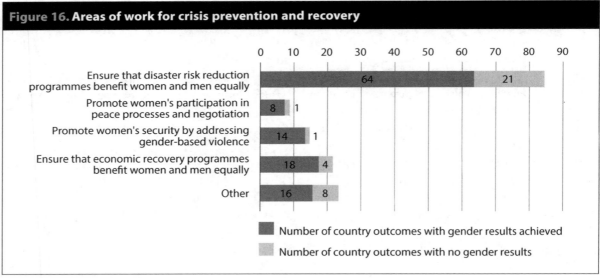

Figure 16. Areas of work for crisis prevention and recovery

Ensure that disaster risk reduction programmes benefit women and men equally: 64, 21
Promote women's participation in peace processes and negotiation: 8, 1
Promote women's security by addressing gender-based violence: 14, 1
Ensure that economic recovery programmes benefit women and men equally: 18, 4
Other: 16, 8

■ Number of country outcomes with gender results achieved
▨ Number of country outcomes with no gender results

Source: UNDP ROARs 2012 and 2013

145 Data reflect expenditure-rated gender marker 2 (significant objective) and gender marker 3 (principal objective) extracted from the programme overview in December 2014.

146 Evaluation sample results: The findings were derived from country visits and ADR results and from secondary research and reviews of global and regional evaluations. Results are illustrative but not representative of changes UNDP made in the area of conflict prevention and recovery.

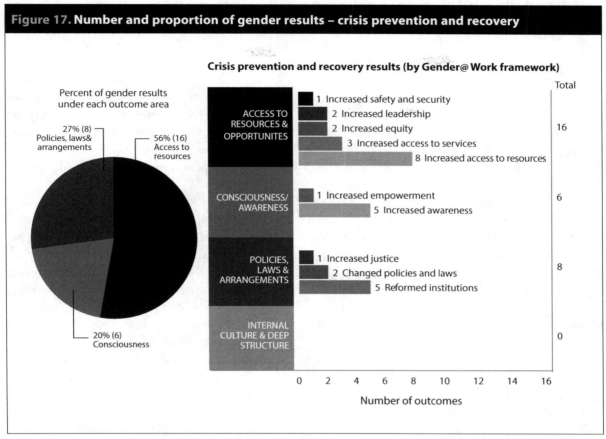

Figure 17. Number and proportion of gender results – crisis prevention and recovery

Crisis prevention and recovery results (by Gender@ Work framework)

Percent of gender results under each outcome area

27% (8) Policies, laws& arrangements

56% (16) Access to resources

20% (6) Consciousness

ACCESS TO RESOURCES & OPPORTUNITES

- 1 Increased safety and security
- 2 Increased leadership
- 2 Increased equity
- 3 Increased access to services
- 8 Increased access to resources

Total: 16

CONSCIOUSNESS/ AWARENESS

- 1 Increased empowerment
- 5 Increased awareness

Total: 6

POLICIES, LAWS & ARRANGEMENTS

- 1 Increased justice
- 2 Changed policies and laws
- 5 Reformed institutions

Total: 8

INTERNAL CULTURE & DEEP STRUCTURE

Total: 0

Number of outcomes

Source: ADRs and country visits. Figure by Impact Mapper

35 percent of project beneficiaries, despite the fact that reconstruction is generally considered men's work. Due to lack of evidence it is unclear whether any deeper normative shifts occurred through this initiative; it appears that results have remained at the 'targeted' level to date.

Similarly, a strong gender mainstreaming model evolved in the joint UN Inter-agency Programme in Nepal, which addressed the integration and rehabilitation of former Maoist fighters. It called for 38 percent of all beneficiaries to be female. There was no gender analysis at the start of the programme, resulting in a focus on reintegration and "assisting girls and young women to re-adapt to traditional norms in the society rather than encourage them to be agents of change". Women

participants, who had been part of the Maoist insurgency, pushed back against traditional gender roles. Accordingly, the programme shifted strategies and activities, enabling the women to participate in the labour force in more empowering ways. This was documented as a lesson learned on GEWE work in the disarmament, demobilization and reintegration context.[147]

In Sri Lanka, the Transition Recovery Programme was rated as particularly effective in targeting women, not only in terms of economic empowerment but also in securing women's networks and increasing their involvement in community welfare and village development. The programme mainstreamed social transformation and cohesion into its livelihood, infrastructure and hous-

---

147 Transition International, 'Independent Evaluation of the UN Inter-agency Programme in Nepal', final report, 21 March 2013, pp. 26 and 35.

ing interventions as a means to bring together communities—who were divided along ethnic, religious, caste, language and other lines—to work towards common village development goals.

Afghanistan provides another example of UNDP's approach to promoting GEWE by supporting the development of grassroots community structures that aid the more difficult and longer term objective of gender-responsive and gender-transformative results. The gains in education and professional and political opportunities for girls and women in Afghanistan represent important achievements, and they have served to reverse some injustices and human rights abuses perpetrated against women under the Taliban regime. (For more information see Box 3.)[148]

In addition, the Law and Order Trust Fund for Afghanistan (LOTFA) was a pooled effort by the country's development partners to support police costs, particularly recurrent costs.[149] This large-scale programme, established in May 2002, had expenditures of $864 million at the time of an evaluation in April 2012. Of particular interest were the positive results of LOTFA's efforts to extend beyond its primary goal of police remuneration by providing benefits such as facilitating the hiring of women. This took place by improving recruitment processes and raising awareness about gender in policing, and the perceptions of the Afghanistan National Police's credibility.[150]

Despite seemingly encouraging results, some negative aspects emerged. Bringing women into the police force apparently put them at risk of abuse from their male colleagues and subjected them to harassment.[151] The lesson for UNDP is the importance of anticipating potential risks and adopting a 'do no harm' approach when working in unstable and transitioning environments. It is particularly important to carry out a gender-specific conflict analysis to understand the potential undesired effects of such programmes.

Finding 32: In terms of promoting women's access to justice, UNDP has had successes in rebuilding legal structures and setting up support for survivors of sexual and gender-based violence. In other instances, there was gender-blind programming that had less positive results.

In Sierra Leone, UNDP took a comprehensive gender-responsive approach to deepening access to justice. It did so by supporting the rebuilding of bodies such as the Attorney General's office, establishing family protection units at police stations and promoting special Saturday courts to address cases of sexual and gender-based violence. In Somalia, a referral system was established (in Hargeisa, Somaliland) allowing clan elders to refer cases of sexual and gender-based violence to formal courts. This resulted in a 44 percent increase in the number of sexual violence cases reaching the formal courts in 2011 compared to the previous year.

Likewise, in Sierra Leone the courts are reducing the backlog of cases involving sexual and gender-based violence while also fostering institutional responses, such as by assigning police focal points to attend court sessions. In Democratic Republic of the Congo, UNDP provided logistical, administrative and technical support to 15 mobile courts, in partnership with other organizations. In 2011 they heard 330 cases, about 70 percent related to sexual violence, and 193 perpetrators were sentenced. This included the country's first-ever convictions of military officers for crimes against humanity on the basis of sexual violence.

---

148   IEO UNDP, Afghanistan ADR report, 2014, p. xii.

149   The key beneficiary institutions are the Ministry of Interior and the Afghanistan National Police. The initial budget was projected at $454 million but the expansion of the police led to expenditures of $864 million for the period September 2008 to December 2010. Phase V of the Fund is supported by 14 donors.

150   Atos Consulting, 'Evaluation of the LOTFA Phase V Report', 17 April 2012.

151   Based on interview for the ADR.

As a result of similar programming in Iraq, there are now five fully operational family protection units, two in Iraq and three in the autonomous Kurdistan region. To increase police investigative capacity, UNDP supported the training of 38 police officers from the Kurdistan region and the central government on interviewing techniques, forensics and the chain of evidence before their deployment to the family protection units. A more lasting result is that the Iraqi Government has allocated land for 14 additional family protection units in different governorates. In addition, UNDP provided technical support to drafting of the domestic violence laws in the Kurdistan region and in Iraq.[152]

Informal justice systems, especially in post-conflict settings, are seen as providing a form of accessible justice for poor people and women, allowing them to have their complaints resolved without having to travel far away to lodge their cases. In Nepal, 36 mediation centres were created, with a total of 432 volunteer mediators (by 2010). However, as these centres are closely linked to social norms and cultural values, they also have the potential to reinforce discrimination and neglect principles of procedural fairness. The Nepal ADR reported that volunteers took on criminal cases that were beyond their capacities, threatening the equity and quality of the justice received. The community mediation process also has limitations for women needing legal advice and support for matters such as violence and rape, as mediators do not have the skills or the legal capacity to deal with these cases.[153]

Finding 33: The UNDP eight-point agenda effectively formed the backbone of GEWE programming in crisis prevention and recovery and contributed to the Secretary-General's seven-point action plan for the UN's delivery of gender-responsive peacebuilding.

The eight-point agenda, launched in 2007, provided a blueprint for the wider United Nations system. However, it has yet to be harnessed as the working gender strategy within integrated missions or used as an effective advocacy and action tool. UNDP supported the task force that conducted the 10-year review of implementation of Security Council Resolution 1325 on women, peace and security. From 2006 to 2008 UNDP also served as chair of the inter-agency initiative UN Action against Sexual Violence in Conflict: Stop Rape Now in support of implementation of the resolution. In this capacity it contributed to coordinated UN efforts to reduce sexual violence in war. In Kyrgyzstan, UNDP supported the development of the National Action Plan on Implementation of 1325. In 2009, UNDP was designated as a leader of UN-wide efforts to implement rule of law and security initiatives under UN Security Council Resolution 1888 on women, peace and security.

UNDP also launched a global programme that placed senior gender advisors in 10 countries facing crisis.[154] This was the first time that UNDP had provided gender expertise at leadership level in crisis countries. The aim was to move away from piecemeal projects to a more holistic, upstream approach to programming. The advisers provided strategic policy and programme advice to UNDP country offices, as well as to partners in the UN system (particularly in integrated missions) and national partners. The Liberia ADR provides evidence of the value of this type of technical expertise. An assessment of the programme also indicated that UNDP's mandate and programming areas provide an ideal entry point for gender mainstreaming, noting

---

152   IEO UNDP, 'Evaluation of UNDP Support to Conflict-affected Countries in the Context of UN Peace Operations', 2013, p. 31.

153   IEO UNDP, ADR Nepal, 2012.

154   Gender advisers were placed in Burundi, Haiti, Iraq, Kosovo, Liberia, Nepal, Papua New Guinea, Sierra Leone, South Sudan and Timor-Leste.

Box 3. Gender mainstreaming interventions in Afghanistan: Gender Equality Project

UNDP's Gender Equality Project in Afghanistan, started in 2009, covered multiple mutually supportive components at national and subnational levels and supported gender mainstreaming in government. It worked on economic empowerment of women, but also, and perhaps more importantly, it engaged in discussions with religious leaders on the role of women in Afghan society. The salient feature was the training of mullahs within the framework of Afghan religious and cultural values. Accordingly 2,130 mullahs participated in trainings in Herat, Blakh and Nangarhar provinces. The project faced strong resistance in Afghanistan, and gender mainstreaming was seen as less important than security sector development and large-scale infrastructure and economic development.*

The project established a working group with the Ministry of Haj and Religious Affairs that included community outreach through the ministry's own newsletter. It also facilitated study tours to countries such as Malaysia and Turkey. All the activities were initiated within the ministry, helping to raise awareness among those from diverse legal traditions. According to an external evaluation of the project (January 2012), "Informants (Mullahs trained) … underline that … a significant amount of information they received in their training and exposure visits was not known to them … Exposure to interpretations within other legal traditions has helped them open their views." This activity was assessed as having laid the foundation for change in the attitudes and behaviours of key leaders in Afghanistan.

People interviewed for the 2013 ADR in Afghanistan noted that the mullah training had positive results, but threats were made against project staff. This suggests that, while the evolution of the political situation entailed risks of setbacks for women's security and rights, UNDP's initiatives were finding the right entry points to start tackling the intricacies of gender relations in a very complex and unstable context. A key lesson was the importance of ensuring that sufficient time is available to establish sustainability and ownership, which cannot be achieved over a three-year project life. The Gender Equality Project was extended for a second phase and specifically targets women entrepreneurs.

* UNDP Afghanistan Assessment of Development Results Report 2013.

that "bringing women's perspectives can fundamentally alter the agenda".[155]

5.2.4 ENERGY AND ENVIRONMENT

Key data

Resources: The environmental focal area includes natural resources management, energy-related programmes, poverty and the urban environment, climate change and what has become defined as resilience. During the evaluation period, the total UNDP expenditure for energy and environment was approximately $3.205 billion, averaging $534 million annually.[156] It is consistently the smallest area of programme intervention by expenditure across the four UNDP focus areas. Despite the critical role women play in the environment, in the period 2010–2013, just over a quarter (27 percent, totalling $622 million) of these expenditures made a 'significant' or greater contribution to GEWE, according to the gender marker tracking system.[157]

Gender results: The energy and environment area averaged 101 gender results per year, a total of 304 ROAR outcomes covering all three years, across UNDP's country operations. This represented an average of 58 percent of the total number of country outcomes reported on energy

---

155 S. Preston Hanssen, 'Towards Transformational Change for Women and Girls in Post-conflict Settings; Case Studies and Lessons Learned from a Global UNDP Initiative', June 2012, pp. 3–5.

156 Source: UNDP Atlas data, 2008–2013.

157 Data reflect expenditure-rated gender marker 2 (significant objective) and gender marker 3 (principal objective) extracted from the programme overview in December 2014.

and environment over the period. This was the second lowest number of gender results reported among the thematic areas. The highest proportion of gender results was reported in the Africa region (69 percent) and the lowest in the Arab States region (45 percent).

Areas of work: The data indicate that most of the gender results in the portfolio were related to 'promoting women's participation and knowledge to protect, sustain and manage the environment and its resources'. Next were activities relating to 'integrating gender perspectives into energy and environment planning, budgeting and policy-making' (Figure 18).[158]

Finding 34. Overall, gender results in energy and environment were limited in all Gender@ Work outcome areas (Figure 19). The results reported were largely gender-targeted increases in 'access to resources and opportunities'. No

change took place in terms of 'internal culture and deep structure', and very few changes in 'policies, laws and arrangements'.

Gender-targeted results focused primarily on women's participation in activities linked to income-generation, food security and conservation. Results from the country visits to Bhutan, Brazil, Cambodia, Nepal and Turkey show that the most results were achieved in increasing access to resources, followed by equal shares of achievement in increased consciousness raising and policy reform.

In Cambodia, a cassava export promotion project involved a value chain study that included analysis of the role of women. In Nepal, women were provided with income-generation opportunities and were trained in operating and maintaining hydropower plants. Over time, however, given the pressure of prevailing social norms (such as

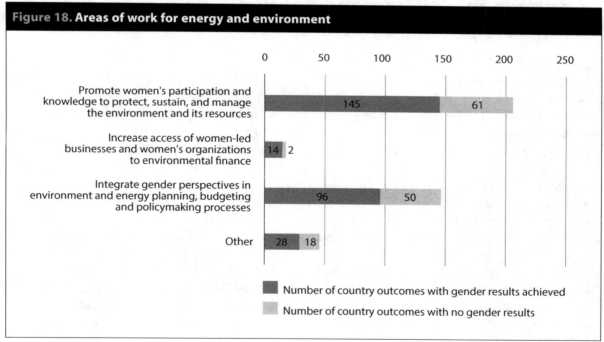

Figure 18. Areas of work for energy and environment

Promote women's participation and knowledge to protect, sustain, and manage the environment and its resources: 145, 61

Increase access of women-led businesses and women's organizations to environmental finance: 14, 2

Integrate gender perspectives in environment and energy planning, budgeting and policymaking processes: 96, 50

Other: 28, 18

■ Number of country outcomes with gender results achieved
■ Number of country outcomes with no gender results

Source: UNDP ROARs 2012 and 2013

---

158 Evaluation sample results: The findings were derived from the country visits and ADR results and from secondary research and reviews of global and regional evaluations. Results are illustrative but not representative of changes UNDP made in the area of energy and environment.

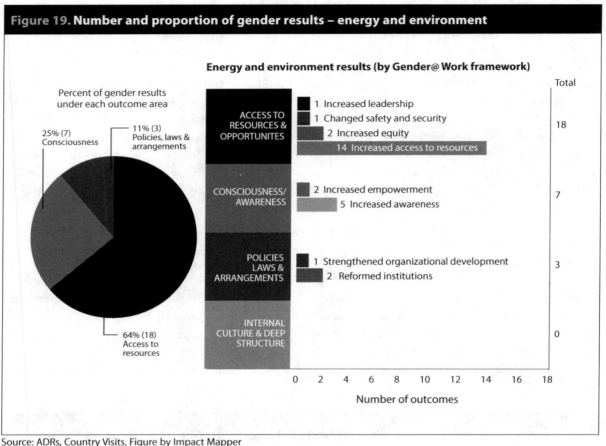

Figure 19. Number and proportion of gender results – energy and environment

Energy and environment results (by Gender@ Work framework)

Percent of gender results under each outcome area

25% (7) Consciousness

11% (3) Policies, laws & arrangements

64% (18) Access to resources

ACCESS TO RESOURCES & OPPORTUNITES
- 1 Increased leadership
- 1 Changed safety and security
- 2 Increased equity
- 14 Increased access to resources

Total: 18

CONSCIOUSNESS/ AWARENESS
- 2 Increased empowerment
- 5 Increased awareness

Total: 7

POLICIES LAWS & ARRANGEMENTS
- 1 Strengthened organizational development
- 2 Reformed institutions

Total: 3

INTERNAL CULTURE & DEEP STRUCTURE

Total: 0

Number of outcomes

Source: ADRs, Country Visits. Figure by Impact Mapper

concerns about having to stay out late at night) these women trained their husbands, who then took over the jobs. This shows the potential for negative consequences when cultural norms are not addressed during project planning.

In Brazil, support provided by UNDP and other agencies to implement the Joint Programme for Food and Nutritional Security of Indigenous Women and Children contributed to positive outcomes. The project improved the food and nutritional security of indigenous women and children and had environmental and social benefits from the eco-stoves developed. The stoves retain heat better than previous models, enabling women to save hours previously spent transporting firewood. This in turn gave them more time for agriculture and livestock production, improving children's nutrition. The stoves also reduced respiratory ailments. However, little consultation and collaboration with stakeholders took

place during project design and implementation, resulting in limited national ownership of results. The minimal engagement of stakeholders also prevented proper identification of institutional strengthening and capacity development needs in the government.

In Turkey, the Energy Efficiency in Appliances Project demonstrates lessons in awareness-building and the importance of selecting gender-aware partners. While UNDP did not take gender into account during the programme design stage, the partnering organization integrated a gender dimension and conducted awareness campaigns on energy efficiency, climate change and energy-efficient products and collected gender-disaggregated data. In Tunisia, a gender analysis was undertaken as part of a climate change resilience study, and some of the resulting activities specifically addressed the needs of particular groups, such as female fishers. Programmatic changes responded largely to women's needs and sought to encourage their inclusion in water management committees. A project in Bhutan strengthened institutional capacity for gender mainstreaming in the energy and environment portfolio (see Box 4).

In terms of consciousness raising and law and policy change, UNDP supported work that increased awareness among politicians and policymakers in 15 countries in the Europe and Commonwealth of Independent States region. Government officials in Bosnia-Herzegovina, Croatia, Kosovo, Kyrgyzstan, Moldova, Romania, Turkmenistan and Uzbekistan became aware that gender should be mainstreamed in all the low-carbon and climate-resilient national strategy documents, and particularly in projects related to climate change.[159] The challenge for UNDP was that the issues under discussion—such as climate resilience, gender and poverty, green jobs and gender equality—were new topics for these individuals. It proved challenging to raise awareness on such diverse and technical topics while also deepening understanding of the need for gender-aware policy implementation.

Self-report data noted that politicians' awareness was strengthened in 15 countries, but action on approving gender mainstreaming strategies varied. As of the end of 2014, five countries were implementing gender mainstreaming. In Uzbekistan, the Government developed a low-carbon strategy and a separate gender mainstreaming policy, an important advancement. On the other hand, a setback occurred in Turkmenistan, where the Government did not want any mention of women or gender, so all gender language was deleted from the policy to address low-carbon and climate-resilient strategies.

Finding 35: In 2012, UNDP adopted an Environmental and Social Screening Procedure that addresses gender and fully complies with the Global Environment Facility (GEF) safeguards policy. GEF standards seek to ensure that programmes and projects do not cause undue harm to people or the environment. It is too early to make a conclusive assessment on whether programming has benefited from the gender dimensions of the screening procedure.

The Environmental and Social Screening Procedure operationalized gender in the project cycle. Some managers find that using the safeguards approach is "more meaningful than the box-ticking exercise of the gender marker because it captures the unequal access and inequality".[160]

As noted in the Gender Report of UNDP-supported GEF-Financed Projects covering the 2010-2012 period, 61 percent of the UNDP-supported GEF-funded projects that were analysed[161] reported having undertaken some work on gender equality or gender mainstreaming. These included project work targeting women and girls; a gender or social needs assessment; collection and reporting of sex-disaggregated data; or gender training for project staff. Of these, 25 percent of projects (89 of 355) reported that they targeted women and/or girls as project stakeholders. In addition, 12 percent (44 of 355 projects) reported having carried out or having

---

159 For a full list and link to the report see www.eurasia.undp.org/content/rbec/en/home/ourwork/environmentandenergy/ Low_emission_development_strategies/.

160 The social and environmental screening template requires participants to describe how the project is likely to improve gender equality and women's empowerment, for example, by addressing the following key issues: (1) Use of gender experts and gender analysis in designing the project, including analysis of gender inequalities; (2) incorporation of age- and sex-disaggregated data and gender statistics and specific, measurable indicators in results framework related to gender equality and women's empowerment; (3) inclusion of actions to address the distinct needs of women and girls, or men and boys; (4) identification of cultural, social, religious and other constraints on women's potential participation and strategies to overcome them. It also includes the instruction to ensure that project scores are 3 or 2 as per the Atlas gender marker.

161 This was 218 out of 355 projects in 2012 and 196 out of 323 projects in 2010-2011 (Source: Gender in Action, 2010-2011 Gender Report of UNDP-supported GEF-financed projects). These projects were all the UNDP-supported GEF-funded projects that submitted annual project reviews (APR/PIRs).

plans to carry out a gender or social needs assessment. These figures show an increase in the number of projects reporting work on gender equality or gender mainstreaming compared to 2011, and a small increase (from 23 percent to 25 percent) in the proportion of projects targeting women or girls as direct beneficiaries.

Whether or not the screening questions pertaining to gender have affected development results is yet to be seen. A meta-assessment[162] of 123 project implementation reviews and annual performance reports concluded that reporting on how GEWE results are contributing to gender equality falls short of capturing development outcomes. Thirty percent of the reports reviewed presented the percentage of women participating in workshops and training programmes. The general trend is that gender results are viewed as equivalent to women participating in project activities, especially attending training events, reflecting the trend of gender-targeted interventions in UNDP. Furthermore, while gender issues were highlighted in 'issues analysis' and 'gender' sections, there was no follow-through in terms of specific actions.

Finding 36: The GEF Small Grants Programme has long reported good results in targeting gender issues. According to a recent evaluation,[163] two thirds of the 30 country programme strategies reviewed had a relatively strong approach to addressing gender. They elaborated the concrete steps that should be taken, such as the inclusion of gender-specific measures in projects.[164]

The GEF Small Grants Programme supports community-based projects covering biodiversity, climate change, land degradation, sustainable forest management, international waters and chemicals. The programme seeks to mainstream gender throughout its portfolio by integrating it as a criterion in the grant approval, project design, needs assessments, implementation, and monitoring and evaluation stages of the project life cycle. According to the data reported, there is evidence of real results in promoting gender equality and contributing to gender empowerment. Of the 103 grant projects that were assessed with respect to gender, more than half were found to have benefited women and men equally, or to have primarily benefited women.[165]

Finding 37: The 2013 evaluation of the Global Gender and Climate Alliance (GGCA)[166] found that significant progress had been made towards delivering its intended outcomes. Gender is also now reflected well in the agreement texts of the United Nations Framework Convention on Climate Change and recognized as an official agenda item of the Conference of the Parties. Gender is also being included in the modalities for financing mechanisms. Furthermore, the foundation has been laid for delivering intended outcomes through capacity building at regional and national levels.

Along with the International Union for Conservation of Nature (IUCN), UNEP and the Women's Environment and Development Organization (WEDO), UNDP sits on the Steering Committee of the GGCA. This network of over 90 civil society organizations, UN agencies and intergovernmental organizations works on gender and climate change issues. UNDP serves as the alliance's administrative body and administers its funding. Through the GGCA, UNDP supports capacity development of governments and civil society in all regions, integrating gender perspectives into decision making on climate change policies, strategies and programmes.

---

162   UNDP, 'Gender Mainstreaming in UNDP's Environment and Sustainable Development Projects: A Compendium of Good Practices and Lessons Learned (in the Asia-Pacific Region)', December 2014.

163   UNDP and GEF, Joint GEF/UNDP Small Grants Programme Evaluation: Preparing for GEF-6, February 2015.

164   Ibid.

165   Ibid.

166   K. Rao and S. Bazilli, 'GGCA Evaluation', 2013.

CHAPTER 5. ASSESSMENT OF UNDP'S CONTRIBUTION TO GENDER
EQUITY AND WOMEN'S EMPOWERMENT DEVELOPMENT RESULTS

Bhutan ranks ninety-eighth out of 146 countries in the Gender Inequality Index, with gender disparities particularly in health, empowerment and labour market participation. Though a 2014 gender equality diagnostic study suggests the country compares well with some countries in the region, it faces many gender challenges. These are particularly significant in political participation and decision-making, literacy, participation in tertiary education and rates of employment, with most women working in the informal sector including in agriculture. Gender-based violence and social stereotyping—particularly among younger males who perceive women as less capable—is a warning sign of future discrimination, given that the median age of Bhutan's population is 25 years.

In 2012, the UNDP country office undertook an exercise to teach how to incorporate gender concerns in programming related to climate change. The point was to raise awareness on gender equality and women's empowerment and on improving the skills of those associated with the design and implementation of five projects in the energy and environment sector. The initiative involved project staff as well as government and civil society counterparts.

Prominent among these projects were the Bhutan Sustainable Rural Biomass (SRBE) Project and the Capacity-Building in Disaster and Climate Resilient Construction (CDRC) Project. The SRBE promotes active participation by women in disseminating efficient cook stoves in poor rural areas. Learning to construct the stoves taught the women masonry skills, providing them with employment in this male-dominated trade. The CDRC has successfully involved women in construction and in promoting disaster-resilient construction methods that can be applied at household level. From their inception, both projects identified gender as a cross-cutting issue.

The SRBE project document highlighted the following aspects of gender relations: (1) Access and control over resources (the need to ensure that women and men have equal opportunities to acquire the technical skills to construct and install cook stoves); (2) impacts on women's health (the introduction of efficient cook stoves could on one hand reinforce socially determined gender roles, but on the other could improve women's situation and health); (3) women's role in community decision-making (by helping to create an environment where women take part in decision-making, addressing their more strategic needs); and (4) skills training (the need to analyse the gender division of labour in stove-related activities and other project interventions, so that the skills trainings are imparted in the most relevant manner and women are engaged more actively and systematically).

The engagement of women in stove construction raised the masonry skills of a cadre of women who are now employed in this male-dominated trade. The SRBE project partnered with the Bhutan Association of Women Entrepreneurs, an NGO working to empower and improve the lives of rural women. The CDRC project was implemented together with the Ministry of Works and Human Settlements.

While the GGCA is not the only entity working to ensure gender-responsive climate change agreements, policies and interventions, it is a significant actor and is instrumental in the achievement of global progress on gender responsiveness. This is due to the leadership of the feminist climate change NGOs who formed GGCA and of a few key individuals in multilateral agencies. The GGCA has shown that feminist advocacy by well-organized NGOs, working with international agencies such as UNDP, can make significant strides in shifting policies and practices at the global level. The leadership of the IUCN and WEDO, in collaboration with the UNDP Gender Team, is a best-practice model of mobilization, advocacy and strategy.

Finding 38: A recent study[167] concluded that women are not key stakeholders or beneficiaries of UN REDD because of their invisibility in the forest sector. It is largely viewed as a masculine domain despite the fact that women

---

167   By Women Organizing for Change in Agriculture and Natural Resource Management, and others, 2013.

harvest and make use of multiple tree-based products. This finding is validated by an independent evaluation report of UN-REDD as well.

UNDP works in partnership with UNEP and FAO through the UN Collaborative Programme on Reducing Emissions from Deforestation and Forest Degradation in developing countries (UN-REDD). The programme aims to generate sufficient resources to significantly reduce global emissions from deforestation and forest degradation in developing countries. A 2014 evaluation of UN-REDD[168] found that the importance of and need for gender mainstreaming is reflected in most policy and programme documents and guidelines. However, gender mainstreaming activities have not been implemented at country or local level in a cohesive and systematic way, which is crucial for addressing all the drivers of deforestation. Instead, the focus has remained at the gender targeting level, such as on achieving gender parity in programme staffing at institutional level, rather than on substantive programmatic benefits for people's lives.

Based on the limited evidence available, the evaluation found, gender mainstreaming activities were likely to occur "only when a UN-REDD gender-sensitive advocate is 'on the ground' and sensitizing stakeholders on the benefits of gender mainstreaming". The lack of a cohesive gender mainstreaming approach may partially be due to the lack of dedicated gender focal points in the programme at global, regional and country levels (even the UNDP gender focal point has other responsibilities). In addition, many government partners do not see gender as a programme priority requiring immediate attention.

---

168 Alain Frechette, Minoli de Dresser and Robert Hofstade, 'External Evaluation of the United Nations Collaborative Programme on Reducing Emissions from Deforestation and Forest Degradation in Developing Countries (the UN-REDD Programme)', Final Report, UNEP, UNDP and FAO Evaluation Office, July 2014.

Chapter 6

CONCLUSIONS AND RECOMMENDATIONS

This chapter presents conclusions based on the evaluation findings in chapters 4 and 5, along with a set of forward-looking recommendations. The recommendations, targeted at UNDP at multiple levels, note the complexity of the interventions and the management responsibilities at policy and other levels.

6.1 CONCLUSIONS

Conclusion 1. There has been far-reaching change and a marked improvement in the UNDP approach to and implementation of policies to address gender mainstreaming since the last independent evaluation in 2006. UNDP has demonstrated greater awareness that gender matters to institutional and development results. It has produced a series of tools and established a number of institutional arrangements, which have helped to strengthen its contribution to GEWE.

The first UNDP gender equality strategy (2008–2013) was catalytic in promoting a number of instruments, tools and processes new to the organization since the 2006 evaluation of gender mainstreaming in UNDP. The GSIC, which is chaired by the Associate Administrator and involves all bureau heads, demonstrates senior-level attention and accountability. However, the extent to which GSIC deliberations and directions trickle down to influence staff at the regional and country office levels was less clear. While the gender marker achieved global application, its contribution in terms of conveying valid gender-enlightened programming is uneven, since there has been variability in its use and a lack of quality assurance. The Gender Seal certification pilot, which innovatively integrated institutional and programmatic aspects of gender mainstreaming, generated interest and deepened

understanding that GEWE will succeed only when it becomes an intrinsic part of the working life of every staff member.

Conclusion 2. While UNDP corporate messaging has highlighted the centrality of gender equality as having a multiplier effect across development results, it has yet to promote and fully resource gender as a main priority of the organization. Resource allocations dedicated to programming and staff to promote GEWE decreased substantially during the period 2008–2014.

Dedicated resources at the global programme level for gender equality received an initial injection in 2009–2010 and declined in 2013 and 2014. Throughout the evaluation period, core allocations for gender were lower than for other focus areas. Non-core resources were also a significant part of the gender unit programming budget during the period 2008–2013.

While Gender Team staffing reached a high of 23 posts in the early years of the Strategic Plan period, this had shrunk to 8 posts by 2013. In 80 per cent of UNDP country offices, gender is attended to by focal points who devote only 20 per cent of their time to this work. For gender equality to be recognized as a central priority of the organization, it must be consistently upheld as a point of departure for all core operating and programmatic engagements.

Conclusion 3. UNDP was only partially successful in meeting the objective of the gender equality strategy that called for the UNDP development contribution to be gender responsive. The majority of results to which UNDP contributed were gender targeted. Furthermore, the finding that a small portion

of results to which UNDP contributes could be described as gender transformative means that UNDP will need to make the attainment of deeper gender results a central objective of its next strategic plan and beyond. While the focus area of democratic governance has seen the most systematic progress in terms of contributing in a gender-responsive manner, the other three focus areas of poverty and the MDGs, crisis prevention and recovery, and energy and environment will require concerted attention. Moving to resilient gender-transformative change will require a longer lead time. UNDP will need to make a sustained commitment, ensure adequate funding and undertake periodic quality checks and assessments of gender results, if it is to stay the course.

The evaluation found that the majority of UNDP gender results were gender targeted, meaning they most often focused on counting the number of men and women who participated in or benefited from programming in the areas of poverty, crisis prevention and environment. In contrast, nearly two thirds of results in the democratic governance focus area were gender responsive, addressing the different needs of women and men and the equitable distribution of benefits, but not the deeper root causes of inequalities in their lives. Very few gender-transformative results emerged from the analysis. This is understandable given that such results, which address the roots of inequalities and power imbalances, require time.

In terms of development results, UNDP had the most systematic approach and made the biggest difference in results in the areas of democratic governance and women's participation in political processes. Democratic governance had the most coverage in the four Gender@Work categories, which provides a promising foundation for contributing to more gender-transformative results in the future.

The other three focus areas will require concentrated support and attention to make progress on the continuum from gender-targeted to gender-transformative contributions supported by UNDP. In terms of poverty reduction, most results were gender targeted in nature, limited to mentioning the percentage of women and men who had benefited. Attention was focused on women's economic empowerment at an individual level and in a few instances on the integration of gender considerations in the MDG processes.

Of the four focus areas, crisis prevention and recovery had the lowest number of gender results reported. Along with contributions in gender-targeted economic recovery, the integration of gender equality considerations in disaster risk management and attention to sexual and gender-based violence appear to be the most consistent areas of attention in the crisis prevention and recovery portfolio. The area of energy and environment reported the second lowest number of gender results. In community-based energy and environment projects, gender has not received broad-based, even attention. It generally has been limited to the participation of women.

While UNDP has made progress since the 2006 evaluation and has moved beyond the 'islands of success' it found, there is still much to do. GEWE is at the heart of the UNDP vision of eradicating extreme poverty and substantially reducing inequality and exclusion. However, in practice, work is often done from a targeting perspective that addresses practical needs through service delivery and access to resources, but not at the deeper level of strategic needs, which addresses structural change and the roots of discrimination and inequalities. Moving to transformational results is context specific, takes time and requires a long-term programming perspective and approaches to monitoring, assessment and learning. Care should also be taken to expand partnerships with gender-aware and women's rights organizations at the global, regional and country levels. UNDP is well positioned to contribute given its sustained commitment to the countries where it works, as well as its political neutrality/impartiality when addressing what is often a very sensitive issue.

Conclusion 4. Pathways to achieving gender results are complex and depend on a variety of institutional and contextual factors. The evaluation learned that demonstrating a direct correlation between UNDP institutional reforms and development results was challenging for a number of reasons. Data constraints posed a key problem, but the far more important factor was the complexity of gender programming. Complexity is intrinsic to such programming, which addresses issues that are deeply rooted in cultural mores, values and belief systems at both individual and societal levels, and where much of the achievement of results is dependent on factors outside the control of UNDP.

At a basic level, when gender mainstreaming was integrated into programming and addressed the differential needs, status and roles of women and men, it was more likely that the programme yielded gendered development results. When gender analysis and mainstreaming were lacking, it was more likely that gender-negative, gender-blind or gender-targeted results occurred.

Internal factors associated with gendered development results were attributable to leadership commitment, particularly at the country level, and to accountability structures, gender-enlightened staff with a rights-based mindset and dedicated gender units promoting and monitoring performance. Other examples of the link between institutional and gendered development results were seen in programming that explicitly recognized and developed capacities to ensure that all stakeholders could consider themselves gender experts, which then were applied to programming and policy work.

These programmes also actively sought to engage community members and women's groups in programme design and activities. Other programming elements included selecting gender-aware partners and strategically adapting programming based on the changing needs on the ground. An analysis of assessment of development results reports of 10 country offices with institutional results classified as gender responsive or gender transformative, found that eight of these country offices also had gendered development results. In all of these cases, gender-responsive or gender-transformative results were in the democratic governance focus area.

The evaluation found that some of the external factors of prime importance to gendered development results beyond the direct influence of UNDP included the socio-political context, national and donor interest and the presence of opportunities as well as backlash (which often affected the timing and trajectory of progress on results). Working in a country context where the government was open to or supportive of GEWE created an enabling environment for gendered development programming. This was considered a factor in some of the countries that were early winners of the Gold Seal in the Gender Seal certification pilot. The presence of strong women's movements and civil society groups that advocated on behalf of gender issues was also key to gains in terms of development results that promoted GEWE.

Conclusion 5. UNDP has yet to develop a firm corporate policy making gender analysis mandatory in all programming. The lack of gender analysis explains to some extent why so many UNDP gender results are gender targeted, gender negative or gender blind. The tools and processes to make GEWE relevant to the work of staff members in programme design, implementation, and monitoring and evaluation have also not been sufficiently developed and applied. The gender marker and the results-oriented annual report, as well as monitoring and evaluation, require further refinements and a more consistent application if UNDP is to increase the quality of its gender interventions and reporting and the assessment of its contributions.

Programming for GEWE requires strong, context-specific analysis in order to identify possible unintended effects and understand the potential for backlash when advances are made. These analyses should be evident at the country programme level and also in individual programme and project interventions. In this connection, the gender marker has the potential to play a useful role at the design and appraisal stage and during monitoring, assessment and evaluation.

Although the gender marker is used primarily to track overall trends in gender mainstreaming in UNDP programmes, it also aims to improve UNDP reporting and accountability on gender equality through tracking of budgeting and expenditures for gender equality results. However, as currently used, it does not capture financial expenditures and allocations in a consistent and reliable manner. Aggregation of the amounts of resources dedicated to gender equality does not provide a clear enough picture of how the resources are allocated and used. If it is to fulfil the goal of tracking expenditure, improving accountability and enhancing transparency, UNDP has yet to develop clear guidelines on how to allocate gender marker ratings at the project and country programme outcome levels, and ensure there is a clear, organization-wide understanding of how to apply this guidance. Better gender analysis and consistent gender marker practice could help to ensure that both the decentralized and independent evaluation functions, as well as audit, have a sounder basis for assessing the contribution of UNDP to GEWE.

Conclusion 6. UNDP has demonstrated that the goal of gender parity is important, although results up to this point remain at a gender-targeted level. Gender parity has been successful in terms of equitable numbers of men and women occupying the lowest and highest positions in the organization. However, at the critical middle levels (P-4/P-5 and D-1/D-2), parity has not been achieved. Men enter the organization at higher levels and get promoted more quickly than women. The culture and unwritten rules about who gets promoted and valued, and whose voices are heard, require deeper attention to truly achieve gender equality.

Although the Gender Parity Strategy is a step in the right direction, there is a lack of deeper analysis. Reflection that goes beyond a parity focus will be necessary if the organization is to arrive at a more complete picture of the power relationships and gender dynamics at play. The data from the annual global staff surveys consistently show that there are gaps between men's and women's experiences with respect to empowerment, professional growth, openness, fairness/respect, work-life balance and office management. Gender parity is generally reported at the aggregate level at both the regional and headquarters levels, which may obscure a more differentiated picture of the situation in individual country offices and units.

Conclusion 7. Although UNDP has a historically close and often collaborative relationship with UN-Women that has matured as UN-Women has reorganized its organizational footprint globally, there is room for further clarification of partnership arrangements. UNDP has yet to define and communicate its comparative strengths on gender issues to ensure that its interventions are strategic and add value. The headquarters of both agencies could facilitate the clarification process, which ideally should also take place in the regional and country contexts.

Formally clarifying the relationship between UNDP and UN-Women and specifying each agency's comparative strengths and different entry points could help to ensure smoother working relationships at all levels of both organizations. This should help both agencies to establish working arrangements, particularly in areas where they address similar development challenges and can add significant value to each other's initiatives. The establishment of improved working arrangements needs to acknowledge that a one-size-fits-all approach will be inadequate and that partnership is based on mutual understanding and a clear appreciation of contextual factors. Successful cases of joint initiatives could inform this process. They could also provide an opportunity for UNDP to communicate its thought leadership on and contributions to GEWE to national governments, partners and donors.

6.2 RECOMMENDATIONS

Recommendation 1. UNDP should align its resources and programming with its corporate message on the centrality of supporting GEWE as a means to 'fast forward' development results. Gender mainstreaming should also go beyond providing sex-disaggregated data for all results areas of the Strategic Plan. In this connection, the merits of integrating the Gender Equality Strategy as part of the next strategic plan (2018 onwards) should receive serious consideration.

Given that the vision of UNDP is to achieve the simultaneous eradication of poverty and significant reduction of inequalities and exclusion, the organization should systematically undertake programming that addresses all facets of gender-based discrimination. UNDP needs to make further efforts to institutionalize a more complete understanding of gender, GEWE that goes beyond targeting so it can report accurately on financial allocations and expenditures on gender. If the gender marker is not suited for this level of specificity, it is recommended that a new tracking and benchmark system be established. Furthermore, as specific financial benchmarks have been established in the current GES, covering 2014–2017, these should be closely monitored and reported to the Executive Board.

Moreover, UNDP should assess the merits and demerits of integrating the Strategic Plan and the GES and making key gender results mandatory. Additionally, guidance documents that promote alignment between the Strategic Plan and country programme documents should require preparation of a gender analysis for all programming developed within country programmes that set out medium-term objectives (over a 5–10 year period) along with other contextual analyses. The gender analysis prepared in the country programme context should have corresponding indicators and monitoring, assessment, and evaluation mechanisms at the programme and project levels.

Deeper attention to gender equality issues and gender mainstreaming is required, especially in the focus areas on conflict prevention and recovery and energy and environment, which saw the lowest number of gender results and the highest rates of targeting. Work in the focus areas on poverty and the MDGs and democratic governance can deepen intentions and action towards gender-responsive and gender-transformative results. All UNDP programming and policies should be attentive to framing women as agents and active citizens. If UNDP aims to contribute to transformative change, it will need to accelerate efforts in all focus areas to more strategically target the roots of inequalities, structures of unequal power, participation and relations, and address and transform unequal norms, values and policies.

Recommendation 2. Given the uneven performance in the four focus areas of the Strategic Plan 2008–2013 in promoting gender development results, UNDP should ensure that future assessments pay specific attention to the progress, effectiveness and quality of gender development results in the seven outcome areas of the current Strategic Plan.

The upcoming midterm review of the Strategic Plan for 2014-2017 presents an opportunity to set in place a framework for such an assessment. The assessment can build on the limited data from the Integrated Results and Resources Framework report cards, which summarize UNDP progress and performance in 2014 and include a deeper, qualitative analysis of the UNDP contribution to gender results on the ground. Preliminary lessons of the Gender Equality Seal certification process, which has been completed in 28 country offices (and implemented on a non-certification basis in others), could also be a rich source of information.

Recommendation 3. UNDP should focus on refining tools, instruments and processes developed during the period 2008–2013 and focus on further internalizing the centrality of GEWE to the achievement of all development goals among staff. Specific recommendations

on these improvements and possible new areas of intervention are discussed below.

(a) **Gender analysis should become mandatory in all programming and be linked with justification of the gender marker rating of each UNDP intervention.** Revised gender marker guidance (2014) indicates that ideally a gender analysis should be done during the project design, before the coding, to determine the most effective strategies in a particular context and to identify results that support gender equality. In addition it should be a required first step. This would contribute to more context-specific gender assessment and minimize inaccurate gender marker ratings, enhancing the credibility of this tool. Furthermore, such analysis should specify the areas of change and UNDP's role and contribution in the change process, on the spectrum from gender blind to gender transformative;

(b) **The gender marker should track allocations in a way that provides reliable aggregated data at different stages of the project cycle.** It should be subject to random external checks and be systematically assessed by internal audit exercises. The new guidance should be monitored and assessed on an annual basis to make the marker a reliable instrument for measuring progress in UNDP programming. Furthermore, if the gender marker is not suited for tracking expenditures with a credible level of specificity at the project and outcome levels, it is recommended that consideration be given to developing a new tracking and benchmark system. Such a system could also be more useful for resource mobilization, accountability, gender-responsive budgeting and gender-informed management decision-making;

(c) **The Gender Seal requires senior management's attention in terms of its future role as a corporate certification initiative.** To facilitate this process, the Gender Seal pilot should be assessed by a team of independent advisers to guide its application as it enters a critical post-pilot phase. Such an assessment could be of value in documenting and assessing the pilot process, including aspects such as the methodology, the resources required and the sustainability of the Gender Seal country interventions (including recertification), and explore institutionalizing different options in addition to the standard gold, silver and bronze seals. The focus should be on lessons learned that should inform the choices, costs, opportunities and downsides the Gender Seal may encounter as it moves into post-pilot implementation. The Gender Seal approach could also be extended to national ministries and partners where opportunities, interest and needs are expressed;

(d) **Stronger attention should be placed on using the GSIC forum as a venue for organization-wide learning, problem-solving and sharing of instructive practices.** All key organizational entities in UNDP should provide reports on progress in promoting GEWE and participate in discussions during annual 'gender days'. The GSIC should play a more active role in assessing UNDP reporting to the UN-SWAP and taking stock of feedback received (from UN-Women) on UNDP performance in the UN-SWAP process. This should facilitate the review of instructive practices from other organizations that may be applied in UNDP. Additionally, there is a need to revitalize the functioning of regional GSICs as envisaged in the GES. Consideration should be given to having a regular, mandatory agenda item in regional bureau cluster meetings;

(e) **The GSIC should ensure that the Gender Parity Strategy is revised and a roll-out programme is articulated.** Attention should be paid to addressing the concerns expressed in the global staff surveys and the gaps between men's and women's positive experiences with respect to empowerment, professional growth, openness, fairness, respect, work-life balance and office management. Annual reports to the Executive Board should include more detailed information on problems and progress in achieving parity targets and actions. It may also help to rename the strategy to signal a 'beyond parity' approach to addressing staff culture and morale;

(f) **UNDP should strengthen capacity development processes that focus on gender mainstreaming so they are relevant and apply to staff's daily work and needs.** Online training courses should be independently assessed to determine whether they are useful and should be continued. In addition, the mentorship programming implemented in the regional bureaux for Africa and Asia and the Pacific and the leadership programmes being made available are examples of targeted investments with coaching and benchmarks. The efficacy and impact of these recent initiatives should be carefully tracked, assessed and reported to the GSIC. Other initiatives for capacity-building and awareness development could include unit or country office training plans with focused gender sessions that encourage lively and open discussions and debates. They could include critical analysis of the portrayal of men and women in the media, discussion of current events and guest lecturers;

(g) **UNDP should consider exploring new frontiers for engaging in gender issues that go beyond women's issues, for example the 'masculinity' agenda.** UNDP should engage more fully in working with men and other populations that suffer from gender discrimination and consider undertaking research that addresses how exclusion negatively affects progress in development.

Recommendation 4. Country offices should prepare gender plans that identify gaps and needs in technical support, capacity-building, joint action and advocacy and collective monitoring that facilitate stronger gender programming. These plans should also help to identify areas where UNDP can draw on expertise and leverage the existing capacities of other United Nations agencies active on gender issues at the country level. This process should be supported, monitored and reported upon annually by the respective regional bureaux to the GSIC.

Gender-capacity benchmarks have been set by the Executive Board in terms of in-country gender expertise. This is a welcome development that should promote better gender analysis, programming and results in the 40 countries that meet the criteria. However, to ensure more even attention to all countries and because country offices are expected to prepare gender plans, it is suggested that regional bureaux take specific measures to support the preparation of these multi-year, country-specific gender plans and monitor and report on their formulation and implementation to the GSIC. This process will provide an opportunity for offices to assess their needs and gaps at the country level and to articulate expectations for support from the regional service centres in terms of promoting GEWE.

Additionally, these plans may also provide an opportunity for UNDP to define its comparative strengths in terms of contributing to GEWE and to explore partnerships with United Nations agencies, in particular UNICEF, UNFPA and UN-Women (see Conclusion 7 for more details with reference to UN-Women).

Recommendation 5. UNDP currently does not have a measurement standard to systematically track the type, quality and effectiveness of its contribution to gender results that also captures the context of change and the degree of its contribution to that change. In order to address this issue, UNDP should codify the way it wishes to monitor, report, evaluate and audit its contributions to gender, and this framework should be used for rigorously tracking results for GEWE at the country, regional and global levels.

UNDP is currently using a number of different metrics, which may confuse rather than clarify future efforts for GEWE. Action should be taken to harmonize various assessment scales in a manner that is most meaningful for corporate programming, reporting, evaluation and audit. These elements should be embedded in iterative learning systems that go beyond linear performance frameworks, which are limited to reporting on indicators focusing on sex-disaggregated data.

More attention to the quality of gender results and the context within which changes happen is required in UNDP monitoring and assessment systems. UNDP may want to reflect on the usefulness of having quality and type measures such as the gender results effectiveness scale and Gender@Work frameworks used in this evaluation. This will help in moving beyond the tendency to focus on numbers of women and men and targeting strategies to more responsive and transformative results. The practice of gender audits should also become a more standard feature throughout the organization.

While UNDP has made significant improvements in tracking gender results at the country level through the results-oriented annual report, the system has limitations in capturing diverse and non-linear change, which is often characterized as 'two steps forward, one step back'. UNDP should start systematically tracking the types of organizations with which it partners to provide a comprehensive picture of its partnerships at global, regional and country levels. Monitoring and assessment should include tracking of backlash and efforts to maintain past gains and identify accelerators and barriers to change. This would help to better contextualize change processes and help the organization learn from what is working under different conditions and contexts. This will help UNDP to articulate its role, most importantly at the country level, which will remain the primary unit of analysis in assessing UNDP's short-, medium- and long-term contribution to GEWE.

Annex 1

TERMS OF REFERENCE

INTRODUCTION

In 2014, the Independent Evaluation Office (IEO) of the United Nations Development Programme (UNDP) will conduct a thematic evaluation of the contribution of UNDP to gender equality and women's empowerment (GEWE). The frames of reference for the evaluation will be the UNDP Strategic Plan (2008–2013) and the Gender Equality Strategy (2008–2013). As the second Evaluation Office exercise dedicated to the theme, this evaluation will assess the overall performance of UNDP in mainstreaming gender and the organization's contribution to development and institutional change in GEWE. The mandate for this evaluation is found in decision 2010/15 of the UNDP Executive Board approving the Evaluation Plan for UNDP in June 2010 (DP/2010/19).

BACKGROUND

Gender equality and the empowerment of women are recognized as integral to successful human development and fundamental aspects of women's human rights. They are major themes in the global commitments emerging from the world conferences of the 1990s and first decade of the 21st century, including the Fourth World Conference on Women and its follow-up, the Millennium Declaration and Millennium Development Goals and their reviews, Security Council Resolution 1325 and the UN World Summit of 2005.

In line with these commitments, UNDP adopted gender mainstreaming in all its activities across the board and developed a Gender Equality Strategy[169] (GES) for the period 2008-2013, which aimed to:

(a) Develop capacities, in-country and in-house, to integrate gender concerns into all programmes and practice areas;

(b) Provide gender-responsive policy advisory services that promote GEWE in the four focus areas of the Strategic Plan; and

(c) Support specific interventions that benefit women and scale up innovative models.

PURPOSE

The purposes of the evaluation are to: provide substantive support to the Administrator's accountability function in reporting to the Executive Board; support UNDP accountability to stakeholders and partners; serve as a means of quality assurance for UNDP interventions; and contribute to learning at corporate, regional and country levels.

OBJECTIVES

The primary objectives of the evaluation are to assess UNDP's contributions to GEWE during the period 2008-2013; assess the extent to which the GES was used and successfully functioned as guidance to UNDP programming in the implementation of the Strategic Plan; and provide recommendations with respect to UNDP's new Gender Equality Strategy (2014 – 2018), considering lessons learned and findings from the previous strategy and changes already made to the new one.

---

169   The Gender Equality Strategy was developed largely in response to an independent evaluation conducted by IEO and published in 2006, 'Evaluation of Gender Mainstreaming in UNDP', which concluded that UNDP had not effectively engendered its development programmes.

SCOPE

The scope of the evaluation is aligned with the 2008-2013 Strategic Plan's vision of advancing gender equality through, (1) initiatives that support gender equality and the empowerment of women, and (2) mainstreaming gender throughout the four UNDP focus areas of poverty reduction, democratic governance, crisis prevention & recovery, and environment &energy at the global, regional and country levels. It will cover two distinct but inter-linked results areas: (1) development results and (2) institutional results. The evaluation will also assess the extent to which the GES functioned as "an integrating dimension of UNDP's work"[170] in the implementation of the Strategic Plan[171].

More specifically the evaluation is being scoped to cover:

1. **Assessment of development results:** This component will assess UNDP's development contribution against the goals established during the period of the first GES in relation to the (a) strategic intents as expressed in the outcomes of the Strategic Plan as well as (b) the gender-responsive indicators presented in the GES. It will also asses the cross-cutting development issues set out in the Strategic Plan and GES (i.e., national ownership, capacity development, South-South Cooperation, effective aid management, etc.) to see if and how these issues affected performance. In addition, and where possible, the evaluation will assess UNDP's performance in different development contexts (i.e. least-developed countries [LDCS], small island developing States, landlocked countries and middle-income countries).

2. **Assessment of institutional change:** This component will assess how UNDP has used the GES to promote gender responsive change in UNDP at the technical, policy and cultural levels within the organization. It will also assess the accountability frameworks for gender equality, gender parity results, the community of practice and knowledge management frameworks and its communication and advocacy efforts. Attention will also be paid to the extent possible to progress on gender equality strategies spearheaded by Resident Coordinators and UN country teams.

EVALUATION QUESTIONS AND CRITERIA

The evaluation questions below will be assessed using the four evaluation criteria of relevance, effectiveness, efficiency and sustainability:

1. **Has UNDP contributed to gender equality and women's empowerment development results?**

   ■ How effective has UNDP been in contributing to development results being gender responsive[172]?

   ■ To what extent has UNDP contributed to development results being gender transformative[173]?

   ■ What is UNDP's value added in promoting GEWE results?

   ■ How has UNDP used partnerships to promote GEWE at global, regional and national level?

---

170 UNDP, Gender Equality Strategy 2008–2013, p. 2.

171 It should be noted that this is not an evaluation of the content of the GES as a stand-alone document. Instead it is an inquiry of the extent to which the GES was effective in guiding the institutional and devel¬opment contributions UNDP made to gender equality and women's empowerment during the implementation of the 2008-2013 Strategic Plan.

172 Gender responsiveness implies consciously creating an environment that reflects an understanding of the realities of the lives of women or men within their social setting.

173 Making results gender transformative means considering not only symptoms of gender inequality but also how to produce results that address the social norms, behaviours and social systems that underlie them.

2. **Has UNDP integrated gender equality across the institution at the programme, policy, technical, and cultural levels during the period 2008-2013?**

   ■ How effective has UNDP been in implementing gender mainstreaming and contributing to institutional change results?

   ■ How effective has UNDP been in building in-house gender equality capacity and accountability frameworks?

   ■ To what extent is gender equality a priority in the culture and leadership of the organization?

3. **Where have UNDP's institutional change results been the most and least successful in improving gender equality and women's empowerment development results?**

   ■ To what extent has UNDPs gender mainstreaming strengthened the link between development results and institutional change?

   ■ What are the key factors contributing to successful GEWE results?

   ■ To what extent has UNDP learned from past evaluation findings to strengthen gender equality results at the programme and institutional levels?

The evaluation will consider the following factors that may have influenced UNDP's performance, within the context of the GES: (i) cultural and political environment; (ii) power relations; (iii) national context; (iv) conflict; (v) national ownership of initiatives and results; (vi) use of national capacities; (vii) Middle Income Country status; (viii) South- south and triangular cooperation; (viiii) global agendas; and (ix) participation and voice in pursuit of equitable access to opportunities and gains. During the data collection process other factors will be identified.

MANAGEMENT ARRANGEMENTS

1. **Management Team, IEO Evaluation Office**

   The evaluation will be the responsibility of 2 IEO staff that will function as Evaluation Manager (EM) and Associate Evaluation Manager (AEM). Aside from managing the overall evaluation, the EM and AEM, together with an Institutional Change & Gender Mainstreaming Consultant, will engage in assessing the institutional results component of the thematic evaluation.

   Two short-term consultants will support the evaluation as follows: first an Evaluation Methodologist to guide and quality assure the data collection and synthesis aspects of the evaluation exercise. Second, a research consultant will support the evaluation process, and produce synthesis reports on (1) benchmarking gender mainstreaming efforts in other UN and non-UN organizations and (2) results from key IEO thematic evaluation reports and Assessments of Development Results in UNDP. In addition, this consultant will also provide knowledge management and communications support for the overall evaluation.

2. **Independent Consultants**

   The EM/AEM will work with five independent consultants who will have specific expertise in gender evaluation and provide thematic expertise in the areas of poverty, governance, crisis prevention, environment, and institutional change. Each consultant will prepare a separate chapter covering their respective area of expertise. The independent consultants will work closely with the EM/AEM, with specific guidance from the Methodologist, to synthesis these chapters into a draft evaluation report. The EM and AEM will be responsible for preparing the final evaluation report.

3. External Advisory Panel

Two high-level development experts will serve as an external advisory panel at key points during the course of the evaluation. These experts are directly accountable to the Director of IEO and will provide quality assessment of the final report.

4. Technical Reference Group

A reference group composed of representatives from Office of human resources (OHR, Executive Office of the Operations support Group (OSG) and regional representatives from each level of UNDP's gender architecture has been consulted during the pre-scoping and design phase of the evaluation. Members of this group and other external experts familiar with UN system gender issues will constitute a technical reference group to advise, facilitate access to sources of information, and comment on the evaluation products for factual corrections and errors of interpretation or omission.

Additionally, the draft terms of reference and draft report will be made available to the UNDP Organizational Performance Group (OPG) to review and provide comments. OPG will also receive the final report so a management response can be prepared.

EVALUATION APPROACH AND METHODOLOGY

The evaluation will be a transparent, participatory process involving development stakeholders at the corporate, regional and country levels. It will be carried out within the framework of the *UNDP Evaluation Policy* and the *United Nations Evaluation Group Norms and Standards*.

The evaluation will seek to obtain data from a range of sources, including document analysis, surveys, as well as stakeholder consultations through semi-structured interviews and focus groups at UNDP headquarters and in a range of programme countries, Regional Service Centres (RSC) and other relevant institutions or locations. The rationale for using a range of data sources (data, perceptions and evidence) is to triangulate findings in a situation where much of the data, due to the very nature of GEWE, is qualitative and thus interpretation is critically dependent on evaluator judgment.

Where possible and appropriate, the evaluation should seek to obtain counterfactual evidence as to what may or may not have occurred in the absence of the GES. Some of UNDPs programmes or modalities may not, due to the very design of the GES, have benefited from its application. Such programmes or modalities may thus serve to provide insights into the relative value added of the GES.

A detailed evaluation design will be developed during the inception phase of the evaluation. The evaluation design will include an evaluation matrix to link the evaluation criteria and questions with data collection methods and sources of data and verification of evidences.

THEORY OF CHANGE

In launching the evaluation, an important initial exercise will be to develop a theory of change for UNDPs planned contribution to GEWE during the time frame under evaluation (2008-2013), taking into account: i) Strategic Plan results; (ii) expected outcomes of GES; (iii) any strategic or operational changes introduced during the implementation process; and (iv) key milestones and achievements, as outlined in progress reports. The Theory of Change will serve to highlight the logic underpinning UNDP's approach to GEWE, its assumptions and risks. The exercise of developing a theory of change should also help the evaluation team identify, at an early stage, any challenges or bottlenecks that may affect *evaluability*.

DATA COLLECTION

After the theories of change have been validated with key stakeholders, the data collection approach will comprise:

1. **Stakeholder analysis.** An important initial exercise will be the conduct of a stakeholder analysis in order to identify, *inter alia*, the institutional entities and individuals within UNDP involved in planning, management and implementation of UNDP GEWE activities; the primary target groups of different UNDP GEWE initiatives; and different partners and beneficiaries.

2. **Documentation reviews.** Due to the wide scope of UNDPs GEWE activities, a very large number of documents and reports (published and unpublished) will be collected. Some may be the subject of only a general review, while others will be subjected to detailed review. Some of the key sources of information will comprise: (i) global and regional programme documents and results frameworks, project documents, monitoring and financial reports, evaluations, as well as key project outputs; (ii) Thematic Trust Fund and related documentation (as above); and (iii) strategic partnership documentation.

3. **Country/regional visits.** The evaluation team will use country and regional visits to complete triangulation of evidences, validate what has been found in other sources of information, (e.g. reports and evaluations) and explore some other topics as identified in the inception phase to strengthen internal and external validity of findings (See Annex I for the country visit selection process and criteria). One possibility that will be explored is the preparation of detailed background paper/s by local consultants, contracted by IEO through Country Offices. The broad scope of the evaluation will not permit the selection of a methodologically appropriate number of country visits or case studies that could be considered a representative sample of UNDP initiatives for generalized judgments. Therefore, the evaluation will use a purposive sampling approach and try to assess a broad range of global, regional and country level initiatives, looking at different practice areas, design and implementation modalities to check the theory of change principles and hypothesis. A set of parameters will be developed based on the Theory of Change models and preliminary analysis of the thematic portfolios for more in-depth coverage of particular issues (i.e., representation of women in elections, gender-based violence approaches, Gender Equality Seal Initiative, etc.).

4. **Consultations.** Structured, semi-structured and unstructured interviews and consultations will be conducted. The results of these consultations and interviews are to be documented for internal team analysis. Structured interview methods are also to be used for other consultations. In some cases, focus-group discussions may be held to capture the dynamic of information sharing and debate and to increase validity of findings. Where possible, the evaluation team will consider conducting interviews by telephone or skype/tele/video conference to cover as many country examples as possible and evidences as needed.

The Evaluation Team will select countries and stakeholders to be visited based on criteria to be finalized in consultation with the Independent Evaluation Office and key UNDP stakeholders (see Annex I). Surveys of project managers, policy advisers, selected practice focal points, Resident Coordinators/Country Directors and national counterparts may also be carried out. Additional consultation will also be considered early in the evaluation process to identify perceptions of UNDP staff and help point in the direction of credible and factual sources of information.

TIME FRAME AND EVALUATION PROCESS

The evaluation process will be conducted as follows:

Time frame for the evaluation process – tentative		
Activity	**Responsible**	**Proposed time frame**
Pre-scoping and launch phase		**December – February 2013**
Terms of reference developed and reviewed by Advisory Panel and OPG, and approval by the IEO	EM / EAM	February
Desk review and inception phases		**March – August 2014**
Preparatory desk review and analysis	EM/AEM/Consultants	March – June
Data collection piloting (Armenia and Uruguay)	EM/AEM/Consultants	May – June
Recruitment of evaluation team members	EM/AEM/Consultants	July – August
Preliminary review of available data and context analysis	EM/AEM/Consultants	August
Inception workshop and design of data collection and analysis plan	EM/AEM/Consultants	August – September
Data collection and analysis phases		**September – November 2014**
Data collection, including country/regional visits	EM/AEM/Consultants	September – November
Synthesis workshop and draft evaluation chapters on development results and institutional	EM/AEM/Consultants	October – November
Report finalization and review phase		**December 2014 – April 2015**
First draft; clearance by IEO	EM and AEM	December
Semi-final draft; review by Advisory Panel	EM	January – February
Stakeholder workshop; final draft presented to Technical Reference Group	EM	February
Final report editing and formatting	IEO	March
Production, presentation and follow-up phase		**May – September 2015**
Management response	UNDP Management	May
Executive Board paper and informals	IEO, Management	April – May
Issuance of the final report		May
Evaluation presented to the UNDP Executive Board Dissemination of the final report	IEO	September

Appendix 1 to the Terms of Reference

CRITERIA TO SELECT COUNTRIES TO BE VISITED

1. OVERVIEW

While most of the assignments will be home-based, it is envisaged that the Evaluation Team will be required to conduct field visits to 12 countries (approximately 3 country visits for each focus area).

It should be noted that the evaluation design envisages the country and regional visits not as in-depth case studies but as an important data verification exercise which will contribute to triangulation of evidence and help to validate what has been previously reviewed, reported and evaluated in depth during the Inception phase, through different sources of data (e.g. evaluations, monitoring reports, surveys). In addition, the country and regional visits will provide an opportunity to explore specific topics (i.e., a review of the Gender Seal[174] process countries, review of the experience of women's parliamentary caucuses, women in elections, women in conflict settings, etc.) as identified in the inception phase, to help strengthen internal and external validity of findings. The evaluation will use a purposive sampling approach and try to assess a broad range of global, regional and country level initiatives, looking at different practice areas, design and implementation modalities to check the theory of change developed and related hypotheses.

Based on a preliminary desk review, the Evaluation Team (IEO) has established the parameters below for country visit selection. A minimum of twelve countries will be selected for visits that meet the following criteria:

2. SELECTION CRITERIA

Regional coverage: At least two country visits per region (i.e. Africa, Arab States, Asia and the Pacific, Europe and Central Asia, Latin America and the Caribbean)

Thematic coverage: Approximately three country visits per focus area, with no less than two per focus area (i.e. democratic governance, poverty reduction and MDG achievement, crisis prevention and recovery, energy and environment)

Development contexts: A balanced representation of development contexts (e.g. special development situations, least developed countries, low-income countries, lower middle income countries, upper middle income countries, net contributor countries)

Gender equality context: Gender inequality rankings will be taken into consideration

Programme coverage: A purposeful representation based on the following criteria:

■ Outliers from the gender marker rating system in each focus area of programme expenditures rated GEN2 and GEN3 (See table 1 for an explanation of the gender marker rating system)

■ Countries with top percentage of programme expenditures rated in the gender marker system as GEN0

■ Representation from Gender Seal pilot countries

---

174 The UNDP Gender Equality Seal is a corporate certification process that recognizes good performance of UNDP country offices, regional service centres and headquarters in delivering gender equality results.

- Countries most cited in annual reports (2008-2013) to the Executive Board on implementation of the Gender Equality Strategy

- Countries identified as learning opportunities (positive and negative)

Note: Data will be collected from the 2014 ADR countries (e.g. Armenia, Malaysia, Somalia, Tanzania, Uruguay, Zimbabwe)[175] in addition to the 12 country visits outlined above.

Table 1. UNDP Gender Marker

Background

In 2005, UNDP commissioned a review of the organization's financial system, Atlas, in order to identify possibilities for enhancing reporting on expenditures expected to contribute to gender equality. The review concluded that the existing approach was not reflecting the full extent of UNDP's expenditure on gender equality.

In 2007, as a response to the UNDP Executive Board's request, UNDP configured Atlas to better track financial allocations and expenditures for gender mainstreaming and women's empowerment. In 2009, after two years of piloting in 17 countries, the gender marker was rolled out to all UNDP country offices. The methodology is based on the OECD/DAC gender marker.

What is the gender marker approach?

The approach aims to score the contribution of investments and expenditures in respect of both gender mainstreaming and targeted interventions on women's empowerment.

- The scoring is done at the output level (project ID level in Atlas). Every single output of each office must be rated on gender equality against a four-point scale that ranges from 0 (no gender impact) to 3 (gender equality as the main objective).
- The rating is based on the nature of the output, not on the amount of resources allocated to it.
- A special 'gender attribute' has been added to the Atlas system to record this rating.

What do gender marker scores mean?

As noted above, each output must be allocated a gender score of 0, 1, 2 or 3, as such:

Score	Meaning
3	Outputs that have gender equality as the main objective
2	Outputs that have gender equality as a significant objective
1	Outputs that will contribute in some way to gender equality, but not significantly
0	Outputs that are not expected to contribute noticeably to gender equality

What does the gender marker in the Atlas tell us?

The gender marker enables us to:

- Track the trend and pattern of resource allocation and financial expenditures in each programme/project and how it contributes to the achievement of gender equality results across all UNDP focus areas, country office and regions as identified in the UNDP Strategic Plan.
- Improve our gender responsive planning, budgeting and policy decision making to ensure that those who need UNDP's support will be benefit from resource allocation.

---

175 The IEO will be conducting six ADRs in 2014. The methods consultant will work with the AEM to devise a core set of questions and data (by end-March 2014) to be gathered by the Evaluation Managers of each ADR and this data for the gender thematic evaluation will be collected in the ADR countries visited by IEO staff/consultants.

Annex 2
PEOPLE CONSULTED

ARGENTINA

Ansotegui, Mercedes, Democratic Governance, UNDP

Ascerald, Flora, Women's Office, Supreme Court of Justice

Aschultz, Monique, President, Women in Equality

Balzano, Andrea, Gender Team, UNDP

Bohorquez, Paola, Inclusive Development Cluster, UNDP

Bottino, Gabriel, Justice Houses Coordinator, Inclusive Development Cluster, UNDP

Combi, Maria Eugenia, Small Grants Programme, UNDP

De Leon, Gimena, Inclusive Development Cluster, UNDP

Fuertes, Flavio, Democratic Governance, UNDP

Galindez, María Eugenia, Democratic Governance, UNDP

Gamarra, Liliana, First Years Coordinator, National Training Plan for Food Security (PNSA)

Garcia, Alejandra, Gender Team, UNDP

Garcia, Virginia, Communications Officer, UNDP

García, Alejandra, Democratic Governance, UNDP

Gras, Mariana, President, Project ARG 09016, National Women's Council

Irizar, Manuel, Inclusive Development Cluster, UNDP

Luzi, Nora, Coordinator, Democratic Governance, UNDP

Majdalani, Carla, UN Gender Theme Group

Marchen, Luciana, UN Gender Theme Group

Mayocchi, Valeria, Justice Houses Coordinator

Momeno, Ivan, Coordinator, Microcredit Project, UNDP

Monferrer, Analia, Office of Domestic Violence, Supreme Court of Justice

Mottet, Matias, Justice Houses Coordinator

Pallares, Ulises, Project Coordinator, DIPECHO Project, DRR, UNDP

Pizani, Moni, Resident Representative, UN-Women

Rangone, Miriam, Coordinator, Food Security Progamme

Repetto, Fabian, Coordinator, CIPPEC

Rodriguez, Benigno, Deputy Resident Representative of Programmes, UNDP

Rodriguez Gusta, Ana Laura, Gender Expert, Academic, National Scientific and Technical Research Council and University of San Martin

Russo, Stella, Inclusive Development Cluster, UNDP

Sastre, Francisco Lopez, Coordinator, Small Grants Programme

Stella, Alberto, Resident Representative, UNAIDS

Thourthe, Manuela, UN Gender Theme Group

Tomassini, Daniel, Justice Houses Coordinator

Turbiner, Natalia, National Technical Assistance Director, Project ARG 09016, National Women's Council

Valdes, Rene Mauricio, Resident Representative, UNDP

BANGLADESH

Ali, Ynus, Chief Conservator, Forests Department, Government of Bangladesh

Asaduzzaman, Sardar, Project Manager, Village Courts Project

Azizul, Sarder H., Women Empowerment Officer, Upazila Governance Project and Union Parishad Governance Project, UNDP

Begum, Ferdousi, Sultan Gender Specialist, UNDP

Beresford, Nick, Deputy Country Director, UNDP

Bithika, Hasan, Programme Officer, Human Rights Commission

Brandao, Gerson, Humanitarian Affairs Advisor, UN Office for Coordination of Humanitarian Affairs

Cela, Blerta, Assistant Country Director, Results and Resources Monitoring, UNDP

Chowdhury, Naved, Poverty Advisor, UK Department for International Development

Dales, Eric, International Consultant, Poverty Reduction

Dewan, Jhuma, Gender Specialist, Chittagong Hill Tracts Development Facility, Bangladesh

Goran, Jonsson, Senior Programme Adviser, REOPA Programme

Hajer, Begum, Gender Focal Point, FAO

Haq, Majeda, Gender Focal Point/Programme Analyst, Poverty Reduction Cluster, UNDP

Hasan, Md.K., Programme Officer, Civil Service Change Management Programme

Hasina, Mushrofa, Socioeconomic Expert/Town Manager, Dhaka North City Corporation, Urban Partnerships for Poverty Programme

Hasmi, Quazi, Sarwar, Director, Planning Department of Environment, Government of Bangladesh

Hossain, Alamgir, Programme Analyst, Energy and Environment, UNDP

Hunter, Christine, Country Representative, UN-Women

Islam, Monowar, Secretary, Ministry of Power, Energy and Natural Resources

Jonsson, Gorann, Senior Programme Advisor, UNDP

Kanti Das, Palash, Assistant Country Director, Poverty Reduction Cluster, UNDP

Khan, Shaila, Assistant Country Director, Local Governance Cluster, UNDP

Larsen, Henrik, Director, Chittagong Hill Tracts Development Facility

Mansur, Elizabeth, Wildlife Conservation Society, Bangladesh

Molla, Sydur, Rahman, Programme Analyst, UNDP

Namji, Narantuya, Head of Human Resources, UNDP

Nandy, Paramesh, Project Manager, Community-based Adaptation to Climate Change through Coastal Afforestation Project, UNDP

Nazrul, Islam, Programme Analyst, Local Governance, UNDP

BHUTAN

Carlson, Christina, Resident Coordinator, UNDP

Choden, Phintsho, Director General, NCWC

Chokey, Sonam, Gross National Happiness Commission

Choki, Pema, Department of Local Governance, Ministry of Home and Cultural Affairs

Dema, Chencho, Programme Manager, Lhak-Sam, Bhutan Network of People Living with HIV & AIDS

Dema, Tshering, Operations Unit, UNDP

Dorji, Karma, National Assembly Member

Dorji, Kezang Dolkar, SAARC Business Association of Home Based Workers

Dorji, Pema, Climate Change Policy Specialist, UNDP

Dorji, Sherub, Bhutan Center for Media and Democracy

Dorji, Singay, Global Environment Facility Small Grants Programme, UNDP

Dorji, Tashi, Programme Analyst, UNDP

Dorji, Tshelthrim, Operations Unit, UNDP

Hadzialic, Hideko, Country Director, UNDP

Khandu, Sangay, National Council Member

Lhamo, Chencho, Election Commission of Bhutan

Palden, Tshering, Procurement Associate, UNDP

Rabgye, Sonam Y, Programme Assistant, UNDP

Rai, Meenakshi, RENEW non-governmental organization

Rapten, Karma L, Portfolio Manager, UNDP

Salonen, Annamari, Inclusive Governance, UNDP

Tenzin, Pema, National Council Member

Tobden, Jamba, RUB

Tshering, Gem, ECB

Tshering, Phurpa, Partnership & Assistance Unit, UNDP

Wangchuk, Namgay, Inclusive Governance, UNDP

Wangchuk, Namgay, JSP Project Manager/Sr. Planning Officer, Gross National Happiness Commission

Wangmo, Tandin, Senior Programme Coordinator, Gross National Happiness Commission

Zangpo, Niduk, National Assembly Member

BRAZIL

Amaral Fontes, Maria Teresa, Social Policies Project Officer, UNDP

Ambrozio, Alessandra, Brazilian Cooperation Agency, Ministry of External Relations

Baioni, Maristela, Assistant Resident Representative of Programmes, UNDP

Borges, Eunice, Program Assistant, UN-Women

Bosi, Andrea, HIV/AIDS Project Officer, UNDP

Chediek, Jorge, Resident Coordinator, UNDP

Dieguez, Rose, Environment Project Officer, UNDP

Freire, Moema, Project Officer, Justice/Disaster Risk Reduction, UNDP

Furst, Daniel, Project Officer, South-South Cooperation, UNDP

Massimo, Erica, Project Officer, Governance, UNDP

Ornellas, Nayara, Human Resources, UNDP

Paiva, Joaquim, Social Policies Project Officer, UNDP

Pires Terto, Angela, Project Officer, Transgender/HIV, UNDP

Rebouças, Leila, Technical and Policy Coordination, Feminist Centre for Studies and Advisory Services (CFEMEA)

Sarita Schaffer Simone, Secretariat of Policies for Women, Government of Brazil

Wenceslau, Juliana, Gender Focal Point, Monitoring and Evaluation, UNDP

CAMBODIA

Chevillard, Julien, Trust Fund Administrator, Cambodia Climate Change Alliance, UNDP

Coultridge, Phillip, Adviser, Council for the Development of Cambodia, UNDP

Gaveglia, Enrico, Deputy Country Director (Operations), UNDP

Hing, Phearanich, Policy Analyst (Environment), UNDP

Ker, Munthit, Communication Officer, UNDP

Khim Chamreoun, H.E., Secretary of State, Ministry of Women's Affairs

Navarro, Napoleon, Deputy Country Director (Programme), UNDP

Nihm, Sakal, Project Manager, Strengthening Democracy Programme, UNDP

Popovic, Velibor, Governance Specialist and ACD (a.i), UNDP

Sok, Lang, Programme, Analyst (Poverty Reduction), UNDP

Sok, Sann, Human Resources Manager, UNDP

Thy, Sum, Director, Climate Change Department, Ministry of Environment

Tin Ponlock, H.E., Ministry of Environment, Secretary General of Green Growth Council

Van der Vaeren, Claire, UN Resident Coordinator, UNDP

Yamazaki, Setsuko, Country Director, UNDP

DEMOCRATIC REPUBLIC OF THE CONGO

Amawamya, Esther, Director, Ministry of Gender, Kinshasa

Bapu, Marie, Gender Focal Point, UNDP

Bucopi, Fabien Mweze, Chief of Cabinet, Ministry of Health Provincial Minister, Bukavu

Cigwerhe, Jean-Claude, Chief of Office, UNDP

Gajraj, Priya, Country Director, UNDP

Hartmann, Nick, Deputy, Programmes (2010-2014), UNDP

Kangi Muya, Victor, Director, Ministry of Gender, Kinshasa

Meta, Christina, Governance and Gender Focal Point, Goma, UNDP

Mohsen, Neveen, Bioenergy for Sustainable Rural Development Project Officer, UNDP

Moussa, Adama, Deputy Director, UN-Women

Mundere, Drosila, Gender Equality Programme Manager, CARE International, Goma

Mutayongwa, Josaphat M., Congolese National Police, Commander's Assistant, PNC PEVS Unit, Goma

Namvura, Justine, Gender and Health Advisor, Provincial Ministry

Ngengele Ishilungu, Jacky, Division Chief, Bukavu

Nilsson, Marie, First Secretary, Swedish Embassy

Sebagenzi Kanze, Marie-Therese, Chief, Gender Division, Goma

Wasso, Valérie Nambula, Coordinator, House of Women, Goma

EGYPT

Artaza, Ignacio, Country Director, UNDP

Abbas, Rafaat, General Manager, Central Non-Financial Services Sector, SFD

Abdelazim, Nazly, Legal Aid Programme Manager, UNDP

Al Batouty, Gehan, Counsellor, Chief Judge and National Project Director, Support to Legal Aid and Dispute Settlement Offices, Family Courts Project

Dahroug, Hoda, National Projects Director, Egypt Information and Communication Technology Trust Fund

Gohar, Nihad, Programme Manager, UN-Women

Grout-Smith, Sam, First Secretary, Arab Partnership British Embassy

Handousa, Heba, Head, Egypt Network for Integrated Development Project

Hoshino, Akie, First Secretary, Japanese Embassy

Howaidy, Ghada, Director, Institutional Development, School of Business, American University in Cairo, Women on Boards Programme

Ibrahim, Naglaa, Head, International Cooperation, National Council for Women

Khalifa, Ghada, Citizenship Lead, Microsoft Egypt

Mohsen, Neveen, Bioenergy for Sustainable Rural Development Project Officer, UNDP

Morsy, Maya, Gender Practice Team Leader, Regional Centre Cairo, Regional Bureau of Arab States, UNDP

Nirody, Anita, Resident Representative, UNDP

Nilsson, Marie, First Secretary, Embassy of Sweden

Rifaat, Noha, Results-Based Management and M&E Officer, Head of Quality Assurance Unit, UNDP

Rizk, Heba, Project Manager, Women Citizenship Project, Ministry of State for Administrative Development

Shalaby, Azza, Head, Gender Unit, Social Fund for Development

Taché, Michel, Head of Aid, Canadian International Development Agency

Wafa, Heba, Gender Focal Point, UNDP

Yassin, Fatma, Communications Officer, UNDP

HAITI

Alysee, Kettly, President, Haitian National Association of Women and Protection of Children (ANAPFEH)

Argueta, Katnya, Deputy Country Director, UNDP

Augustin, Elisabeth, Communication Officer for the Development of Haiti

Balutansky, Edwige, Senior Project Advisor, International Institute for Democracy and Electoral Assistance

Baptiste, Irvyne, Jean, Programme Director, Zafen, FonKOZE

Barreau, Bateau, Raphaelle, Network of Youth Parliamentarians

Belizaire, Pablo, Sociologist, National Directorate of Water Supply and Sanitation

Bellegarde, Frantz, Director, Regional Offices, National Directorate of Water Supply and Sanitation

Calixte, Barbara, Project Manager (16/6 Programme), UNDP

Ceran, Ronel, Consultant, Action Aid, and Former Small Grants Programme Head

Chery, Léane, Gender Specialist, Canadian Cooperation

Christie, Karen, First Secretary (Development), Embassy of Canada

Colas, Bernatho, Network of Youth Parliamentarians

Davila, Roly, Technical Advisor, Elections, UNDP

Deschamps, Marie-Marcelle, Haitian Group for the Study of Kaposi's Sarcoma and Opportunistic Infections

Dimanche, Jean, Parnell, Small Grants Programme, UNDP

Elvariste, Myriame, UNHCR Haiti

Felix, Olga, Haitian Women's Solidarity (SOFA)

Fleurant, Rose, General Director, Ministry of Women's Affairs

Guillemard, Julien, Programme Specialist, UNDP Rule of Law project

Hirakawa, Atsuko, Elections and Gender Specialist, UNDP

Hurtig, Jane, Country Director, National Democratic Institute

Josephe, Kinder, Heidegge, Project Director, Fund for Economic and Social Assistance (FAES)

Kenley, Talmer, Network of Youth Parliamentarians

Lassègue, Marie-Laurence, Jocelyn, Director, International Institute for Democracy and Electoral Assistance

Lormeus, Nikette, Social Protection, UNDP

Lunecey, Désouvré, Marie, Network of Youth Parliamentarians

Marinescu, Simona, Chief, Professional Development Impact, UNDP

Morrison, Jessica, Democracy & Governance Office, USAID

Neptune, Ked, Regional Coordinator, Director, Department of Environment for South Haiti, Ministry of Environment

Paccaud, Lea, Employment and Gender Focal Point, UNDP

Philistin, Jocie, Commission of Women Victims for Victims (KOFAVIV)

Ramirez, Victoria, Independent Consultant

Rossi, Alessandra, Director, International Foundation for Electoral Systems

Russo, Sandra, Zafen Project Business Owner

Santich, Carolina, Gender Specialist/Focal Point, European Union

Sciarra, Rita, Head of Unit, UNDP

Senatus, Dorothy, Executive Director, Femmes en Démocratie (Women in Democracy)

Serrador, Borja, Climate Change Specialist, UNDP

Sinicimat, Esther, General Director, Ministry of Women's Affairs

Solda, Paola, Debris Project, UNDP

Sparos, Helen, Independent Consultant

Stevenson, Soliné, Network of Youth Parliamentarians

Theodate, Marie, Pascale, Member of Cabinet, Ministry of Commerce and Industry

Thermesi, Maître, Director General, School of Magistrates

Wismick, Jean, Charles, Vice Rector, University of Notre-Dame of Haiti

KENYA

Averbeck, Carolin, Team Leader, Inclusive Growth & Social Development Unit, UNDP

Chokerah, Julius, Strategic Planning and Advisory Unit, UNDP

Deletraz, J.C., Lieutenant-Colonel, Chief of Staff, International Peace Support Training Centre

Ferguson, Hanna, Programme Analyst, Democratic Governance Unit, UNDP

Frechette, Alain, Evaluation Specialist

Frischin, Dimitry, Programme Officer, United Nations Volunteers

Githingi, J.K., Colonel, Research Department, International Peace Support Training Centre

Keating, Maria-Therese, Country Director, UNDP

Kipyego, Nicholas, Research Associate, Strategic Advisory Unit, UNDP

Knutsson, Per, Head, Office of the Resident Coordinator, Strategic Advisor, United Nations

Kumari, Krishna Waiba, Secretary, Beyond Beijing Committee

Kuria, Paul, Commission Secretary/CEO, National Gender and Equality Commission

Lokaale, Ekitela, Programme Specialist, UNDP

Maili, Gideon, Director, Enablers Coordination Department, Ministry of Devolution and Planning

Mweni Dzame, Caroline, Economist, National Treasury

Ngatia, Sheila, Assistant Country Director and Team Leader, Democratic Governance Unit, UNDP

Ngugi, Nyambura, Programme Specialist, Strategic Planning & UN Coordination, UN-Women

Njoba, Susan, Manager, Business Development, KenInvest

Nyamweya, Pauline, Judge, Kenya High Court, and former Lecturer in Law, Nairobi University

Nyathi, Clever, Peacebuilding Adviser, UNDP

Ranja, Timothy, Programme Analyst, Energy, Environment & Climate Change, UNDP

Reeves, Wilmot, Economics Advisor, UNDP

Smith, David, Manager, Africa Poverty and Environment Initiative, UNEP-UNDP

Sorvald, Marit, Gender Specialist, Nordic Consulting Group

Teya, Beatrice, Disaster Risk Reduction and Recovery Team Leader, UNDP

Vwamu Mudindi, Joan, Programme Officer, Democratic Governance Unit, UNDP

W. Njoba, Susan, Manager, Business Development, Kenya Investment Authority

KYRGYZSTAN

Abdrahmanova, Busaira, NGO Akniet 2005, Osh region

Abdykalykova, Gulnara, Project Coordinator, UNDP-UNEP Poverty-Environment Initiative

Achikeeva, Cholpon, Peace and Development Programme, UNDP

Addullaeva, Gulfia, National Implementation Consultant, Kyrgyz Resident Mission, Asian Development Bank

Alieva, Gulsara, former Chief, Personnel Department, Ministry of Internal Affairs

Ashiralieva, Aidai, Programme Associate, Programme and Policy Support Unit, UNDP

Avanessov, Alexander, Resident Representative, UNDP

Bedelbaeva, Aidai, Gender Mainstreaming Specialist, UNDP

Bekkoenova, Ainura, Democratic Governance Dimension Chief, UNDP

Bokoshova, Ilima, National Programme Officer, UN OHCHR

Borombaeva, Toktokan, Deputy, Ombudsman Institute

Choroeva, Jyldyz, Programme Associate, Programme and Policy Support Unit, UNDP

Djangaracheva, Mira, Socio-Economic Dimension Chief, UNDP

Dospaeva, Saltanat, Operations Manager, UNDP

Dunganaeva, Asel, Gender Expert, UNDP

Ferenci, Beatrix, Human Rights Officer, UN OHCHR

Hock, Claudia, Project Manager, Operations section, Delegation of the European Union to the Kyrgyz Republic

Imankulova, Aizhan, Human Resources Associate, UNDP

Isaeva, Burul, Head, National Network 'People with HIV'

Isakunova, Taalaikul, Gender Expert

Isakzhanova, Marina, Specialist, Strategic Planning and Informational-Analytical Department and Secretary, Gender Commission, Ministry of Emergency Situations

Isalieva, Venera, Head, Department State Agency on LSG and Interethnic Relations (Gender Focal Point)

Jorobaeva, Ziyada, Territorial Council Ishkavan Kyzyk-Kyshtak LSG, Osh Region

Junusova, Dinara, Head, Social Development Department, Government Representative, office for Naryn Region

Kasybekov, Erkinbek, Assistant Resident Representative, UNDP

Kayimov, Talant, Mayor's Office, Osh City

Kochorbaeva, Zulfia, Gender Expert

Koricic, Andreja, JPO Gender Focal Point, Delegation of the European Union to the Kyrgyz Republic

Kuramaev, Baikadam, Chief, Directorate of International Cooperation, Humanitarian Assistance and Information, Ministry of Social Development

Kuvatova, Jyldyz, Communications Officer, UNDP

Kylychev, Kumar, Environment Protection Dimension Chief, UNDP

Machl, Sabine, Representative, UN-Women

Macini, Laura, Human Rights Officer, UN OHCHR

Mamayusupova, Dilbarkan, women's NGO 'Iret', Osh Region

Mamytova, Aina, Agency on Modernization and Development NGO, Bishkek City

Nurmambetova, Gulzat, Educational Project's Naryn Agency NGO, Naryn Region

Ogay, Nelya, Chief, Strategic Planning and Informational – Analytical Department and Deputy Chair, Gender Commission, Ministry of Emergency Situations

Ormonbekova, Lilia, M&E Officer, Gender Focal Point, UNDP

Orozbaeva, Kanykei, Head, Environmental Statistics and ICT, National Statistics Committee

Patscher, Katinka, Human Dimension Officer, Organization for Security and Co-Operation in Europe, Bishkek

Polotova, Jyldyz, Deputy Minister, Social Development

Rakisheva, Zhypar, National Project Officer, UN Office on Drugs and Crime

Sarandrea, Lucio Valerio, CTA on Rule of Law, UNDP

Sharshenova, Nazgul, Disaster Risk Management Coordination Specialist, UNDP

Shishkaraeva, Elmira, Country Programme Gender Coordinator, UNDP

Soltoeva, Eilen, Programme Finance Associate, UNDP

Stenbaek, Johannes, Madsen, Head of Operations Section, Delegation of the European Union to the Kyrgyz Republic

Ten, Lubov, Advisor, Minister of Economy

Tilekov, Edil, HIV Officer, UNICEF

Tkachenko, Olga, Monitoring and Evaluation Officer, UN Office on Drugs and Crime

Toktorbaeva, Jyldyz, Chief, International Department, Ministry of Emergency Situations

Toktoshev, Askarbek, Director, Drinking Water Supply and Sanitation Department, State Agency on Architecture and Construction, and Executive Secretary, Coordination Commission on Climate Change Problems

Usubalieva, Jumagul, Department of Diseases Prophylaxis and State Sanitary and Epidemiological Surveillance, Ministry of Health

NEPAL

Adhikari, Suresh, Joint Secretary, Ministry of General Administration

Adhikari, Krishna R., Assistant Country Director, Operations, UNDP

Bhattarai, Anjani, former Focal Point for HIV and AIDS, UNDP

Bhusal, Padam, Programme Manager, Livelihoods, Australian Aid Programme, Department of Foreign Affairs and Trade

Diana, Massimo, Head, Resident Coordinator's Office, Strategic Planning Adviser, UNDP

Gurung, Tara, Director, Development Policy and Programmes, Australian Aid Programme, Department of Foreign Affairs and Trade

Kemkhadze, Sophie, Deputy Country Director, UNDP

Khadka, Heema, Assistant Country Director, Poverty and Inclusion Unit, UNDP

Kujala-Garcia, Marianne, Counsellor, Development, Embassy of Finland

Kumari, Yam, Khatiwada, Joint Secretary, Ministry of Industry

Lignell, Pia, Programme Manager, Swiss Agency for Development and Cooperation

Marasini, Prerana, Information and Communications Officer, RIDA International

Margar, Binda, Gender Focal Point, UNDP

McGoldrick, Jamie, Resident Representative, UNDP

Onta-Bhatta, Lazima, Assistant Country Director, Strategic Planning Unit, UNDP

Prasad, Ramji, Neupane, National Project Manager, MEDEP Programme, UNDP

Pun, Lakshman, Chief Technical Adviser, MEDEP Programme, UNDP

Ristimaki, Silla, Programme Specialist, UN Peace Fund for Nepal, UNDP

Shrestha, Nabina, Programme Analyst, Poverty and Inclusion Unit, UNDP

Singh, Vijaya, Assistant Country Director, Energy Environment & Climate, Disaster Risk Management Unit, UNDP

Singh, Gitanjali, Deputy Representative, UN-Women

Tamata, Tek, Programme Analyst, Justice and Human Rights, UNDP

TUNISIA

Andersen, Reidun, Vice Consul, Royal Consulate-General of Norway

Ayachi, Saide, President, Tarmil Association for the Development of Gafsa

Baldo, Rabab, Gender Specialist, Political Participation, Elections Support Programme

Barranca, Ricardo, Project Coordinator, Support to the Electoral Process

Boubizi, Hend, President, Tounissiet Association

El Mounir, Mohamed, International Expert on Civil Society, Parliamentary Support Programme, UNDP

Jerbi, Meriem, Project Coordinator, Centre of Arab Women for Training and Research

Joudane Saiji, Leila, Assistant Representative, UNFPA

Lopez-Mancisidor, Eduardo, Programme Analyst, UNDP

Madhkour, Mohamed, Principal Technical Counsellor, UNDP

Murphy, Jonathan, Chief Technical Advisor, Support to the Constitutional Process, Parliamentary Development and National Dialogue

Rasmussen, Anne Margrethe, Senior Advisor, Ministry of Foreign Affairs, Denmark

Robbana, Aida, Coordination Specialist, United Nations

Sassi, Hanen, Member of the Tunisian National Constituent Assembly and member of the Free Patriotic Union (UPL) party

Skhiri, Hela, National Programme Officer, UN-Women

Tabet, Mounir, Resident Representative, UNDP

Trabelsi, Ihsen, Free Woman Sfax Association

Yamadjako, Selomey, Deputy Resident Representative, UNDP

Zaaraz, Anis, Gender Specialist, Political Participation Elections Support Programme

TURKEY

Adam, Olivier, Deputy Regional Director, UNDP

Akcadag, Goknur, General Directorate of Status of Women

Albayrak, Birce, Project Associate, Energy Efficiency in Appliances, Inclusive and Sustainable Growth portfolio, UNDP

Bag, Aysegul, Project Associate, Innovations for Women's Empowerment in Southeast Anatolia, UNDP

Baran, Berna Bayazit, Manager, Poverty Reduction, UNDP

Canalp, Ekrem, Directorate of Local Authorities, Ministry of Interior

Canbay, Feyhan, Evitan, Project Manager, Democratic Governance, UNJP for Promoting Women's Human Rights

Carrington, Daniela, Climate Change Policy Advisor, UNDP

Cethlaya, Naz, Human Resource Associate, UNDP

Danilova-Cross, Elena, Programme Specialist, Poverty & Inequality, UNDP

Dimovska, Matilda, Deputy Resident Representative, UNDP

Galvanlova, Barbora, Regional Gender Practice Focal Point, Knowledge Management, UNDP

Gelz, Daniele, Poverty Reduction Manager, UNDP

Gullu, Canan, Federation of Women Association of Turkey

Hasirci, Hediye Nur, Project Associate, UNDP

İncesoz, İlknur, Chairperson of Equal Opportunities Commission

Kurt, Nermin, Gender-responsive budgeting in Eskişehir Project, Eskişehir Soroptimist Club

Lateckova, Barbora, Programme Specialist, Czech Trust Fund, UNDP

Macauley, John, Regional HIV, Health and Development Programme Specialist, UNDP

Malhotra, Kamal, Resident Coordinator, UNDP

Mariassin, Dmitri, UNDP

Ozbagdatlı, Nuri, Project Manager, Climate Change Portfolio, UNDP

Ozberk, Ebru, UN Joint Programme Coordinator, UN-Women

Ozdemir, Tolun, Human Resources Manager, UNDP

Ozguç, Naz, Monitoring and Evaluation Officer, Climate Change Portfolio, UNDP

Ozturk, Arit Mert, Project Administrator, Inclusive and Sustainable Growth Portfolio, UNDP

Ozturk, Pelin, Programme Monitoring, UNDP

Palova, Elena, Coordination, UNDP

Pogrebnyak, Andrey, Operations Manager, UNDP

Rieken, Joern, Trade Policy Specialist, UNDP

Sadasivan, Bharati, Regional Gender Advisor, UNDP

Semiz, Nesrin, Chairperson, Man Grant Project, Capital City Women's Association

Şen, Leyla, Portfolio Manager, Inclusive and Democratic Governance Portfolio, UNDP

Tadic, Slobodan, UNDP

Ten, Marina, Results-based Management Specialist, UNDP

Unaldi, Zeliha, Gender Specialist, Unone

Vrbensky, Rastislav, Centre Manager, UNDP

Yalcm, Usame, Operations Manager, UNDP

Yarali, Deniz Seyma, Conference Interpreter

Yorukoglu, Gokce, Programmatic Partnerships Associate, UNDP

UNDP HEADQUARTERS AND REGIONAL MEETING/INTERVIEWS, JANUARY 2015

ASIA-PACIFIC REGIONAL CENTRE, BANGKOK

Behuria, Radhika, Gender and Inclusion in Peace-Building Specialist

Gasparikova, Daniela, Results-based Management Specialist

Johnson, Gordon, Practice Leader, Energy, Environment and Climate Change

Lang, James, Regional Adviser, Ending Violence against Women

Miyaoi, Koh, Gender Team Leader, RBAP

Rossellini, Nicholas, Regional Director

Velumail, Thiyagarajan, Regional Advisor, Energy

Wiessen, Caitlin, Head, Policy and Regional Programmes,

Yamamoto, Yumiko, Programme Specialist, Poverty Reduction Practice

UNDP HEADQUARTERS, NEW YORK

Akhtar, Tehmina, Deputy Global Manager, Small Grants Programme

Bennett, Nancy, Results Management Adviser, UNDP-GEF

Bernabeu, Neus, RBLAC Programme Specialist, Gender, Poverty, Decent Work and Employment, and Social Protection

Bernardini, Jean-Philippe, Partnership Development Specialist, RBLAC

Bhattacharjea, Roma, former Gender Advisor, Bureau of Crisis Prevention

Cossee, Olivier, ADR Afghanistan Evaluation Manager, Independent Evaluation Office

Cote, Marjolaine, Development Solutions Team Coordinator, BPPS

Daniels, Ciara, Gender Focal Point, UNDP-GEF

Davis, Randi, Director, Gender Team, BPPS

Diaz, Ana Maria, Strategic Planner, RBLAC

Farnsworth, Mark, Officer in Charge, Chief of Talent Management, Office of Human Resources

Ghazal, Jacqueline, Gender Focal Point, RBAS

Gitonga, Stephen, Policy Adviser

Goni, Orria, Policy Specialist, RSCSA

Hansen Dam, Susanne, Strategic Planning & Management Advisor, RBAS

Jahan, Selim, Director, Human Development Report Office

Kabaya, Odette, Programme Gender Advisor, Ethiopia, RBA

Kumpf, Benjamin, Innovation Specialist, BDP

Lagunas, Raquel, Cluster Leader, Gender Team, UNDP

Lemarquis, Bruno, Crisis Response Unit, BDP

Lex, Christa, Inspection and Evaluation Officer, Inspection and Evaluation Division, Office of Internal Oversight Services, United Nations

Liv Ostergaard, Jeannette, Programme Specialist, RBAP

Lusigi, Angela, Gender Focal Point, RBA

Marinescu, Simona, Chief, Development Impact Group, UNDP

Mazzacurati, Cécile, Gender Focal Point, Peacebuilding Support Office

McDade, Susan, Deputy Director, RBLAC

Mehrotra, Aparna, Senior Adviser, Coordination, and Focal Point for Women in the UN System

Menon-Sen, Kalyani, Feminist Learning Partnerships (Gender Seal Consultant)

Morsy, Maya, Gender Team Leader, RBAS

Muir, Jan, Inspection and Evaluation Officer, Inspection and Evaluation Division, Office of Internal Oversight Services, United Nations

Ndeye Sarr, Rose, Regional Desk Specialist, OSQAB/Programme Division, UNFPA

Oliveira, Marielza, Manager, Performance Analytics & Monitoring, Organizational Support, UNDP

Ruedas, Marta, former BCPR Deputy Director, current Afghanistan Country Director

Saeedi, Nika, Governance and Peacebuilding, BPPS (formerly BCPR)

Sanchez Mugica, Jesus, Consultant, Institutional Effectiveness, Gender Team

Sandhu-Rojon, Ruby, Deputy Director, RBA

Sekhran, Nik, Chief of Profession, Sustainable Development, BPPS

Singla, Radha, Programme Specialist

Smith, Tammy, M&E Expert, Peacebuilding Support Office

Stavenscaia, Irina, Head, Engagement Unit, Integrated Talent Management Team

Sultanoglu, Cihan, Assistant Secretary-General, Assistant Administrator and Director, RBEC

Suppiramaniam, Nanthikesan, Monitoring and Evaluation Advisor, RBA

Wahba, Mourad, Acting Deputy Assistant Administrator and Deputy Director, RBAS

Xu, Haoliang, Assistant Secretary-General, Assistant Administrator and Director, RBAP

DOCUMENTS CONSULTED

Andersson, K.P. and Ostrom, E., 'Analyzing Decentralized Resource Regimes from a Polycentric Perspective', *Policy Science*, 2008.

Arutyunova, A. and Clark, C., 'Watering the Leaves and Starving the Roots', Association for Women in Development, 2013.

Avila, J. Y., 'Scalability Study of the UNDP-Korea Trust Fund Project Technical Report: Empowerment of Vulnerable Women through Livelihoods and Micro-Enterprise Creation in Earthquake-affected Areas of Port-au-Prince and Environs', UNDP, 2014.

Blattman, Jamison, Green and Annan, 'The Returns to Cash and Micro-Enterprise Support among the Ultra Poor: A Field Experiment', May 2014.

Blerta, C., 'Tracking Gender-Related Investments in UNDP', PowerPoint presentation, 2010.

Brondizio, S., Ostrom, E. and Young, O. R., 'Connectivity and the Governance of Multilevel Social-Ecological Systems: The Role of Social Capital', *Annual Review of Environment and Resources*, Vol. 34, 253-278, 2009.

Byron, G. and Ørnemark, C., 'Evaluation of Sida's Contribution to Gender Equality', Sida Evaluation Series, Swedish International Development Cooperation Agency, 2010.

CAWTAR/IDRC, Formes Traditionelles, Formes Nouvelles de L'engagement Politique des Jeunes Femmes en Context de Transition: Le Cas de la Tunisie', July 2013.

Cecelski, E., and Soma, D., 'Mainstreaming Gender in Energy Projects: A Practical Handbook', European Union Energy Initiative, Partnership Dialogue Facility (EUEI PDF), c/o Deutsche Gesellschaft für Internationale Zusammenarbeit (GIZ) 2013

Chant, S., *Gender Generation and Poverty: The Feminisation of Poverty in Africa, Asia and Latin America*, Cheltenham Glos, UK: Edward Elgar, 2007.

Chant, S., 'Re-Thinking the Feminisation of Poverty', London School of Economics and Political Science, July 2006.

Charlesworth, H., 'Not Waving but Drowning: Gender Mainstreaming and Human Rights in the United Nations', *Harvard Human Rights Journal*, Spring 2005.

Cleaver, F., *Masculinities Matter! Men, Gender and Development*, Zedbooks, 2002.

Cox, T. and Blake, S., 'Managing Cultural Diversity: Implications for Organizational Competitiveness', *Academy of Management Executive*, Vol. 5, No. 3, 1991.

Daniels, C., 'Gender in Action 2010–2011, Gender Report of UNDP-supported GEF-financed Projects, UNDP and GEF, June 2012.

Danielsen, K., 'Gender Equality, Women's Rights and Access to Energy Services: An Inspiration Paper in the Run-Up to Rio+20', Ministry Of Foreign Affairs, Denmark, February 2012.

Dumazert, P., 'Strengthening of Capacities for Sustainable Management of Lands, Haiti', GEF/UNDP – Terminal Evaluation Report, June 2012.

Equality Now, 'The Impact of Discrimination in Law and Legal Processes on Women and Girls – Some Case Examples', submission to the Working Group on the Issue of Discrimination against Women in Law and Practice, New York, 2012.

Equality Now, 'Discrimination against Women in Law: A Report Drawing from the Concluding Observations of the Committee on the Elimination of Discrimination against Women', New York, May 2011.

European Bank for Reconstruction and Development, 'Country Assessment Tunisia', September 2012.

Fukuda-Parr, Sakiko, 'What Does Feminisation Mean For Poverty?' (abstract, undated).

GEF, 'GEF Medium-Sized Project Brief: Linking and Enhancing Protected Areas in the Temperate Broadleaf Forest Ecoregion of Bhutan', April 2001.

GEF, 'GEF Policy on Gender Mainstreaming PL/SD/02', May 2012.

GEF, 'Review of GEF Agencies on Environmental and Social Safeguards and Gender Mainstreaming', November 2013.

Government of Haiti, 'Annex to the Action Plan for National Recovery and Development of Haiti, Haiti Earthquake PDNA: Assessment of Damage, Losses, General and Sectoral Needs', 2010.

Government of Haiti, GEF and UNDP, 'Strengthening Adaptive Capacities to Address Climate Change Threats on Sustainable Development Strategies for Coastal Communities in Haiti', 2013.

Greenberg and Zukerman, 'The Gender Dimensions of Post-Conflict Reconstruction: The Challenges in Development Aid', Gender Action, 2009.

Governance and Social Development Resource Centre, 'Topic Guide on Political Systems: Sections on Gender and Participation, and Women in Political Parties', 2015.

Huffer, E., 'Desk Review of the Factors that Enable and Constrain the Advancement of Women's Political Representation in Forum Island Countries, Fiji', 2006.

Institute for Democracy and Electoral Assistance (IDEA), Haiti, 'Favoriser le Dialogue Entre les Partis Politiques et le Conseil Électoral', Haiti, 2013.

IDEA, 'Les Partis Politiques Haïtiens dans la Construction de la Démocratie', International IDEA, Port-au-Prince, Haiti, 2014.

IUCN, 'The Environment and Gender Index 2013 Pilot', 2013.

Kenya, Ministry of Devolution and Planning, 'Review of the Implementation of the Beijing Platform for Action', 2014.

Kenya National Gender and Equality Commission, '2013 General Elections Observation Report', Nairobi, April 2013.

Kenya National Gender and Equality Commission, 'A Guide for County Government Leadership: Integration of Gender Equality and Inclusion in Community Development', Nairobi, 2013.

Kenya National Gender and Equality Commission, 'The Long Journey to Inclusion of the Most Vulnerable in Society in Political Representation at the County Level', Nairobi, 2013.

Kimani, K., 'The Gender Rule Quagmire: Implementing the Two-Thirds Gender Principle in Kenya', Institute For Education in Democracy, Kenya, 2013.

Lampietti and Stalker, 'Consumption Expenditure and Female Poverty: A Review of Evidence', World Bank, April 2000.

Lister, S., 'Emerging Trends in Democratic Governance', Oslo Governance Forum, UNDP, 2011.

Mansour, A., Deveaux, K. and Chouaib, M., 'Mid-Term Evaluation of Support Project to the Constitutional Process, Parliament and National Dialogue', Tunis, 2014.

Medeirios, M. and Costa, J., 'What Do We Mean by the Feminisation of Poverty?' International Policy Centre, July 2008.

Mersch, S., 'Tunisia New Coalition Government Cabinet – Gender Equality?', *Sada Journal*, 2015.

Moser, C., 'Asset-Based Approaches to Poverty Reduction in a Globalized Context', The Brookings Institute, November 2006.

Moser, A., 'Overview Report on Gender and Indicators', Building Resources in Democracy Governance and Elections, 2007.

Msimang, S., 'The Backlash against African Women', *The New York Times*, 10 January 2015.

Nelson, Gay Lee and Cooper, Jennifer, 'Two Roads: One Goal'. MDG Achievement Fund / UN-Women, 2013.

Niner, S., Parashar, S. and George, N., '2012 Women's Political Participation Report Asia-Pacific', SSRC Conflict Prevention & Peace Forum, University of Queensland, 2012.

Norwegian Agency for Development Cooperation (NORAD) and International Law and Policy Review, 'Review of Norwegian Support to Strengthening Citizens' Political Influence in Haiti through the National Democratic Institute', November 2012.

NORAD, 'Report on Lessons Learned from Gender Reviews of Norwegian Embassies', November 2012.

NORAD, 'Gender and Development – A Review of Evaluation Reports 1997–2004', 2005.

Ostrom, E., *Understanding Institutional Diversity*, Princeton University Press, 2005.

Oxfam Canada, 'Resilience in Times of Food Insecurity: Reflecting on the Experiences of Women's Organizations', September 2014.

Pape, J.W., Severe, P., Fitzgerald, D.W. and Deschamps, M.M, et al., 'The Haiti Research-based Model of International Public Health Collaboration: The GHESKIO Centres', NIH Public Access Author Manuscript, National Institute of Health, Haiti, April 2014.

Peebles, D., 'The A To Z of Gender Mainstreaming: How to Set Up, Manage, Monitor and Evaluate the Integration of Gender Equality in the UN System' (draft), UN Office of the Special Adviser to the Secretary-General on Gender Issues and Advancement of Women, 2006.

Peebles, D., 'IFAD Gender Architecture Review', International Fund for Agricultural Development, 2011.

Peebles, D., Sachdeva, N. and Tezare, K., 'Challenges to Gender Mainstreaming Facing the UN System: A Discussion Paper and Review of Key Issues', UN Office of the Special Adviser to the Secretary-General on Gender Issues and Advancement of Women, New York, 2008.

Posh Raj Pandey, 'Some Reflections on MDG Acceleration Framework in Nepal', PowerPoint presentation, February 2013.

Ramalingam, B. and Jones, H., et al., 'Exploring the Science of Complexity: Ideas and Implications for Development and Humanitarian Efforts', Working Paper 285, Overseas Development Institute, 2008.

Rao, K., Prasada, B. and Bazilli, S., 'Gender-Responsive Climate Change Initiatives and Decision-Making. Global Gender and Climate Alliance – GGCA, Evaluation Report', UNDP, IUCN and WEDO, December 2013.

Rao, K., Prasada, B., Ipsen, N. and Jorgensen, P., 'Final Programme Evaluation: Africa Adaptation Programme (AAP), UNDP, April 2013.

Rector, I., Hagemann, S. and Salgado Silva, C., 'Africa Adaptation Programme: Terminal Report', prepared by the Inter-Regional Technical Support Component, UNDP-AAP, March 2013.

'Strategic Plan for the Ministry of Justice, 2012-16', Republique d'Haiti, Fonds pour L'Environnement Mondial, Programme de Micro Financements and UNDP, Haiti, 2013.

Republique d'Haiti and UNDP, 'Fonds pour L'Environnement Mondial et Programme de Micro Financements, Stratégie Nationale de Programme', August 2008.

Risby, L.A. and Todd, D., 'Mainstreaming Gender Equality: A Road to Results or a Road to Nowhere? An Evaluation Synthesis', African Development Bank Group, Tunis, 2011.

Schwensen, C. and Ørnemark, C., 'Revenue Watch Institute Regional Knowledge Hub Program Evaluation', Orbicon, Denmark, March 2013.

Secretariat of the Pacific Community, Secretariat of the Pacific Regional Environment Programme, PACC, Australian Aid, UNDP, UN-Women, Duetsche Gesellschaft Fur Internationale Zusammenarbeit (GIZ) and German Cooperation, 'Pacific Gender and Climate Change Toolkit: Tools for Practitioners' (draft), 2013.

Sen, G. and Mukherjee, A., 'No Empowerment without Rights, No Rights without Politics: Gender Equality, MDGs and the Post-2015 Development Agenda', April 2014, *Journal of Human Development and Capabilities,* Routledge, 23 July 2014.

Sheller, M., Galada, H. C., Montalto, F., Gurian, P.L., Piasecki, M., Ayalew, T. B. and O'Connor, S., 'Gender, Disaster, and Resilience: Assessing Women's Water and Sanitation Needs in Leogane, Haiti Before and After the 2010 Earthquake', *Wh2o: The Journal of Gender and Water*, March 2013.

Svågsand, L., 'International Party Assistance: What Do We Know about the Effects?', University of Bergen, Expertgruppen För Biståndsanalys, Sweden, 2015.

The American Academy in Berlin, 'Global Trends in the Quality of Governance and Democracy', 2012.

The Economist, 'Democracy & Equality: The Mayoress of Mecca', 2011.

United Kingdom Department for International Development (DFID), 'Accountability Briefing Note', 2008.

UK DFID, 'Annual Report and Accounts 2013–2014', 2014.

UK DFID, 'Governance Portfolio Review Summary 2004–2009', 2011.

UN Task Team, 'The Post-2015 UN Development Agenda: A Discussion Note', March 2012.

UN-Women, 'Addressing Inequalities: The Heart of the Post-2015 Development Agenda and the Future We Want for All. Achieving Gender Equality through Response to Climate Change: Case Studies from Local Action to Global Policy', November 2012.

UN-Women, UNDP, UNICEF, 'Informal Justice Systems: Charting a Course for Human Rights-based Engagement', 2012.

UN-Women, 'UN System Wide Action Plan for Implementation of CEB United Nations Policy on Gender Equality and the Empowerment of Women', 2012.

UN-Women, 'UN-SWAP Technical Guidance Note', 2014.

UN-Women, 'Women's Leadership and Political Participation', 2012.

UN Department of Economic and Social Affairs, 'The World's Women 2010: Trends and Statistics', 2010.

UNCT Tunisia, 'Observations sur le Projet de Constitution du 1er Juin 2013 à la Lumière des Engagements Internationaux de la Tunisie', informal working document presented to the Tunisian Government, June 2013.

UNDP, 'Mainstreaming Gender in Water Management', 2006.

UNDP, 'Strategic Plan 2008–2013', 2007.

UNDP, 'Sustainable Energy Services: The Why and How of Mainstreaming Gender', 2007.

UNDP, 'The Why and How of Gender Mainstreaming in Sustainable Land Management', 2007.

UNDP, 'Empowered and Equal: Gender Equality Strategy 2008–2011', 2008.

UNDP, 'Gender Thematic Trust Fund Annual Report', 2008.

UNDP, 'GES Addendum: Guidance for Integrating Gender Equality Results in UNDP's Strategic Plan 2008–2011', 2008.

UNDP, 'Strategic Plan 2008–2011: Accelerating Global Progress on Human Development', May 2008.

UNDP, 'Africa Adaptation Programme, Consolidating Gains and Building Momentum, Knowledge, Transformation and the Human Legacy of the Africa Adaptation Programme', 2009.

UNDP, 'Baseline Report on Learning and Capacity Development for Gender Equality Strategy 2008–2011', 2009.

UNDP, 'Gender Parity Action Plan 2009–2013', 2009.

UNDP, 'Of Supporting Country-led Democratic Governance Assessments. Practical Note', 2009.

UNDP, 'Resource Guide on Gender and Climate Change', 2009.

UNDP, 'The Gendered Dimensions of Disaster Risk Management and Adaptation to Climate Change: Stories from the Pacific', 2009.

UNDP, 'Tracking Gender-Related Investments and Expenditures in Atlas, Guidance Note', 2009.

UNDP, 'Gender, Climate Change and Community-Based Adaptation. A Guidebook for Designing and Implementing Gender-Sensitive Community-Based Adaptation Programmes and Projects', 2010.

UNDP, 'Briefing Note, Pilot Phase of the UNDP Gender Equality Seal Initiative: Lessons Learned', 2011.

UNDP, 'Democratic Governance Thematic Trust Fund Annual Report' for 2010, 2011 and 2012.

UNDP, 'Gender Mainstreaming Guidance Series, Chemical Management: Chemicals and Gender', 2011.

UNDP, 'HIV, Health and Development Strategy Note 2012–2013', 2011.

UNDP, 'Instructions on How to Generate Gender Marker Report', 2011.

UNDP, 'Mid-Term Review of the UNDP Gender Equality Strategy 2008–2013', 2011.

UNDP, 'UNDP Community-Based Adaptation to Climate Change and Gender', 2011.

UNDP, 'UN Collaborative Programme on Reducing Emissions from Deforestation and Forest Degradation in Developing Countries, National Programme Document, Cambodia', May 2011.

UNDP, 'UNDP Country Programme for Bangladesh (2012–2016)', September 2011.

UNDP, 'Environment and Energy: Promoting Climate Resilient Water Management and Agricultural Practices in Rural Cambodia', December 2011.

UNDP, 'Haiti Rebuilds', December 2011.

UNDP, 'Country: Cambodia. Project Document', 2012.

UNDP, 'Gender and Climate Change – Africa: Gender and Adaptation', policy briefs and training modules, 2012.

UNDP, 'GSIC Progress Reports on Implementation of Gender Equality Strategy: UNDP Haiti and Ministry of Environment', Haiti, 2012.

UNDP, 'Report on the Regional Dialogue on Women's Political Leadership', Kenya, 2012.

UNDP, 'Seeing beyond the State: Grassroots Women's Perceptions on Corruption and Anti-corruption', 2012.

UNDP, 'The Future We Want: Biodiversity and Ecosystems – Driving Sustainable Development. United Nations Development Programme Biodiversity and Ecosystems Global Framework 2012-2020', 2012.

UNDP, 'UNDP Assessment of the Gender Marker: Successes, Challenges and the Way Forward', 2012.

UNDP, 'UN-SWAP Report 2012', 2012.

UNDP, 'Mainstreaming Climate Change in National Development Processes and UN Country Programming: A Guide to Assist UN Country Teams in Integrating Climate Change Risks and Opportunities', February 2012.

UNDP, 'Discussion Paper: Measuring Democracy and Democratic Governance in a Post-2015 Development Framework', August 2012.

UNDP, 'Haiti Strides Forward: Women Speak', December 2012.

UNDP, 'A User's Guide to Measuring Gender-Sensitive Basic Service Delivery', 2013.

UNDP, 'Annual Report 2013, UNDP Pacific Centre', 2013.

UNDP, 'Cambodia Annual Report 2012', 2013.

UNDP, 'Debris Management: The Door to Development. Systemization of the Debris Management Programme, Haiti 2010-2012', 2013.

UNDP, 'Democratic Governance Group: Bureau for Development Policy, 2012 Annual Report', 2013.

UNDP, 'Democratic Governance Thematic Trust Fund, Evaluation Summaries', 2013.

UNDP, 'Gender Parity Strategy 2013–2017', 2013.

UNDP, *Human Development Report: The Rise of the South and Human Progress in a Diverse World*, 2013.

UNDP, 'UN-SWAP Report 2013', 2013.

UNDP, 'Implementation of UNDP GES 2008–2013', background paper to the UNDP Executive Board, January 2013.

UNDP, 'Accelerating Progress and Sustaining Results', September 2013.

UNDP, 'Haiti Country Programme Document 2013–2016, Costed Evaluation Plan', November 2013.

UNDP, 'Annual Report 2013–2014', 2014.

UNDP, 'Biodiversity for Sustainable Development. Delivering Results for the Asia and the Pacific Region, 2014.

UNDP, 'Changing With the World. UNDP Strategic Plan: 2014–17', 2014.

UNDP, 'Democratic Governance: Promoting Gender Equality in Electoral Assistance: Lessons Learned in Comparative Perspective 2011-13', 2014.

UNDP, 'Expanding Access to Modern Energy Services for the Poor. Multifunctional Platforms: Fighting Energy Poverty and Empowering Woman to Accelerate the Achievement of the MDGs', 2014.

UNDP, 'Gender Equality Briefing Package', 2014.

UNDP, 'Gender in the New Tunisian Constitution – UNDP fact sheet', Iknow Politics Platform, 2014.

UNDP, 'Gender Mainstreaming: A Key Driver of Development in Environment & Energy', 2014.

UNDP, 'Global Programme for Electoral Cycle Support: Summary of Achievements 2009-2013', 2014.

UNDP, 'Global Report on Gender Equality in Public Administration', 2014.

UNDP, 'Guidelines, Democratic Governance Trust Fund, Country Projects', 2014.

UNDP, *Human Development Report 2014: Sustaining Human Progress: Reducing Vulnerabilities and Building Resilience*

UNDP, 'Promoting Gender Equality in Electoral Assistance: Lessons Learned in Comparative Perspective (2011–2013)', 2014.

UNDP, 'UNDP Gender Equality Strategy 2014–2017. The Future We Want: Rights and Empowerment', 2014.

UNDP, 'Mid-Term Review: Building Adaptive Capacity to Address Climate Change Threats for Sustainable Development Strategies in Coastal Communities of Haiti', January 2014.

UNDP, '2008–2013 Gender Equality Strategy, Mid-Term Review', 2011.

UNDP, 'Briefing Note: UNDP Gender Equality Seal Initiative', 2010.

UNDP Asia-Pacific Regional Centre, 'APRC Annual Report 2012', February 2013.

UNDP Asia-Pacific Regional Centre, 'Achieving Sustainable Energy for All in the Asia-Pacific Region', August 2013.

UNDP Bangladesh, 'Mid-Term Evaluation of Community-based Adaptation to Climate Change through Coastal Afforestation in Bangladesh', January 2012.

UNDP Bangladesh, 'Resilient Bangladesh: UNDP Bangladesh Annual Report 2013 – 2014', 2014.

UNDP Bhutan, 'Report On Mainstreaming Gender in the Energy & Environment Portfolio of UNDP Bhutan', June 2014.

UNDP Cambodia, 'Annual Project Report 2012: Promoting Climate-resilient Water Management and Agricultural Practices in Rural Cambodia', 2012.

UNDP Cambodia, 'Annual Project Report 2011: Promoting Climate-resilient Water Management and Agricultural Practices in Rural Cambodia', UNDP and GEF, 2011.

UNDP Cambodia, 'Annual Project Report 2012: Promoting Climate Resilient Water Management'.

UNDP and Energia, 'Mainstreaming Gender in the Environment and Energy Portfolio of UNDP Cambodia', Gender Mainstreaming Workshop, Cambodia, March 2011

UNDP Cambodia, 'Annual Project Report: Strengthening Sustainable Forest Management and Bio-Energy Markets to Promote Environmental Sustainability and to Reduce Greenhouse Gas Emissions in Cambodia', December 2012.

UNDP Executive Board, 'UNDP Country Programme Document for Haiti (2009–2011)', December 2008.

UNDP Executive Board, 'Draft Country Programme for Kenya (2014–2018)', Annual Session, June 2014.

UNDP Haiti, 'Haiti en Avant: Paroles de Femmes', 2013.

UNDP Haiti, 'Rapport Mission de Suividans le Departement du Sud-Est', 2014.

UNDP IEO, 'Assessment of Development Results: How-to Note on Gender', 2014.

UNDP IEO, 'UNDP Focus Area Overview: Energy and Environment', 2014.

UNDP IEO, 'Kenya Assessment Of Development Results', April 2014.

UNDP IEO, 'Evaluation of UNDP Contribution to Poverty Reduction', January 2013.

UNDP IEO, 'Evaluation of the Fourth Global Programme', May 2013.

UNDP IEO, 'Evaluation of the Regional Programme for Asia and the Pacific', May 2013.

UNDP IEO, 'Evaluation of UNDP Contribution to the Strengthening of Electoral Systems and Processes', 2012.

UNDP IEO, 'Bangladesh Assessment of Development Results', 2011.

UNDP IEO, 'UNDP's Contribution to Strengthening Local Governance', 2010.

UNDP IEO, 'Gender Equality: Evaluation of Gender Mainstreaming in UNDP', January 2006.

UNDP IEO, 'Evaluation of the Democratic Governance Thematic Trust Fund', May 2008.

UNDP IEO, 'Evaluation of UNDP's Role and Contribution in the HIV/AIDS Response in Southern Africa and Ethiopia', May 2006.

UNDP Kenya, 'Amkeni Wakenya Profile 2014', 2014.

UNDP Kenya, 'Young Women in Politics: Experiences of 2013 General Election', 2014.

UNDP Kenya, 'Access to Rights Programme: Empowering the Communities of Kenya', UNDP Kenya and Embassy of Sweden to Kenya, 2011.

UNDP REDD+, 'Annex 6: Readiness Preparation Proposal (R-PP) Assessment Note on the Proposed Project with Cambodia for REDD+ Readiness Preparation Support', 2014.

UNDP Tunisia, 'Consolidating the Democratic Transition in Tunisia: Concept Note for UNDP Support to the Tunisian Parliament 2015-2019', 2014.

UNDP Tunisia, 'La Constitution et la Question du Genre et des Droits Humains en Tunisie, PNUD-Tunisie Project d'Appui À l'Assemblée Nationale Constituante (ANC)', A Comparative Study of Four Versions of the Draft Constitution, 2013.

UNDP and UNCDF, 'Haiti: Economic Empowerment of Vulnerable Women in Earthquake-affected Areas, Poverty Reduction and MDG Achievement', 2011.

UNEP, UNDP and FAO Evaluation Office, 'External Evaluation of the United Nations Collaborative Programme on Reducing Emissions from Deforestation and Forest Degradation in Developing Countries (UN-REDD Programme), Final Report', July 2014.

United Nations, *The Millennium Development Goals Report 2014*, 2014.

United Nations, 'United Nations Development Assistance Framework for Bangladesh 2012–2016', 2011.

United Nations, 'United Nations Development Assistance Framework for Kenya 2014-18', 2014.

UNEP, Ministry of the Environment, Haiti, and Quisqueya University, 'Geo Haiti 2010 – State of the Environment Report 2010', 2010.

UNEP, UN-Women, PBSO and UNDP, 'Women and Natural Resources: Unlocking the Peacebuilding Potential', November 2013.

United Nations, Tunisia, 'Plan Cadre d'Aide au Développement Tunisie 2015–19', Republic of Tunisia 2014.

UN-REDD, 'The Business Case for Mainstreaming Gender in REDD+', December 2011.

UN-REDD, 'Annual Report 2012, Cambodia Programme', March 2013.

Van De Bold, M., Quisumbing, A.R. and Gillespie, S.,' Women's Empowerment and Nutrition: An Evidence Review', IFPRI Discussion Paper, October 2013.

Wilson-Grau, R. and Brit, H., 'Outcome Harvesting', Ford Foundation, Egypt, 2012.

World Economic Forum, 'Global Gender Gap Report', October 2013.

Annex 4

COUNTRY VISIT SELECTION AND PROCESS

The country visits were purposively selected using multiple criteria, including (a) at least two countries per region were visited; (b) equitable variation in countries per region, LDC status and country type; (c) variation in how each thematic area delivered on gender results; and (d) equitable representation of Gender Seal countries versus non-Gender Seal countries. See Table 1 for the first two set of criteria and Table 2 for the second two.

The sample also was selected based on participation in the Gender Seal exercise. The three original pilot countries that took part in the Gender Seal process from 2010-2012 (Argentina, Kyrgyzstan and Bhutan) were included in the

country visit sample, as well as countries in the current phase (2013–2014). The sample is more positively biased because the team was interested in visiting countries with some level of gender results to ensure efficiency of evaluation expenditures. As such, the team did not want to travel to places with no or few gender results.

In order to address that positive bias, the IEO undertook a scan of the annual reports to the Executive Board and produced a table on presence of gender results being reported (at least two times) in each thematic area, which was taken under consideration in the final sample selection. This allowed the team to visit a variety of countries—countries that appeared to be

Table 1. Profile of country visits, country offices and regional bureaux

Country	Region	LDC Status	Country type
Country offices			
Kyrgyzstan	RBEC	Non-LDC	Stable LIC
Turkey	RBEC	Non-LDC	MIC
Bangladesh	RBAP	LDC	Stable LIC
Bhutan	RBAP	LDC	MIC
Cambodia	RBAP	LDC	Stable LIC
Nepal	RBAP	LDC	Stable LIC
Egypt	RBAS	Non-LDC	MIC
Tunisia	RBAS	Non-LDC	MIC
Kenya	RBA	Non-LDC	Stable LIC
Democratic Republic of the Congo	RBA	LDC	SDS
Brazil	RBLAC	Non-LDC	MIC
Haiti	RBLAC	LDC	SDS
Argentina	RBLAC	Non LDC	MIC
Regional bureaux			
Bangkok, Thailand	RBAP	n/a	n/a
Cairo, Egypt	RBAS	n/a	n/a
Istanbul, Turkey	RBEC	n/a	n/a

performing well in all four thematic areas, or only in two or three thematic areas. This acted as a natural control technique—holding UNDP leadership constant at the highest levels as well as the country context—allowing the evaluators to better parse out what some of the drivers of institutional and development results shifts were (see Table 2).

The sample coverage of countries included in this analysis is over 50 percent of all UNDP countries. Data were gathered from all 136 UNDP country offices in terms of contributions to gender results and implementation of key gender mainstreaming practices, such as gender focal points or teams, engagement in gender thematic groups, gender parity work, etc.

Country	Conflict prevention and recovery	Democratic governance	Energy & environment	Poverty & MDGs	Gender Seal countries
Argentina			x	x	Yes (pilot)
Bangladesh			x	x	No
Bhutan			x		Yes (pilot)
Brazil					No
Cambodia		x		x	Yes
Democratic Republic of the Congo	x			x	No
Egypt		x	x	x	Yes (2015)
Haiti	x			x	No
Kenya		x		x	No
Kyrgyzstan		x			Yes (pilot)
Nepal	x	x	x	x	Yes
Tunisia		x			No
Turkey				x	No

Table 2. Coverage of gender results in country results and Gender Seal participation

Annex 5

DATA COLLECTION AND ANALYSIS

SCOPING THE EVALUATION

The pre-evaluation concerns included exploring feminist evaluation and practically addressing OECD DAC evaluation criteria of relevance, effectiveness, efficiency and sustainability through this lens.

The UNDP IEO core evaluation team referenced external sources for ideas on how to approach the evaluation. This included Podem's summary of six tenets of feminist evaluation in 'Feminist Evaluation and Gender Approaches: There's a difference?' (2010) and Batliwala & Pittman's 'Capturing Change in Women's Realities: Critical Overview of M&E Frameworks' (AWID).

The evaluation team then commissioned an occasional paper on historical developments, UNDP's response and feminist approaches and tools authored by Alex Pittman. Following this, a scoping workshop was conducted. It was attended by 30 staff members, including gender advisers from regional centres, senior management, gender focal points and representatives from UN-Women. The workshop resulted in the key evaluation questions that guided the report. The terms of reference for the evaluation were structured around UNDP's Gender Equality Strategy for 2008–2013 and were reviewed by UNDP's Evaluation Advisory Panel members.

CYBERMETRIC ANALYSIS

The team assessed 20 global and regional UNDP publications (4 publications in each thematic area plus institutional change) with 1,812 URL references obtained from a series of systematic Bing searches based upon the publication title. Of these, a random subset of 372 were subject to an in-depth assessment, with a maximum of 20 per UNDP publication or knowledge product.[176] In terms of UNDP knowledge platforms, the study examined 15 UNDP and benchmarking websites with 30,050 URL references. The team also extracted data from Teamworks, showing overall trends in terms of the main topics discussed, such as 4,821 gender-related keywords used during the evaluation time frame. In terms of Twitter, the team combined 7 UNDP corporate Twitter accounts with 211 UNDP staff accounts, and analysed 125,737 tweets.[177]

OUTCOME HARVESTING

The country visit sample was used to engage country office staff in an outcome-gathering exercise and to dig deeper to validate certain results. As part of the preparation for the country visits, gender results were extracted from the ROARs 2011–2013. Other background information was collected, such as country programme documents, programme assessments and gender marker data, along with other relevant reports or financial data as available.

To ensure consistency in country visits, typically two consultants visited each country, gathering basic information from all four thematic areas and the institutional area through an initial focus group meeting. This allowed the evaluation team to gather basic data on all four thematic areas

---

176   A full list of the URLs is available at: http://cybermetrics.wlv.ac.uk/audit/UNDPgender/

177   The complete list of 125,737 tweets cannot be given due to Twitter terms of service prohibiting data sharing, but the top tweets are reported.

that had been judged by country office staff as a most significant change (or a change they wish had happened but didn't) in order to refine validation and triangulation efforts. Consultants were then asked to validate and triangulate at least one outcome from each thematic area with external stakeholders, such as beneficiaries, government, or civil society.

A brief survey was distributed at the beginning of each focus group session (with a sample of UNDP staff members) to get an idea of how participants understand and work with gender mainstreaming and gender equality in the office and programming. The data gathered from this activity directly contributed to answering the main evaluation questions, focusing on the extent to which UNDP contributes to gender-responsive and gender-transformative results; the extent to which institutional changes occurred through gender mainstreaming architecture, systems and processes; and to explore if there were links in certain country offices related to better gender mainstreaming and achievement of development results.

Interviews and site visits with beneficiaries were undertaken to a limited extent with the intent of validating emerging results and to gain qualitative data on the nature of change that had occurred. It was done to the best of the consultants' ability given their limited time in country. In some cases this was challenging to undertake for all thematic areas due to the short (five days) duration of field visits. Some examples of beneficiaries reached include former women's political caucus members in Nepal, members of a weaving and farm cooperative in rural Nepal, a youth network in Haiti, members of a village free of female genital mutilation in Egypt, and women who were part of governance projects in the Democratic Republic of the Congo and Bangladesh.

Coding scheme for results analysis of 62 ADRs and outcomes gathered from 14 countries

Coverage of gender result:
- *Superficial*: Result that lists gender among other issues, such as women and marginalized populations, or a gender project was described but there was no evidence of results;
- *Minimal*: Few and minor references of gender result in text, typically a few sentences at most.
- *Moderate*: Some elaboration of gender results, typically a paragraph or two, but without comprehensive supporting evidence.
- *Thorough*: Comprehensive coverage of the gender issues in the result area with supporting evidence.

Type of result:
- *Gender negative*: Resulted in a negative outcome;
- *Gender blind*: No attention to gender in the results;
- *Gender targeted*: number of women, men or marginalized populations have been targeted in the result;
- *Gender responsive*: Results address differential needs of men or women and address equitable distribution of benefits, resources, status, rights, etc.;
- *Gender transformative*: Result contributes to changes in norms, cultural values, power structures and the roots of gender inequalities and discriminations.

Gender@Work framework: an analytical tool that is divided into four quadrants:
- *Consciousness*: Changes that occur in women's and men's consciousness, capacities and behaviour;
- *Access*: Changes that occur in terms of access to resources and services;
- *Policies, institutions, arrangements*: Formal rules/ adequate and gender equitable policies and laws that are in place to protect against gender discrimination;
- *Cultural norms*: Changes in deep structure and implicit norms, undergirding the way institutions operate, often in invisible ways.

STRATEGY FOR COUNTRY VISIT RESULTS AND ADR META-ANALYSIS

In total 64 countries are represented in the analysis of country visits and the ADR meta-analysis (47 percent of all UNDP country programmes). Gender result data from the country visits and outcome harvesting focus groups[178] were coded in **Impact Mapper** using the Gender@Work framework. This same process was used for the ADR meta-analysis gender results as well. For both the outcome-gathering exercise and the ADR meta-analysis, detailed result data were categorized and validated in country visits and ADR results according to the following five-point scale (see text box).

For the meta-analysis of the 62 ADRs only, we also categorized according to depth of the coverage of the gender results. Results from this analysis

---

Diverse approaches to programming and diverse outcomes

It is important to note that gender results—even those addressing the same subject, such as women's political participation, economic empowerment, or even service delivery—can yield very different results depending on the socio-political context, in terms of how repressive or open it is, the strategies being implemented, the presence of backlash and whether and how gender analysis was used.

The examples below, from the democratic governance area, highlight a programme with the similar goal of increasing the number of women in political positions through campaigning and election trainings. However, it shows how the strategies, approaches and contextual elements used in implementation can yield very different results. This means that GEWE programming often requires more iterative learning cycles allowing monitoring of progress and contextual events to feed back into programme development and refinement.

- *Gender-transformative result*: More women gender champions have gained power and access to decision-making spaces to advocate for their constituency's needs after participating in a political participation and campaigning programme. Political structures have changed to accommodate equitable women's participation. There may also be a critical mass of gender and women's rights advocates built within or across party lines.

- *Gender-responsive result*: More women gender champions are elected to office and have the skills and support systems in place to navigate discrimination they may face after taking part in a political participation and campaigning programme. However, women are still peripheral in terms of power, status and access to the key decision spaces. Political structures and people limit women's equitable contributions and power distribution.

- *Gender-targeted result*: More women are elected to office after participating in political participation and campaigning programme that exclusively targeted women. Women gained technical electoral and policymaking skills in the programme. However, there was not attention to the real challenges and discrimination that women would face when elected, and no exploration of support strategies to assist women in navigating political access challenges, power differentials and other barriers they may face once elected, leaving women more isolated and without important networks. Elected women may or may not be gender champions.

- *Gender-blind result*: A share of more women and men get elected to office after attending a political participation and campaigning training. The training did not address gender differentials or inequalities in terms of access to political spaces and power or target women specifically. The sustainability of this result would be under question given the depth of existing inequalities and discrimination present in the political system. Elected women may or may not be gender champions.

- *Gender-negative result*: More women are elected to office after attending a political participation and campaigning training. However they are used as tokens to show gender equity in a political party. Women run for office with the agreement that they will follow the advice and agendas of the powerful political leaders in the party. Women have no real voice, power or access to decision-making power. Often, if women challenge this status quo, threats, violence or intimidation are common. Elected women may or may not be gender champions.

---

178   Outcome data that were triangulated or easily verifiable, such as gender units being set up in offices.

found that 70 of the 288 results were superficial, and these were excluded from deeper analysis using the Gender@Work framework and type of results categorizations.[179] Gaining this sort of nuance was critical to this evaluation as it was important to tell a story about the evolution of attention to gender equality in the institution. In order to do that, it was necessary to differentiate gender results along a spectrum.

Of course, results are not static over time, and may evolve. That means that gender-targeted or gender-responsive results have the potential to become transformative over time or that transformative shifts contain possibilities for reversal or backlash precisely because they deal with the difficult issue of tackling underlying power structures.

As noted by Sheela Patel, co-founder of SPARC & Slum/Shack Dwellers International (1987): "When you work for women's interests, it is two steps forward - and at least one step back. And those steps back are… often evidence of your effectiveness; they represent the threat you have posed to the power structure, and its attempt to push you back. Sadly, even our 'success stories' are sometimes nothing more than ways the power structure is trying to accommodate and contain the threat of more fundamental change by making small concessions to us."

The issue of sustainability of results thus comes to the forefront when we are addressing gender equality results, and the importance of tracking instances of backlash. Gender analysis and monitoring the evolution of gender results (including pushbacks and steps forward) as it evolves within a context is crucial to developing more effective programming. The objective of using a more in-depth process for analysing results in this evaluation is to support UNDP in reflecting more critically about its intended results, strategies and analyses and how all of this, along with the context, affects progress on gender equitable results.

A range of different analysis techniques were experimented with for this evaluation. Specifically, this included experimentation with some feminist approaches to evaluation, such as focusing on contribution methods of analysis and more in-depth gender analysis tools, such as the Gender@ Work framework (see text box below), to see if they could be useful in the UNDP context.

The democratic governance and poverty and MDGs areas deliver the highest number and proportion of gender results.[180] The conflict prevention and recovery and energy and environment areas were quite weak comparatively in terms of reported gender results (11 percent and 9 percent respectively). Poverty and MDGs had a significant number of gender results (29 per cent) (see table).

Democratic governance ADR results had better coverage of results at the moderate and thorough levels as coded. Energy and environment results were more superficially covered. Both the conflict prevention and recovery and poverty and MDGs thematic areas had an equal (or near equal) distribution of superficial—minimal and moderate—thorough coverage of gender results.

---

179 The meta-analysis of 62 ADRs in the evaluation time period revealed that across all thematic areas, nearly one quarter (24%) of the 288 gender results assessed were reported in a superficial way, mentioning gender without supporting evidence. Almost a third (29%) of the results shared (n=84) had minimal coverage—a few sentences related to gender results with little supporting evidence, such as number of women with increased incomes. This means that 53% of the results mentioned were superficial or minimal in nature without in-depth evidence or description of shifts. The other 47% of ADR gender results had moderate (n=94, 33% of gender results) to thorough (n=40, 14%) coverage. Given that superficial results were dropped from the more detailed analysis, this resulted in analysis of only 218 gender results. There were also a fair number of results (29%) that were classified as minimal coverage and that used gender-related without fully unpacking them or providing in-depth evidence.

180 This finding is confirmed with the ADR and country visit result sample and in terms of ROAR analyses for all 136 country programmes presented in Chapter 3. Not only was the democratic governance area delivering more gender-responsive results than other areas, but it also had the highest number of reported results (52%) across both the ADRs and the country visits.

Countries with the greatest coverage of gender and the highest number of gender results in the ADRs (7-8 gender results) include Sierra Leone (2013), Kenya (2013), Côte d'Ivoire (2013), Liberia (2012), Egypt (2012), Nepal (2012), Democratic Republic of the Congo (2012), Papua New Guinea (2011), Bangladesh (2011), Lao People's Democratic Republic (2011), Somalia (2010), Zambia (2009 and 2010), Maldives (2010), Afghanistan (2009) and Barbados (2009). Only one ADR mentioned that gender was not a priority for the country.

Using the Gender@Work framework to classify country visit and ADR gender results

The Gender@Work framework is a gender analysis tool that helps institutions reflect on the types of changes they should be making when trying to achieve gender transformation and awareness through gender mainstreaming. Typically, the framework has been used for planning purposes, but more recently some have adapted the model for evaluation purposes and specifically to visualize where the concentration of outcomes fall in the four quadrants. In this evaluation, in order to gain more information from the type of gender results present in ADRs and country visits and understand the areas in which UNDP is making the most change, we classified all results from this sample according to the following four categories: (1) Changes in women's and men's consciousness; (2) access to resources; (3) formal rules and policies; and (4) Internal culture and deep structure (norms).

The framework proposes that, for deep and transformative changes in gender equality to occur, changes must occur in women's and men's consciousness, capacities and behaviour, for example, in the way that they understand, communicate and prioritize gender. Changes must occur in terms of access to resources and services. Adequate and gender-equitable policies and laws must be in place to protect against gender discriminations.

Of particular importance is the fourth quadrant, which focuses on changes in deep structure and the implicit norms that undergird the way institutions operate, often in invisible ways. This may be in terms of whose voice matters in meetings, who is rewarded in the institution, and who has power and influence, and in what ways. Changes in this quadrant are normative and often may take longer to surface in interventions. However, this area goes to the heart of any change process, the internalization of new cultural rules and norms. It can occur at institutional or societal levels.

Annex 6

MANAGEMENT RESPONSE

<table>
<tr>
<td colspan="3">

Recommendation 1.

UNDP should align its resources and programming with its corporate message on the centrality of supporting gender equality and women's empowerment as a means to 'fast forward' development results. Gender mainstreaming should also go beyond providing sex-disaggregated data for all results areas of the Strategic Plan. In this connection, the merits of integrating the gender equality strategy as part of the next strategic plan (2018 onwards) should receive serious consideration.
</td>
</tr>
<tr>
<td colspan="3">

Management response:

The UNDP Strategic Plan, 2014-2017 has strongly integrated gender equality across its Integrated Results and Resource Framework (IRRF). In addition to a dedicated outcome for accelerating gender equality, it has mainstreamed gender equality across all other outcomes. The new gender equality strategy, 2014-2017 is an accompaniment to the Strategic Plan and looks at how to mainstream gender in all outcomes of the plan. The strategy, which was approved by the Executive Board, has made financial and human resource commitments to ensure that gender mainstreaming is adequately resourced. This includes as a principal objective meeting the United Nations system-wide financial target of allocating 15 per cent of the organization's resources towards gender equality by 2017. The gender marker is tracking UNDP investments on gender and is aligned to UN-SWAP principles and standards. The gender marker is now being used as an accountability tool in the GSIC to track progress towards the 15 per cent target. UNDP will integrate the 15 per cent financial commitment into the guidelines for trust fund allocations, work with IEO to improve their evaluation of gender outcomes and draw on the gender marker findings. The merits of integrating the gender equality strategy into the next strategic plan (2018 onwards) will be considered as part of the midterm review of the current Strategic Plan, 2014-2017. Additionally, new quality assurance tools are being developed to ensure that gender analysis is integrated in all country programmes and programme documents. The text under this recommendation also suggested that UNDP strengthen its work on the crisis prevention and recovery and energy and environment focus areas. Tools and work processes will be developed (please refer to the key actions below) to address this recommendation.
</td>
</tr>
<tr>
<td>

Key action(s)
</td>
<td>

Time frame
</td>
<td>

Responsible unit(s)
</td>
</tr>
<tr>
<td>

1.1 UNDP will expand the GSIC forum to include all central and regional bureaux, the Human Development Report Office and all professional homes, and utilize tools such as the gender marker to monitor compliance with corporate mandates and resource targets. The gender marker data will be broken down by region and Strategic Plan outcomes and outputs to be a more precise monitoring tool. The gender marker data will also be incorporated into the corporate planning system. Improvements will be made to the gender marker to improve accuracy (please see key actions under recommendation 3).
</td>
<td>

By December 2016
</td>
<td>

Executive Office, Bureau for Policy and Programme Support (BPPS)/ Gender Team, regional bureaux
</td>
</tr>
<tr>
<td>

1.2 The merits of integrating the gender equality strategy into the strategic plan from 2018 onwards will be considered based on findings of the mid-term review of the Strategic Plan, 2014-2017.
</td>
<td>

By December 2017
</td>
<td>

Executive Office
</td>
</tr>
<tr>
<td>

1.3 UNDP standard operating procedures in crisis contexts, surge and express staff rosters (terms of reference, capacities, training) and crisis response tools all are being reviewed to ensure that gender equality and women's empowerment can be addressed at the onset of crises.
</td>
<td>

By June 2016
</td>
<td>

BPPS/Gender Team, Crisis Response Unit
</td>
</tr>
<tr>
<td>

1.4 To support the integration of gender in energy and environment programming, UNDP will develop: (a) a toolkit for UNDP staff on mainstreaming gender in environment programming; (b) a gender toolkit for GEF projects; and (c) tools for integrating gender into disaster preparedness and response.
</td>
<td>

By December 2016
</td>
<td>

BPPS/Gender Team, BPPS/ Climate Change and Disaster Risk Reduction Team
</td>
</tr>
</table>

Recommendation 2.

Given the uneven performance in the four focus areas of the Strategic Plan, 2008-2013 in promoting gender development results, UNDP should ensure that future assessments pay specific attention to the progress, effectiveness and quality of gender development results in the seven outcome areas of the current Strategic Plan.

Management response:
UNDP welcomes this recommendation and will develop guidelines for integrating gender development results in thematic assessments including reviews, and will work with IEO to improve the integration of gender in all evaluations.

Key action(s)	Time frame	Responsible unit(s)
2.1 Guidelines for integrating gender in reviews, assessments, decentralized and independent evaluations (drawing on existing tools including the IRRF, gender marker, etc.,) will be developed.	By December 2016	BPPS/Gender Team, IEO

Recommendation 3.

UNDP should focus on refining tools, instruments and processes developed during the period 2008-2013 and focus on further internalizing the centrality of gender equality and women's empowerment to the achievement of all development goals among staff. Specific recommendations on these improvements and possible new areas of intervention are discussed below:

3.1 Gender analysis should become mandatory in all programming and be linked with justifying the gender marker rating of each UNDP intervention.

3.3 The gender marker should track allocations in a way that provides reliable aggregated data at different stages of the project cycle. It should be subject to random external checks and also be systematically assessed by internal audit exercises.

3.3 The Gender Seal requires senior management's attention in terms of its future role as a corporate certification initiative.

3.4 Stronger attention should be placed on using the GSIC forum as a venue for organization-wide learning, problem-solving and sharing of instructive practices.

3.5 UNDP should strengthen capacity development processes that focus on gender mainstreaming so they are relevant and apply to staff's daily work and needs

3.6 UNDP should consider exploring new frontiers for engaging in gender issues that go beyond women's issues, for example the 'masculinity' agenda.

Management response:
UNDP management appreciates the recognition of past efforts, and notes that UNDP will continue to refine tools, instruments and processes with a focus on internalizing gender equality and women's empowerment towards the achievement of development goals.

3.1 Gender analysis should become mandatory in all programming and be linked with justifying the gender marker rating of each UNDP intervention.

UNDP will ensure that gender analysis is linked with the gender marker rating of every UNDP intervention by integrating this analysis in existing and upcoming mandatory programme/project planning, monitoring and assessment processes such as programme/project quality assurance, social and environmental screening and revision of the project document.

3.2 The gender marker should track allocations in a way that provides reliable aggregated data at different stages of the project cycle. It should be subject to random external checks and also be systematically assessed by internal audit exercises

UNDP welcomes this recommendation and will include in the revised gender marker guidance note provisions for random assessments and integrated into internal audit exercises.

3.3 The Gender Seal requires senior management's attention in terms of its future role as a corporate certification initiative. To facilitate this process, the Gender Seal pilot should be assessed by a team of independent advisors to guide its application as it enters a critical post-pilot phase.

Management appreciates the recognition that the Gender Equality Seal approach can be of value to national ministries. UNDP welcomes and agrees with the recommendation for independent assessments to review, document and improve upon the experiences of the Gender Equality Seal.

3.4 Stronger attention should be placed on using the GSIC forum as a venue for organization-wide learning, problem-solving and sharing of instructive practices.

UNDP appreciates the recommendation for the GSIC to become a venue for learning, finding solutions and sharing of practices. UNDP has expanded the membership of the GSIC and for the first time in 2015, all UNDP bureaux reported gender equality progress and results, shared lessons learned and identified overall and bureau-specific recommendations to take forward.

3.5 UNDP should strengthen capacity development processes that focus on gender mainstreaming so they are relevant and apply to staff's daily work and needs

UNDP agrees on the importance of capacity development for gender mainstreaming and will improve existing and upcoming training tools by including gender content.

3.6 UNDP should consider exploring new frontiers for engaging in gender issues that go beyond women's issues, for example the 'masculinity' agenda.

UNDP will consider exploring new frontiers for engaging in gender issues that go beyond women's issues, for example the 'masculinity' agenda.

Key action(s)	Time frame	Responsible unit(s)
3.1.1 Mandatory environmental and social screening procedures established for all projects above $500,000 to ensure they have gender equality as a key principal.	Continuous	BPPS/Gender Team, BPPS/ Development Impact Team, regional bureaux and regional service centres
3.1.2 Gender analysis is a requirement of the mandatory project quality assurance process.	Continuous	
3.1.3 Quality assurance guidelines for all country programmes and global/regional programmes will address gender equality and women's empowerment.	By December 2016	
3.2.1 The gender marker guidance note will be revised to provide more specific guidance to improve gender marker accuracy.	By December 2016	BPPS/Gender Team
3.2.2 The gender marker rating will be included in the cover note for project documents and integrated in the quality assurance guidelines.	By December 2016	BPPS/Gender Team, BPPS/Development Impact Group
3.2.3 A sample of random gender marker audits will be undertaken each year to improve accuracy (ensuring regional balance).	By December 2016	BPPS/Gender Team, regional bureaux
3.2.4 Guidelines for integrating gender in reviews, assessments, evaluations and audits (drawing on existing tools including IRRF, gender marker, etc.) will be developed.	By December 2016	BPPS/IEO/Office of Audit and Investigations
3.3 Independent assessment will be undertaken of the Gender Equality Seal to review, document and improve the tool.	By June 2016	BPPS/Gender Team
3.4.1 The GSIC will continue to be strengthened with all bureaux reporting. Accountability tools such as the gender marker, results-oriented annual report data and gender parity data will inform the GSIC meetings. GSIC recommendations will be presented to the Executive Group and they will be reviewed for implementation by the GSIC.	Continuous	All UNDP
3.4.2 GSIC will refresh the UNDP gender parity strategy with a view to achieving a more holistic approach to gender parity issues in UNDP.	By November 2015	GSIC, with support from Office of Human Resources

3.5 UNDP to review and improve training tools for policy and programme staff on gender mainstreaming in programming, monitoring and reporting with greater focus on improving capacity for gender analysis, accuracy and consistency in gender marker ratings and gender in areas of profession.	By December 2016	BPPS/Gender Team
3.6 UNDP to undertake research on 'masculinities' to better understand the linkages between masculinities and gender inequality, specifically gender-based violence.	By December 2016	BPPS/Gender Team, Regional Bureau for Asia Pacific

Recommendation 4.
Country offices should prepare gender plans that identify gaps and needs in terms of technical support, capacity-building, joint action and advocacy and collective monitoring that facilitate stronger gender programming. These plans should also help to identify areas where UNDP can draw on expertise and leverage the existing capacities of other United Nations agencies active on gender issues at the country level. This process should be supported, monitored and reported upon by the respective regional bureaux to the GSIC on annual basis.

Management response:
The Gender Equality Seal certification is the primary tool for strengthening country office capacity and ensuring collective monitoring for stronger gender programming. Currently, 29 countries have undertaken the Gender Seal certification process. This will be expanded to more countries. Regional bureaux and the GSIC will draw upon the GSIC benchmarking to measure progress.

Key action(s)	Time frame	Responsible unit(s)
4.1 The Gender Equality Seal benchmarking to be completed by all country offices in Africa and utilized as a tool for monitoring gender capacity.	By December 2015	BPPS/Gender Team/Regional Bureau for Africa
4.2 The next phase of the Gender Equality Seal certification initiative will be launched with approximately 30 country offices being certified.	By December 2016	BPPS/Gender Team/ regional bureaux and country offices

Recommendation 5.
UNDP currently does not have a measurement standard to systematically track the type, quality and effectiveness of its contribution to gender results that also captures the context of change and the degree of its contribution to that change. In order to address this issue, UNDP should codify the way it wishes to monitor, report, evaluate and audit its contributions to gender and this framework should be used for rigorously tracking results for gender equality and women's empowerment at the country, regional and global levels.

Management response:
UNDP believes that it has a range of tools for measuring progress that are used for different purposes. These comply with a range of different inter-agency standards. Taken together, these give a good view of the gender mainstreaming taking place in a given business unit. However, management will take forward the recommendation to consider adopting measures such as the Gender@Work framework to move beyond a focus on numbers of women and men towards more transformative results is worth consideration.

Key action(s)	Time frame	Responsible unit(s)
5.1 UNDP will begin an internal dialogue bringing experts from the Gender@Work network to explore how the organization can move beyond a focus on numbers of women and men towards more transformative results. This will include the development of a capacity- building strategy to support country offices and accelerate changes.	By December 2016	BPPS/Gender Team
5.2 In developing its monitoring policy, UNDP will integrate provisions for systematic tracking of the type, quality and effectiveness of its contribution to gender results.	By December 2016	Executive Office, BPPS/Development Impact Group/Gender Team, regional bureaux

5.3 UNDP will bring the Gender@Work framework to be discussed at the Gender Steering and Implementation Committee meetings.	By December 2017	Executive Office, BPPS/Gender Team, regional bureaux
5.4 The feasibility of the Gender@Work framework to become part of the UNDP results-based management policy and processes to be considered in the midterm review of the Strategic Plan, 2013-2017.	By December 2016	Executive Office, BPPS/Development Impact Group